# PRAISE FOR *THE SECRETS OF CHARACTER*

"There are plenty of books on the craft of writing. But there's only one Matt Bird, the ultimate writing coach: smart, funny, insightful, and armed with a toolbox of innovative tips for creating characters readers will love. Whether you're new to writing or a seasoned pro, you need this classic-in-the-making."

—Katherine Applegate, Newbery Award–winning author of
*The One and Only Ivan*

"*The Secrets of Story* instantly became one of my favorite writing guides. This follow-up dives under the water to take an even more in-depth look at the iceberg of character development. Meticulously researched and brimming with examples, it offers advice that is both precise and actionable. It reveals the genre-spanning patterns of memorable and resonant characters in an easy-to-access reference format that makes for both fun reading and a great tool to keep on your desk for easy thumb-through inspiration."

—K. M. Weiland, author of *Creating Character Arcs* and
*Structuring Your Novel*

"Matt Bird has done it again! *The Secrets of Character* is a book you want next to you when you write. From revealing what gatekeepers look for in your first ten pages to sharing powerful writing tricks from 150 years ago through today, this is a book to read with your laptop nearby. You'll see what your writing needs, and it's sure to inspire you to write!"

—Torrey Maldonado, author of *What Lane?* and *Tight*

"All the great ideas in the world don't matter if you don't hook your audience out of the gate. In Matt's new book, he lays it out plain and simple, practical advice for making readers grab on to your protagonists and never let go. *The Secrets of Character* is the perfect companion to *The Secrets of Story*, another essential writing guide from Matt Bird."

—Lou Anders, Hugo-winning editor and author of
*Once Upon a Unicorn* and *Star Wars: Pirate's Price*


"Who says there are no shortcuts to success? Matt Bird's marvelous *The Secrets of Character* offers indispensable, easy-to-implement story hacks that guarantee your character will grab readers' attention—and ensure you have a story worth writing."

—Keir Graff, author of *The Three Mrs. Wrights* and
*The Swing of Things* (writing with Linda Joffe Hull as Linda Keir)

# THE
# SECRETS
# OF
# CHARACTER

*Writing a Hero Anyone Will Love*

## MATT BIRD

WRITER'S
DIGEST
BOOKS

**WRITER'S
DIGEST
BOOKS**

An imprint of Penguin Random House LLC
penguinrandomhouse.com

Trade paperback ISBN 9780593331224
eBook ISBN 9780593331231

Printed in the United States of America
2nd Printing

Book design by Ashley Tucker

To Lily and Jack

# TABLE OF CONTENTS

## Part I

# BELIEVE, CARE, INVEST

# PREFACE

S O HERE'S THE THING: I GET LETTERS.

A few years ago I wrote a book called *The Secrets of Story: Innovative Tools for Perfecting Your Fiction and Captivating Readers.* Most of the book consists of a checklist with 122 questions you can ask yourself to improve your story, whether it's a novel, short story, or screenplay. Now I get the occasional email: "I just read your book and I'm rewriting my manuscript, but I can't figure out how to answer yes to one question, so could you give me permission to skip that one?"

I always say yes, of course. And I cringe. Both before and after I deliver the checklist in that book, I insist that any story that checks all 122 boxes will be terrible, but evidently I didn't make that clear enough throughout the book. I made it sound like each item absolutely has to be done, and I inadvertently scared people into seeking an audience with me to ask for a special papal dispensation.

There's a delightful comedic novel called *How I Became a Famous Novelist* by Steve Hely. In the book, the hero decides that he wants to find instant success as a writer, so he does an analysis of every book on the bestseller list, then crafts a book cynically targeted at the broadest possible readership: *The Tornado Ashes Club.*

Once he's finished his manuscript, he sends it to a friend who works in publishing in New York. She soon calls him excitedly, saying it's going to get her promoted. "You thought it was good?" he asks. "Oh, not *good* good," she replies. But she's going to buy it anyway: "Because you meet the checklist!"

She explains that her corporate overlords have dictated that all new manuscripts must check off every box on a checklist of commercial viability, and his terrible novel is the first one she's ever gotten that checks every box, so she's going to make him rich.

Reading this, I was of course horrified: I am that corporate boss! Have I created a monster?

Don't get me wrong, I'm very gratified by the success of my first book. It ended up on the Amazon bestseller list, and it's got a big fan base. And I'm proud of it, as long as I can reassure myself most readers understand that they shouldn't check every box!

So now here we are with a follow-up, but please use these new suggestions à la carte. Pixar says that the advice they give their writers is "Tools, Not Rules." Here's a new toolbox, not a rulebook, this time with a focus on character—what makes them believable, relatable, and unforgettable.

Remember, you don't have to check every box. As the liquor companies say: "Enjoy responsibly!"

# CHAPTER 1

# BASHING YOUR HEAD AGAINST THE GATES

**Y**OU ARE A WRITER. MAYBE YOU'RE WRITING NOVELS, screenplays, TV scripts, memoirs, plays, or comics. One way or another, you've got a hero, and you're asking people to care about them. But you've got a problem: No one is agreeing to read your work. Publishers, movies studios, agents, and managers are all saying no to you.

Then, one day, dawn breaks. A gatekeeper agrees to read your manuscript! You're ecstatic. But then they specify: "I tell you what, just send me the first ten pages, and I'll take a look at those, then I'll have you send me the rest if I'm still interested."

What an ass! Your story doesn't even get going until page seventeen. How can they judge it based on ten measly pages?

Well, before you get too pissed, you should appreciate one piece of good news: This gatekeeper is being honest with you. Anyone who tells you otherwise is lying. No one clears their slush pile by reading every manuscript cover to cover. Everyone just reads the first ten pages, which is enough to eliminate nine out of ten submissions.

So does that mean you should shoehorn your first three plot points into those first ten pages to give them a sense of what's going to happen? Nope. This brings us to a central law of story-telling from my first book: Nobody really cares about your story, they just care about your hero. They're not looking for a great *story* in those ten pages, they're looking for a great *hero*. (In this book, the term "hero" is gender neutral and morally neutral. A hero can be any gender and good or evil.)

They want to fall in love. Once we love a hero, we'll follow her anywhere. It doesn't matter if the story is any good. And if we don't feel that connection, then the best story in the world is just a waste.

My first book was about every possible aspect of writing. That made it easy to write! I just tossed in every thought I had on the subject. I knew that, for this book, I wanted something more focused. Why bury you in notes for your big beautiful manu-script when no one is offering to read it in full? I wanted to write a book focused on surviving that first swing of the axe. I just want to get you into that rarefied club: that one in ten that they keep reading.

## The Three Things You Have to Do

So let's go ahead and get to the central idea of this book. What are the gatekeepers looking for in those first ten pages?

After much consideration and the examination of dozens of great stories, I've come to the conclusion that readers want to do three separate things in those first ten pages.

They want to:

• **Believe** in the reality of the hero

• **Care** about the hero's circumstances

• **Invest** their hopes in the hero to solve this problem

That's it. That's what great stories tend to do in the first ten pages. Actual plot points can wait.

Now some of you may recognize that language. My last book had a Character chapter, and it was divided into three sections: Believe, Care, and Invest. This book will be, in some ways, an expansion of that chapter into a whole book, and it will also be divided into Believe, Care, and Invest sections, but I've substantially reconceived and improved on all three ideas here.

Here's what I've been doing for the last five years since I wrote that book: I revisited all my favorite stories. I reread the first ten pages of lots of my favorite novels and memoirs, and I rewatched the first fifteen minutes of my favorite movies and TV pilots. And I submitted them to the Believe, Care, Invest test.

I found that Believe, Care, Invest was indeed an excellent lens for investigating what made a beginning great. But I did make some adjustments over the years. I have a much better, fuller sense now of what causes us to believe in, care for, and invest in a character. One change that has resulted: Today I'd put under Believe a lot of the questions I had asked under Care and Invest last time. Those of you familiar with the first book will notice that things have shifted around a bit in this book.

And if you haven't read the last book, then great! I know

what I'm talking about a lot more this time, and you're going to get off on the right foot first!

So let's get started with an example. As everyone knows, a writer should always . . .

## Kill the Cat

Of course, there already is a very popular book with a titular piece of advice about how to get us to fall in love with a hero right away: *Save the Cat!* In the late Blake Snyder's book, he suggests that you begin your story with your main character doing something heroic and upstanding. So when I revisited all these great stories, did I find a lot of examples of that?

I did not.

In fact, I frequently found something quite different. Here's the third paragraph of Suzanne Collins's *The Hunger Games*:

> *Sitting at Prim's knees, guarding her, is the world's ugliest cat. Mashed-in nose, half of one ear missing, eyes the color of rotting squash. Prim named him Buttercup, insisting that his muddy yellow coat matched the bright flower. He hates me. Or at least distrusts me. Even though it was years ago, I think he still remembers how I tried to drown him in a bucket when Prim brought him home. Scrawny kitten, belly swollen with worms, crawling with fleas. The last thing I needed was another mouth to feed. But Prim begged so hard, cried even, I had to let him stay. It turned out okay. My mother got rid of the vermin and he's a born mouser. Even catches the occasional rat. Sometimes, when I clean a kill, I feed Buttercup the entrails. He has stopped hissing at me.*

Not exactly loving to the family cat! But hey, you might point out, she decides not to kill the cat, so I guess you could say she's, um, saving it from her own murderous impulses, right? Well, don't worry, a few paragraphs later, she does finally get to kill a cat that just wants her love! She talks about meeting a boy in the forest:

> *My real name is Katniss, but when I first told him, I had barely whispered it. So he thought I'd said Catnip. Then when this crazy lynx started following me around the woods looking for handouts, it became his official nickname for me. I finally had to kill the lynx because he scared off game. I almost regretted it because he wasn't bad company. But I got a decent price for his pelt.*

So what's actually going on? Why do we fall in love with a heroine who literally kills cats? Because, already from this first page, we Believe, Care, and Invest.

**Why do we Believe?** This one paragraph does a great job of showing a thoroughly believable worldview. The syntax is consistently terse ("He hates me. Or at least distrusts me."). Her value judgments show her character ("He's a born mouser" is her ultimate compliment). Her idea of showing kindness is to share the entrails of her kill. She doesn't seem like an accumulation of author-imposed traits. She seems like a fully realized human, albeit an unpleasant one.

**Why do we Care?** She's clearly suffering and doing what she can to survive ("The last thing I needed was another mouth to feed."). If she was living a comfortable life in the suburbs, we would hate her for wanting to kill a cat, but seeing her hunger, our heart goes out to her. We wonder what we would do.

**Why do we Invest?** We definitely trust her to solve whatever challenges this book offers. She's badass, and she's ready to make hard decisions. On page three, she slips through an electrified fence to bowhunt her own food. We've picked the right hero!

*The Hunger Games* is a great example of this model, because it's got Believe, Care, and Invest right away on page one. We commit to reading this whole book, but not because Collins has fired up the central plot right away. She can now take all the time she needs to do that. We commit because we love this cat-killing heroine. And we're now willing to go anywhere with her. It's no surprise to me that this book was such a hit.

So there you go. You have my whole book in a nutshell. So why are you still reading?

Here's why: Because this book will be filled with hundreds of *tricks*.

In Part I, I will look at dozens of tricks to get readers to Believe, Care, and Invest, all backed up with examples from my copious research. You will not only thoroughly understand these three concepts, you will have a cheat sheet for how to use them to fix your first ten pages, right now, today!

Okay, with that first rule set out, let's dive in—no, wait, first I should give . . .

## A Warning Before We Begin

We're about to jump into the heart of this book: But let me make one big admission up front: I will cheat. Ninety percent of these examples will come from the first ten pages of a novel or memoir, or the first fifteen minutes of a movie or television pilot episode. But I'm not going to *strictly* hold myself to that. There will be some examples that come from much later. I make no apologies!

So let's start with Believe.

# CHAPTER 2

# HOW CAN YOU MAKE YOUR READERS BELIEVE IN THE REALITY OF YOUR CHARACTERS?

THEY KNOW YOU'RE LYING.

If you're writing fiction, you're lying. You're claiming that a character exists that doesn't really exist. You just made it all up! You're not fooling anyone.

But so what? They've bought a book or movie ticket, they understand the concept of fiction, so why can't a reader just willingly suspend their disbelief? Well, they are willing to do that, but only if you meet them *halfway*.

You need to *make* your character come to life. You need to trick your reader or viewer into thinking, "Oh, this isn't just some phony character I've seen a million times, this one is *real*! I feel like I *know* this hero."

Your hero will just be a phony construct until you breathe life into her. To do this, you need a strange combination: *Universal* details we identify with, and oddly *specific* details that seem so unusual that they must be real, because no one could make them up.

In this chapter we'll look at dozens of tricks you can use to increase the believability of your characters, starting with . . .

## The First Rule of Believability: Be Repetitive

I'm always a fan of counterintuitive advice, so let me start with this general rule for character believability: The best way to make a character believable is to be *repetitive*. And I don't just mean over the course of your whole story, I mean even in these first ten pages.

Hit their characterization *hard*. As I've said before, writers overestimate a reader's desire to be surprised. Beginning writers assume that the reader wants to say, "I had no idea the hero was going to do that!," but they actually love to say, "I *knew* he was going to do that!"

How quickly do they want to know what the hero will do? Right away! You can give your heroes five different opportunities to show their character in the first ten pages, and readers will love it if they can already start to guess how heroes will react by the time they get to page ten.

Let's look at a good candidate for Great American Novel: *Little Women*. Author Louisa May Alcott sets an especially hard task for herself: She introduces all four sisters at once. She's got to let us know that Jo will really be our primary hero, but that we'll get to know and love all four sisters. Let's look at how she does that swiftly and masterfully.

These are the first four paragraphs:

*"Christmas won't be Christmas without any presents," grumbled Jo, lying on the rug.*

*"It's so dreadful to be poor!" sighed Meg, looking down at her old dress.*

*"I don't think it's fair for some girls to have plenty of pretty things, and other girls nothing at all," added little Amy, with an injured sniff.*

*"We've got Father and Mother, and each other," said Beth contentedly from her corner.*

So right away, we get all four personalities. And then, a few pages later, they discuss getting gifts for their mother:

*Meg announced, as if the idea was suggested by the sight of her own pretty hands, "I shall give her a nice pair of gloves."*

*"Army shoes, best to be had," cried Jo.*

*"Some handkerchiefs, all hemmed," said Beth.*

*"I'll get a little bottle of cologne. She likes it, and it won't cost much, so I'll have some left to buy my pencils," added Amy.*

And then, *still* in that first ten pages:

*The girls flew about, trying to make things comfortable, each in her own way. Meg arranged the tea table, Jo brought wood and set chairs, dropping, over-turning, and clattering everything she touched. Beth trotted to and fro between parlor kitchen, quiet and busy, while Amy gave directions to everyone, as she sat with her hands folded.*

Whew! Just ten pages in, we know these girls *very* well. We're already starting to say, "Oh, that's so *Amy*." We can predict their behavior now, which we love to do. They're already starting to feel like our own family. (Of course, each character will have times they surprise us, but we enjoy that precisely because it *is* a surprise.)

But wait, you say, that novel is 150 years old! That's not how people write today! But little has changed. Celeste Ng's *Little Fires Everywhere* also introduces four siblings at once, and has several versions of this paragraph:

> *Last year it had paid for their trip to Martha's Vineyard, where Lexie had perfected her backstroke and Trip had bewitched all the local girls and Moody had sunburnt to a peeling crisp and Izzy, under great duress, had finally agreed to come down to the beach— fully clothed, in her Doc Martens, and glowering.*

Just as Alcott did, Ng hits their characterizations a few different times in a few different moments in the first ten pages.

Want a book by a dude? *A Game of Thrones* is yet another novel that tackles the difficult task of introducing several siblings at once. Let's just focus on the ward, Theon. Right away in the first chapter, author George R. R. Martin hits Theon's character note over and over.

He's introduced with "Theon was a lean, dark youth of nineteen who found everything amusing." That's a great character description we haven't heard a million times before. Then, after that, we get his same character note repeated three times:

> *He laughed, put his boot on the head, and kicked it away.*

> *Greyjoy was laughing and joking as he rode.*

> *Theon Greyjoy said with wry amusement . . .*

We're already saying, "That's so *Theon*." All three of these books take on the hard task of introducing several siblings at once, but they all rise to the challenge by *repetitively* driving home the characterization of each until we know how they contrast with the others. In all three books, we feel like a member of the family by the end of the first chapter.

Okay, now we can discuss . . .

## The Four Aspects of Believability

So let's preview this chapter. In order to make a hero believable, they must have:

- A full life

- A fully fleshed-out world

- Universal behavior

- A specific personality

Personality will be the big one, so we'll break that down further. Subcategories of personality will include:

- A unique way of talking

- A unique backstory

- Flaws

- Secrets

- Assertiveness

• Beliefs

• Specific tastes and belongings

I'll talk about each one, and then hit you with a ton of examples. A few pieces of advice in this list will be ones that you might be familiar with from my last book, but I'll redefine them, offer original examples, and talk about new twists on each.

Great! So let's start with giving your hero . . .

# A Full Life

First and foremost, your hero must *exist*. They can't just be there to serve the wonderful story you've cooked up. They need to have things they'd be doing if you didn't dump all this crap on their heads.

How do you make your hero a real person? The first trick:

### Give your hero some food

(Again, let me stress that all of this advice will be à la carte. No one should do all of them. Sample just a few, and feel free to spit any of them into your napkin. All clear on that? Okay, let's get back to our regularly scheduled book . . .)

Complete heroes have an id, an ego, and a superego. Hunger is a great way to show their id. This is a person who must live in the world, and is subject to the weaknesses and desires that define our waking days.

I mentioned in my last book that it's always good to put things in your heroes' hands and it's always good to make it clear that they'd be doing something else if this scene wasn't happening. Giving them something to eat in the first scene accomplishes both of these things.

Jack Bauer, the hero of *24*, would soon become famous for his ability to make it through twenty-four real-time hours without eating a thing, but when we first meet him, he's still human enough to have a midnight pudding snack. I hope you enjoy it, Jack, because it's the last food you'll touch for a long time.

Even better are heroes who don't just consume food for fuel, but love their food. Books, especially, love to lavish attention on the many courses of long, delicious meals, whether in Harry Potter, *The Hobbit*, or *The Hunger Games*.

Few characters love food more than FBI Agent Cooper in *Twin Peaks*. As he drives into the titular city to help solve a case, he speaks into his recorder to his assistant, Diane, back at the Bureau: "Lunch was $6.31 at the Lamplighter Inn. That's on Highway 2 near Lewis Fork. That was tuna fish sandwich on whole wheat, slice of cherry pie, and a cup of coffee: Damn good food! Diane, if you ever get up this way, that cherry pie is worth a stop!"

Eating can be a great way to show the hero's relationship to their culture. The Chinese American heroine of *The Farewell* reconnects to her lost culture through food first at her parents' house in America, and then at her grandmother's apartment back in China. *The Sopranos* pilot is all about Tony trying to save his favorite Italian restaurant. His whole family revolves around food. The one line everybody loves from that pilot is where Tony is shipped off to the hospital before a family gathering and his preteen son says, "So what, no fucking ziti now?"

## Give your hero a job

We don't really trust adult heroes who don't work. Our own lives are sharply proscribed by our economic circumstances and we want to recognize that onscreen. A world will seem more real if everything in it has a value, and giving objects a financial value makes that literal.

Think of Luke in *Star Wars*. One great thing about his job is that we don't quite get what's going on. Luke is farming moisture or something? We just shrug and say, "Whatever, this is a big weird world and everybody has their own thing going on, which this movie will never explain." That feels real. The first thing we see Luke doing is haggling with Jawas over the price of new droids. The makers of *The Force Awakens*, never shy about borrowing from the first movie, have Rey mired in economic activity on her own desert planet. In that case, she gets to show her character by refusing money for BB-8, even though we've seen how desperately poor she is.

Even if your world doesn't have cash money, there are going to be lots of jobs to get done. The early montages in *Moana* make it clear that there are about twenty different professions that have to be done to maintain their way of life, and we see each one at work. They may not have money, but they have an economy.

Throughout the book, we'll look for places that cause you to Believe and/or Care and/or Invest at the same time, so let's preview a few of those. In the Care section, we'll look at lots of heroes who get fired. We'll also look at jobs that are particularly humiliating. And in our Invest section, we'll look at a moment that happens in many stories, either early or late, where the hero rises above their economic circumstances and stands up to their boss.

## Give your hero friends

This is a mistake many writers make. It's tempting to have the whole world be set against your hero, but that's not always the best choice. Having friends does a lot of work. This hero has built a support network over the course of their life. Friends complete us, and you want a complete human. Friends are the people who see some value in us, above our economic circumstances, so if you give your hero friends, you're giving them value.

In *Raiders of the Lost Ark*, Indy comes back to the university from his failed mission. We expect stories to maximize the hero's humiliations, so why not have his boss lecture him sternly? Maybe threaten to fire him if it happens again? But the opposite happens: His boss, Brody, is a good friend and assures him that it's fine. Later, they hang out and have a brandy as they discuss the new mission. Indy isn't just a conflict engine. He's got a full life.

Lots of ink has been spilled on the topic of what the Marvel Cinematic Universe is doing right and what the DC films are doing wrong, but this is a big one: Almost every Marvel hero has *friends*, whether it be Rhodey or Bucky or the Warriors Three.

Think of our first scenes with T'Challa in *Black Panther*. T'Challa has a love interest, but he's also got a female warrior whom he's just *friends* with, who joshes him about freezing up when he's around his love interest. ("What are you talking about? I never freeze," he says, unconvincingly.) Most of the DC heroes don't have friends, at least not ones who were friends before the beginning of the movie and remain friends afterward.

We want to be able to try to guess what would have occurred if this story *hadn't happened*. What would the hero *rather* be doing on Friday night?

## Give them something to read

In my last book, I talked about how the simplest way of getting us to identify with a hero is by having that hero read, just like the reader is doing right now. Even better is when they're interrupted and criticized for reading, as in *Pride and Prejudice* and *Jane Eyre*.

The hero of *Matilda* is horribly neglected at home, but she comes alive when she discovers her local public library. At first the librarian steers her toward the children's section, but gradually comes to realize that she can handle adult books. We'll talk later about how lists of the hero's stuff are always good, and

Matilda's extensive reading list allows us to say, "Hey, I've read that one, too! We have something in common!"

*Lady Bird* begins with the title character and her mother driving down a two-lane highway listening to the final scene of *The Grapes of Wrath* on audiobook, both shedding a tear. Then Lady Bird pops the tape out and says, "Our college trip took twenty-one hours and five minutes." I've listened to hundreds of audiobooks, but I'd never seen anybody do so onscreen before, so this felt very real and not made up.

Of course, the reason you don't see it a lot is because it's not very cinematic, but don't worry, the shared moment of emotion quickly falls apart and the two start verbally sparring, resulting in a shocking act we'll discuss later.

(And if we've read the book ourselves, we know that the scene they're listening to is apropos. The Joads were also traveling around California on a futile quest for somewhere to belong, and looking for a mother's succor in all the wrong places.)

Of course, this is definitely one that *not* every hero should do. Often, a story will hit the ground running, and the hero will have no downtime in the first ten pages, which is fine. Reading is a privilege that not everybody has.

OKAY, ONCE YOU'VE given your heroes a full life, you can go further and put them in . . .

## A Fully Fleshed-Out World

When we're watching a movie or TV show, we always want the sense that there's something going on outside the frame. If we suddenly turned around, would we see a sound stage, or would we find that this world is fully immersive? This is equally true of novels. We want the sense that there's a full world here, and our hero is just one part of it.

## Give us sensory information about their world

This is an area where different types of writers get jealous of others. Novelists and memoirists have access to all five senses, but it's harder to directly convey smell and taste in movies, TV, plays, and comics. Nevertheless, in every medium, you must fully engage your reader, and the best way is to fully engage as many senses as you can.

Sound is a sense available to all sorts of storytellers, but great novelists can use similes and metaphors to make it come alive in a way that dramatic writers can't. In *The House on Mango Street*, Sandra Cisneros excels at odd descriptions of sounds. Her heroine Esperanza talks about hearing her own name: "At school they say my name funny as if the syllables were made out of tin and hurt the roof of your mouth." She describes her laugh: "Not the shy ice cream bells' giggle of Rachel and Lucy's family, but all of a sudden and surprised like a pile of dishes breaking." She hears a music box in an old antique store: "Then he starts it up and all sorts of things start happening. It's like all of a sudden he let go a million moths all over the dusty furniture and swan-neck shadows and in our bones."

*Americanah* by Chimamanda Ngozi Adichie begins with a great line: "Princeton, in the summer, smelled of nothing . . ." Later on down the page, the heroine gives us a tour of other places she's lived in America, according to their smells: "Philadelphia had the musty scent of history. New Haven smelled of neglect. Baltimore smelled of brine, and Brooklyn of sun-warmed garbage."

Smell is the sense most linked to memory. Nothing makes the past come alive more than a whiff of something we haven't smelled since we were kids. (For example: That bizarre book glue they used in the '70s.)

Movies can convey unexpected sensory information as well. Before the first image even fades up, *Gravity* begins with a title onscreen: "At 600km above planet Earth the temperature fluctuates between +258 and -148 degrees Fahrenheit. There is nothing to carry sound. No air pressure. No oxygen. Life in space is impossible." Already, from this one title card, we Believe, Care, and Invest. The sensory information makes the setting come alive for us; this information will put our heroes in danger and our heroes will be badasses for going out there anyway.

Movies can even use smell. Imprisoned serial killer Hannibal Lecter sniffs at his FBI visitor Clarice Starling in *The Silence of the Lambs* and shows his masterful powers of perception: "Sometimes you wear L'air du Temps . . . but not today."

## Anthropomorphize nature

This one is pretty much just a trick for prose writers. One great way to make the world come alive is to *actually* make the world come alive. Treat nature like a person.

The first line of Arundhati Roy's *The God of Small Things* is "May in Ayemenem is a hot, brooding month." Then later on in the page, she says "The countryside turns an immodest green." Months brood, colors are immodest—everything is alive in this world, which makes the novel come alive for us.

Likewise, in Tara Westover's memoir *Educated*, we begin with her thinking about leaving her mountain, but as she looks at it, she thinks, "Meanwhile our farm dances: the heavy conifer trees sway slowly, while the sagebrush and thistles quiver, bowing before every puff and pocket of air." We get not just adjectives describing nature, but personified verbs: dance, sway, quiver.

Young Tara will be reluctant to leave this mountain, even after suffering grueling abuse and neglect there, because she loves it like a person. She concludes the paragraph by personifying the mountain: "I can see the dark form of the Indian Princess." She loves the princess, and she feels that the princess loves her back. These details get us to picture the setting vividly and thus believe in the heroine describing them.

## Give them songs and dances

Everyone is part of a culture, of one kind or another, and the easiest way to make your hero's culture come alive is to convey their song lyrics, whether it's a song the hero's family has been singing for generations, or just one that the hero has made up.

Often, when we enter the world of a Disney movie, they're singing songs about their history and culture, whether it's the sailors in *The Little Mermaid* or the ice cutters in *Frozen*.

It's somewhat counterintuitive, but book readers actually love song lyrics even though we don't necessarily know the tune. In *Angela's Ashes*, Frank McCourt's father likes to disappear on drunken jags and then return singing songs about Irish independence. He drunkenly makes his two sons stand up and swear to die for Ireland, then makes them sing songs about the great Irish martyrs Kevin Barry and Roddy McCorley. We already get song lyrics in the first ten pages.

Of course, no writer ever loved song lyrics more than J. R. R. Tolkien. I've recently been reading his books to my daughter, and I can't go five pages without having to make up another tune for a hobbit song (I make them sound like shanties) or an elf song (I make them sound like French ballads). Sometimes they're singing songs from the old days, and sometimes the mood strikes them to compose a ditty themselves.

## Give them unique language, including work jargon and tradecraft

This is one of many pieces of advice that I'll revisit from my last book but expand upon with new examples and permutations.

Every world has its unique jargon, and the better you can capture that language, the more this world will come alive. Your hero lives in a specific world, not a generic one. The people speak and act in ways that combine their cultural history, professional jargon, and unique personalities. You as a writer need to combine voices you know from real life with aspects of this world that you've learned about either from your research or your lived experience.

Authors who have changed professions always have an advantage: They have extensive firsthand knowledge of the worlds in which they used to live and work. John Grisham was a lawyer, and shares with us the lies that lead to such jobs in the opening scene of *The Firm*: Mitch McDeere says in his interview, "I enjoy research." Grisham then tells us, "They nodded and acknowledged this obvious lie. It was part of the ritual. No law student or lawyer in his right mind enjoyed research, yet, without fail, every prospective associate professed a deep love for the library."

If you're not writing about your own lived experience, you can still get lots of details through your own hard work. Paul Attanasio conducted hundreds of hours of interviews while writing *Donnie Brasco*, and found a highly entertaining example of the unique language of this world. FBI Agent Joe Pistone is so deeply undercover in the mafia that he has a hard time dealing with his handlers on those rare occasions that he comes in from the cold. Nevertheless, two of the technicians transcribing his tapes feel they have to tentatively ask him a question: "Hey, can I ask you something? What's 'fugettaboutit'? What is that?"

Donnie is exasperated that he has to explain, but he tries his best:

> *"Fugettaboutit is like, uh, if you agree with someone, y'know? Like 'Raquel Welch is one great piece of ass, fugettaboutit.' But then, if you disagree, like a Lincoln is better than a Cadillac? Fugettaboutit! Y'know? But then, it's also like if something is the greatest thing in the world, like, 'Minghia!, Those peppers, fugettaboutit.' Y'know? It's also like saying 'Go to hell,' too, like, y'know, like, uh, 'Hey Paulie, you got a one-inch pecker,' and Paulie says 'Fugettaboutit!'"*

The technicians thank him, then he adds: "Sometimes it just means fugettaboutit."

Those examples featured language from real life, but if you want to be more ambitious, you can create a whole jargon from scratch. Harrison Ford famously told George Lucas about the script for *Star Wars*, "George! You can type this shit, but you sure can't say it! Move your mouth when you're typing!" This is generally interpreted to mean that the dialogue was too poorly written to perform, but it's always struck me that this was probably Ford complaining that he had to sell so many weird phrases when he didn't know what they meant.

What does it mean to say that a ship is "Corellian"? How is he supposed to react when he's called a "nerfherder"? What does any of this even *mean*? It was understandably a challenge for Ford, but it's what makes the dialogue so *good*. All of the unique language gives us our "first step into a larger world," as Obi-Wan might say.

## Give them internecine conflicts

Your world will feel more real if your heroes spend more time involved in internecine conflicts within their group than conflict with outside groups. In a complex world, the hero is always equally in danger of being stabbed in the back as being stabbed in the front. That's a world we'll recognize.

We may look back now and think, "Oh, the punk era was all about punks vs. preppies," but of course it was just as likely to be about art-punks vs. hardcore punks, as you can see in *20th Century Women*.

The title of *Born a Crime* promises a book about the evils of apartheid, but apartheid is actually abolished when author Trevor Noah is five and he soon faces far more danger from rival ethnic groups: "As the apartheid regime fell, we knew that the black man was now going to rule. The question was, which black man?" The first chapter deals with an incident in which Trevor and his mother, who are Xhosa, are almost killed by Zulu cab drivers.

Sometimes internecine conflicts fall away. The early Harry Potter books are very concerned about the competition for the "house cup." By the time we get to book four, the kids have outgrown caring about that, as they now have far more serious external threats to worry about.

## Give them oddly complicated situations

The whole goal in this chapter is to get the reader to subconsciously think, "No one could make that up." Sometimes, this means that you're getting them to subconsciously think, "No one *would* make that up."

It's a standard piece of writing advice that you should tell simple stories with complex characters, not complex stories with simple characters. But that creates an opportunity for writers. Because the reader is expecting simplified plots, you can make your story feel more real by complicating things.

*The Fighter* is based on a true story, and unlike in many biopics, they didn't simplify the family situation. The family history of boxers Micky and Dicky and their various half-sisters is dizzying when they try (and fail) to sum it up for others. We hear it and we say, "Nobody would make that up."

Don DeLillo's *White Noise*, on the other hand, is pure fiction, but DeLillo knows that complex family structures feel more real than simplified ones. Both the hero and his wife have previous marriages and the house is a confusing mix of kids from various couplings, many of whom live there only part of the year.

*Angela's Ashes* doesn't go the way fiction goes: In stories, immigrants show up in a new country, burn their boats, and endure a trial by fire in this new world. Heroes rarely retrace their steps in fiction. McCourt's parents, however, quickly realize that they can't cut it in America and return to Ireland. (Then by the end of the sequel memoir, everybody ends up back in America.) When things don't move in straight lines, that feels like real life, not fiction.

## Fill their world with meaningful (or meaningless) objects

Objects have always been a big part of my advice (and you'll find a video about them on the Secrets of Story YouTube channel.) It's one thing to just talk about meaning, but it's much more powerful to embody that meaning in an object that the hero can grasp fondly or discard angrily (then desperately fish out of the garbage when their anger subsides).

Objects specific to this world help it come alive for us, such as when Anthony Bourdain tells us about cooks snorting cocaine through uncooked penne pasta in *Kitchen Confidential*.

In *Moby-Dick*, when Ishmael enters a public house in New Bedford, he quickly realizes that his new profession is rather intimidating:

*The opposite wall of this entry was hung all over with a heathenish array of monstrous clubs and spears. Some were thickly set with glittering teeth resembling ivory saws; others were tufted with knots of human hair; and one was sickle-shaped, with a vast handle sweeping round like the segment made in the new-mown grass by a long-armed mower. You shuddered as you gazed, and wondered what monstrous cannibal and savage could ever have gone a death-harvesting with such a hacking, horrifying implement. Mixed with these were rusty old whaling lances and harpoons all broken and deformed. Some were storied weapons. With this once long lance, now wildly elbowed, fifty years ago did Nathan Swain kill fifteen whales between a sunrise and a sunset. And that harpoon—so like a corkscrew now—was flung in Javan seas, and run away with by a whale, years afterwards slain off the Cape of Blanco. The original iron entered nigh the tail, and, like a restless needle sojourning in the body of a man, travelled full forty feet, and at last was found imbedded in the hump.*

Sometimes the heroes' interaction with objects speaks to the theme. In the movie of *How to Train Your Dragon*, Hiccup accidentally defeats Astrid in their dragon-fighting class when her axe gets stuck in his wooden shield. This prefigures how his pacifism will defeat her militarism.

But objects can also be delightfully meaningless in a way that makes this world come alive.

Bless the set designer of *Alien* who added a bizarre drinking-bird toy, the only thing the crew left behind when they cleaned up the ship before going into cryo-sleep. It's just so odd!

## Have them talk about real-world things fictional characters don't usually talk about

Your reader has read a lot of stories. They know the sort of things that usually happen. The goal is to startle them awake, to make them say, "Whoa, this isn't the prettied-up world I'm used to, this has the grit of real life."

Raymond Chandler described his private eye Phillip Marlowe this way: "Down these mean streets a man must go who is not himself mean, who is neither tarnished nor afraid. He is the hero; he is everything. He must be a complete man and a common man and yet an unusual man." That became the template for the genre, but *Chinatown* ripped down that façade. When we first see private eye Jake Gittes, he's mired in the *sordid* side of the business, showing a tuna fisherman pictures of his wife cheating on him. We think, "Oh, this is a *real* private detective, doing the down and dirty work of the profession."

This also applies to stories that get away with being the first story to discuss formerly taboo topics. Judy Blume is of course the queen of this, from scoliosis in *Deenie*, to periods in *Are You There God? It's Me, Margaret*, to the adventures of "Ralph" in *Forever*.

The casual discussion of helping each other get abortions in *Juno* was refreshing. Likewise with *Lady Bird* and masturbation. "Oh," we say with embarrassment, this is set in *our* world, not some phony made-up place. "I never thought I'd get to see the real world onscreen like this."

Okay, so now we've got a real world, so let's talk about the next element of creating a believable hero . . .

## Universal Behavior

Characterization is always a tricky combination of the familiar and the unique. Having some familiar behavior makes us say, "Ah, yes, this resonates with my own life," while unique behavior makes us say, "but this hero isn't exactly like me, she's a specific individual." Let's start with universal behaviors . . .

## Have them prep for conversations

Once you start looking for these scenes, you'll see them all the time. If they prep for a conversation, then you can either have the conversation go how they hoped, which we now know is a gratifying payoff (both for them and for us), or things can not go well, which is a way to ironically upset expectations (both theirs and ours).

Most stories have one hero, but Tolstoy wrote big sprawling sagas with tons of coequal heroes. Nevertheless, before most scenes, one and only one character gets a prep scene, to preestablish their specific intentions. That's the character we know to identify with in that scene.

Jason in *The Bourne Identity* is fished out of the sea with no memory and sails home on a fishing trawler, spending his time in the hold practicing introducing himself when he arrives. This bonds us to him and makes his insecurities real to us.

An example of setting up an ironic reversal: In *Mulan*, Shang practices for the speech he'll give his troops about how they're the pride of China, then steps out of his tent to find them in a massive brawl.

## Have them interrupt themselves when they talk

This is a matter of much debate among writers. Should characters speak in complete sentences? The fact is that people rarely do so in real life, but do readers actually want to read realistic dialogue? Do audiences want to hear it?

I'm sure we all enjoyed the Operation Varsity Blues scandal, where the rich and famous got arrested for various illegal schemes to get their kids into universities (hiring imposters to take their kids' SATs, faking learning disabilities to get more time on the test, photoshopping their heads onto athletes to get recruited, etc.). Well, they released accurate transcriptions of the wiretaps, and they're instructive for seeing how people actually talk.

In my own writing, I've often gotten pushback for how fragmentary my dialogue is, but I always defend it by saying that it's the way we really talk. Well, these strictly faithful transcriptions back me up nicely.

Here's one example:

> Spouse: *So [my son] and I just got back from [U]SC Orientation. It went great. The only kind of glitch was, and I—he didn't—[my son] didn't tell me this at the time—but yesterday when he went to meet with his advisor, he stayed after a little bit, and the— apparently the advisor said something to the effect of, "Oh, so you're a track athlete?" And [my son] said, "No."'Cause, so [my son] has no idea, and that's what—the way we want to keep it.*

Another conversation:

> B. Isackson: *Well, I, I—But if—but they, they—*

> CW-1: *Yes.*

> B. Isackson: *—went the meat and potatoes of it, which a—which a guy would love to have is, it's so hard for these kids to get into college, and here's—look what—look what's going on behind the schemes, and then, you know, the, the embarrassment to everyone in the communities. Oh my God, it would just be—Yeah. Ugh.*

People don't finish their sentences, they lose their train of thought, they rephrase things on the fly, they interrupt each other. These are all highly educated, successful people and every single one talks this way.

So should you write this way? As I said, producers and other note-givers have said I do it too much. It's realistic, but maybe too much so. If your characters are too articulate, injecting some of this realism into your dialogue will make it come alive and feel refreshingly real, but maybe don't take it as far as I did. The goal in writing is to create a sense of the real, but once you've done that you can make everyone a little more articulate than they would actually be.

Looking at the above transcript, you probably wouldn't want to write a sentence exactly like "and here's—look what—look what's going on behind the schemes, and then, you know, the, the embarrassment to everyone in the communities . . ." That's realistic in an annoying way.

But you might well want to write something like the next sentence: "Oh my God, it would just be—Yeah. Ugh." That's realistic in a more appealing way. Not finishing that sentence seems more meaningful than the stumbles in the previous sentence.

Let's look at a great example from fiction. As in some of the examples above, characters can reveal a lot by *where* they interrupt themselves.

In the first scene of *The Hobbit*, Gandalf the wizard visits Bilbo the hobbit for the first time in many years. They discuss the fact that Gandalf used to take hobbits on adventures. Bilbo is torn between his desire for respectability and his repressed desire for adventure. He reveals this by saying to Gandalf: "Bless me, life used to be quite inter—I mean, you used to upset things badly in these parts once upon a time." He starts to say what he means, then corrects himself halfway through to say what he knows he *should* say. We all do this. It's a great way to reveal character.

In Part II, we'll look at an example where a hero interrupts herself constantly in her own *interior* monologue, but no spoilers!

## Have them use language or do things we only know from real life

Prose writers can easily describe tastes or smells that the audience hasn't experienced since childhood. Dramatic writers need to have someone awkwardly describe them out loud. But all sorts of writers can use language the reader hasn't heard in a million years, which will instantly make this feel like real life and not a made-up story.

In the first scene of the pilot of *Community*, the dean loses one of the index cards he's reading from, accidentally turning his rah-rah speech into a harsh put-down. When he realizes this, he gets embarrassed and asks everyone to help him look for the missing card, saying, "Can we all look around our immediate areas?" As surely as if I'd eaten Proust's madeleine, I flashed back to hearing this phrase many times as a child, but I hadn't heard it since.

And any type of writer can provide visuals that we haven't seen since we were kids: The schoolgirls in *An Education* use the sides of their fists to make baby feet on a rainy window, then dot in the toes with a fingertip. I certainly remember doing that in school, but I'd never seen it onscreen before and it made me smile.

Whenever you hear or recall something from your youth that hasn't been done to death by other writers, jot it down and cherish it. Look for ways to reopen doors in your reader's mind.

## Don't let them say what they wouldn't say

You've created your characters and now you can't wait to tell your audience who they are. The easiest way to do that is to have them introduce themselves to the audience, right? The problem is that certain types of characters don't like to introduce themselves. Sometimes, what they don't say speaks volumes.

In the *Sopranos* pilot, Dr. Melfi asks Tony Soprano what he does for a living. He says, "Waste management consultant," then helpfully adds with a little smile and shrug: "The environment." If you write it well, we'll hear the truth through the lie, and we'll believe in the reality of the character more because he was coy.

In *The Bourne Identity*, the head of the evil CIA program wants to find out what his subordinate Conklin has been up to, but Conklin is hardwired to avoid discussing what he's doing, even with his boss. Finally he says, "You're asking me a direct question? I thought you were never going to do that."

Nick in *The Great Gatsby*, like a lot of Ivy League graduates, avoids saying the name of his school, supposedly out of humility, but it always just calls attention to it: "I graduated from New Haven in 1915."

## Write non-written dialogue

One of the most dreaded notes that a dialogue writer can get is "This feels written." We speak differently from how we compose on the page, and writers should keep that in mind when writing dialogue. How is off-the-cuff dialogue different from an essay that someone would compose?

In the pilot of *The Good Place*, Eleanor wakes up to find herself in a cheery waiting room, then is brought into an office for a meeting. The man inside makes polite conversation with her for a while, but she gets confused, and says, "Oh, one question: Where am I, who are you, and what's going on?"

Obviously, if you're writing that, you're going to go back and change that to "three questions," but when someone is speaking, the words just tumble out, and you can't go back and revise. Writing it this way makes it feel non-written.

Another rule for good prose is that you're supposed to avoid using the same word twice in the same sentence. Later in the *Good Place* pilot, Eleanor is telling her soul mate Chidi about her life: "Well, I was born in Phoenix, Arizona, I went to school in Tempe, Arizona, and then I moved back to Phoenix, Arizona." That's a mundane life story reported in a believably mundane way. Real life is mundane.

Likewise, slipping between past and present tense is terrible in prose, but good in dialogue. In *The Big Short*, Mark is talking about an encounter he had at lunch: "And you know what he did? He laughed. He just walks out of the lunch, doesn't say a word." That subconsciously sounds like reality to us, because that's how we really talk, though we would never write it down that way. If we were writing it down, we'd make the tenses agree.

Children's dialogue should always feel non-written. In a Humans of New York photo-story, photographer/interviewer Brandon Stanton talks to little girls and attaches this quote to their picture: "Sometimes we play a game called Bracelets. You put pillows on the ground, sit on them, then play with bracelets."

Okay, once you've established some universal behavior, it's time to get specific.

## A Specific Personality

You need to balance their universal behavior with unique things that only this character would do. This must be an individual. On the one hand, we've all had the experience of seeing someone else do something we thought only we did, and saying, "Oh, good, I'm not the only one." On the other hand, we've all had that dreaded moment of realizing, "Oh crap, I'm the only one, aren't I?"

So how do you establish that this character is a unique

individual? We've got lots of suggestions to go under personality, starting with . . .

## A Way of Talking

Go through your texts and you'll hear your friends talking as you read each one, because they all have different voices. This is even more true of fictional characters, who should always "pop" a little more than people in real life.

We'll start with three that may be familiar, but I'll provide new twists and examples:

### Give them a unique metaphor family

This is the aspect of your characters' lives that determines which metaphors, curses, and exclamations they use. The source of this is usually their job, their home region, or their psychological state.

Sometimes metaphor families can hint at a hidden trait. Obi-Wan Kenobi in *Star Wars* seems like a kindly old monk, but his metaphor family is militaristic:

- One of his first lines could come out of the mouth of Patton: "Quickly. They're on the move."

- When he gives Luke an emblem of his religion, he gives him, of all things, a laser-sword, and he praises it by pointing out that it has superior target accuracy to a laser-gun: "This is the weapon of a Jedi Knight. Not as clumsy or as random as a blaster."

- Later his concern with weapon accuracy continues: "Sand People always ride single file to hide their numbers. And these blast points, too accurate for Sand People. Only Imperial stormtroopers are so precise."

- And there's plenty more general-speak: "But it also obeys your commands." "In my experience, there's no such thing as luck." "No, it's a short-range fighter."

It's not just a matter of his knowledge set; his word choice is inherently militaristic, referring to their "numbers," "blast points," etc.

This isn't to say that Obi-Wan isn't a spiritual character, he clearly is, but if the spiritual wisdom he dispensed was accompanied by a more new age–y metaphor family (which would be the default choice) then we would be more likely to see him as a hoary old stock character. Giving him a metaphor family that speaks to his suppressed former life enriches the character and makes his wisdom seem much more powerful, because it's clearly hard-won.

It's also telling when a character shifts their metaphor family based on the situation. The heroes of both *Get Out* and *Black-ish* are shuttling between all-white and all-Black worlds, and talk differently in each, though it annoys them that they have to do so. They're code-switching.

Dre in the *Black-ish* pilot has to put up with white coworkers at his advertising firm asking him, "How would a Black guy say 'good morning'?" With exasperation, he answers, "Just like that," but later he acts equally exasperated with his family for speaking in a deracialized way at home. They've been trained by their mostly white private school to avoid mentioning race, but he has no patience for that.

### Give them a default personality trait

Characters grow and change throughout a story, and their moods can fluctuate wildly, even within each scene, but whether they're happy or sad or regressed or enlightened, they'll still have some aspects of their personalities that never change.

You can certainly see this in the Marvel movies.

Tony in *Iron Man* completely changes his beliefs. He starts out saying to a reporter, "My old man had a philosophy: Peace means having a bigger stick than the other guy." By the end, he's had a big turnaround. He says to his love interest, Pepper, "I'm going to find my weapons and destroy them. I'm not crazy, Pepper, I just finally know what I have to do, and I know in my heart that it's right."

Nevertheless, his default personality trait *never* changes. When he's a self-serving arms dealer, he acts like a cocky asshole. When he completely abandons arms dealing to become a heroic crusader, he *still* acts like a cocky asshole.

Steve Rogers is told before he transforms into Captain America that they're being careful to reserve the process for someone pure of heart, because the process will only magnify the basic personality of the subject. That's true of all the transformations in Marvel movies.

In the case of *Dr. Strange*, this is a big difference between the comics and the movie: In the comics, when jackass hotshot surgeon Dr. Stephen Strange goes through enlightenment in Tibet, he comes home totally transformed, *including* his personality. He's no longer a jerk at all. But in the movies, perhaps because they feel they can't transform a hero too much over the course of a two-hour movie, he's still pretty jerky after his life-changing encounters. He's a much better person, but his default personality trait shows through.

Now let's get to my favorite moment of personality in this whole book.

In *Thor*, the titular hero is greatly humbled and humiliated by being sent down to Earth without his super-strength or his weapon. For the first time in his life, he is feeling relatively weak and vulnerable when his new human friends take him to a diner.

Nevertheless, when he tries coffee for the first time, he likes it, so he throws his mug down on the floor, shattering it into a dozen pieces, and joyously shouts, "Another!" Clearly, he can only change so much.

### Give them a default argument tactic

Characters should also have hardwired approaches to problem-solving that they keep going back to, no matter how much smarter they get over the course of solving this problem.

In the opening of *Born a Crime*, Trevor Noah recounts how his mother would drag him to three different church services all over town every Sunday. One day, the car won't start, and his mother begins to be discouraged:

> *"It's the Devil," she said about the stalled car. "The Devil doesn't want us to go to church. That's why we've got to catch minibuses."*

> *Whenever I found myself up against my mother's faith-based obstinacy, I would try, as respectfully as possible, to counter with an opposing point of view.*

> *"Or," I said, "the Lord knows that today we shouldn't go to church, which is why he made sure the car wouldn't start, so that we stay at home as a family and take a day of rest, because even the Lord rested."*

> *"Ah, that's the Devil talking, Trevor."*

> *"No, because Jesus is in control, and if Jesus is in control and we pray to Jesus, he would let the car start, but he hasn't, therefore—"*

> *"No, Trevor! Sometimes Jesus puts obstacles in your way to see if you overcome them. Like Job. This could be a test."*

*"Ah! Yes, Mom. But the test could be to see if we're willing to accept what has happened and stay at home and praise Jesus for his wisdom."*

*"No. That's the Devil talking. Now go change your clothes."*

This snarky, legalistic argument tactic will serve Trevor well throughout the memoir, and throughout his life, as anyone who has seen his quick-witted hosting of *The Daily Show* can attest.

### Give them unique syntax

A character's syntax is the quickest and surest way to define their voice. Everyone you know speaks slightly differently, and each voice you write in should be different as well.

The easiest way to give someone unique syntax, of course, is to base it on their culture. Vladek in *Maus* pops right away: "It would take many books, my life, and no one wants anyway to hear such stories." We can hear him say that. His son is assimilated, and speaks with a less unique syntax, but we can still hear his voice, too (partially just because of the italics): "*Please*, pop! I'd rather not hear all that *again*."

When I read novels aloud to my kids, my eye has to jump all over the page. I do different voices for every character, so I have to jump ahead and see who's talking before I open my mouth. This is especially a problem when a piece of dialogue is at the end of one page, then I have to flip the page to find out who's talking. But in well-written novels, I *don't* have to flip ahead, because every character talks differently, and it's obvious from the syntax who is speaking before I flip the page. In the entire Harry Potter series, I don't think there's a single line that Ron and Hermione would phrase in exactly the same way. I always know just from reading the sentences who's speaking.

Of course, for prose writers, it's not just dialogue. *Every* sentence needs to have a voice (even if you're writing in third person).

The most frustrating note for an aspiring novelist to get is, "I think you have issues with voice." Geez, can't you let me just tell the story? Does everything have to have a 'voice'? Mastering voice is tremendously tricky, but once you finally find a unique voice for the character, readers will love them so much more. You want them to say, "I just love to be in this guy's head, seeing the world from his unique point of view."

Whether you're writing description or dialogue, the easiest way to differentiate two characters' syntaxes is the use of commas vs. periods. The more periods, the terser and more badass they sound. Here's the first paragraph of Lee Child's *Killing Floor*, the book that introduced Jack Reacher:

> *I was arrested in Eno's diner. At twelve o'clock. I was eating eggs and drinking coffee. A late breakfast, not lunch. I was wet and tired after a long walk in heavy rain. All the way from the highway to the edge of town.*

We instantly understand Reacher's personality, just from those beautiful periods.

Lots of modern novels have multiple first-person narrators, but writers often do it poorly. Different narrators tell us about different events, but they all do so in the same voice. *Gone Girl* is a notable exception. The first chapter is from Nick's point of view. Nick's a creep, and we start with this wonderfully creepy paragraph, showing the way he looks at the world:

> *When I think of my wife, I always think of her head. The shape of it, to begin with. The very first time I saw her, it was the back of the*

*head I saw, and there was something lovely about it, the angles of it.*
*Like a shiny, hard corn kernel or a riverbed fossil. She had what the*
*Victorians would call a* finely shaped head. *You could imagine*
*the skull quite easily.*

Then the next chapter is from his wife's point of view. This
is how it starts:

*Tra and la! I am smiling a big adopted-orphan smile as I write this.*
*I am embarrassed at how happy I am, like some Technicolor comic*
*of a teenage girl talking on the phone with my hair in a ponytail, the*
*bubble above my head saying:* I met a *boy!*

Her voice could not be more different from his. She has a
totally different personality and it results in a totally different
syntax.
That brings us to their . . .

## Unique Backstory

As I said in my last book, just because your hero has baggage
doesn't mean they have to take it out of the overhead bin during
the flight. Often you want to know more than you show. But if
there's something noteworthy or unexpected about their backstory, then by all means let us know.

### Give them an oddly specific backstory

Most characters will have a backstory that's about what we expect (your cop may come from a family of cops), so there's no
need to tell us that. But you can sometimes make a character
come to life by giving them an oddly specific backstory that feels
true to life.

Annie in *Bridesmaids* gets in trouble at work, and her boss says, "The whole reason you have this job is because your mom's my sponsor in AA and I'm doing you a favor." That feels like an oddly real backstory (and one that's supposed to remain confidential, which makes it even more surprising).

*Mean Girls* is based on a nonfiction work of sociology about hierarchies in modern high schools. Screenwriter Tina Fey figured that the best way to show this was to have a girl entering a school with no previous social skills. So she created a heroine with an oddly specific backstory: Cady has been homeschooled by her anthropologist parents in Africa until age sixteen.

(Of course, as an example of a mean high school, Fey chose the huge public high school in Evanston, Illinois. That's where I live, so my kids will soon be going there. So yay!)

Sometimes their unique backstory gives them a distinct way of talking. Brody in *Jaws* is unlike most sheriffs of New England beach towns: He used to be an NYPD cop (one can imagine he's the same character Roy Scheider played in *The French Connection*). He and his wife, Ellen, wake up in their new house on a New England beach island and hear the kids outside, so Brody looks out the window.

Ellen: *Can you see the kids?*

Brody: *They must be in the backyard.*

Ellen: *In Amity, you say "yahd."*

Brody: *They're in the yahd, not too fah from the cah. How's that?*

Ellen: *Like you're from New York.*

### Give them a legacy, not a prophecy

It's the word I hate the most in all of fiction: prophecy. Prophecies are the laziest form of writing: foreshadowing without any shadows.

I got a horrible sinking feeling at the end of the fifth Harry Potter book when the prophecy was revealed. I at least had some vague hopes that it was a fake out, but, alas, it wasn't. It would have been wonderfully ironic if we found out at the end of book seven that the prophecy was about Neville after all, but alas, it was about Harry, just as it appeared.

Even when the ultimate point is that prophecies are a bad idea, as in the *Star Wars* prequels, they're still coldly alienating to an audience: That usually just means that it comes true in an ironic way, which still implies a predestined universe. We want our heroes to have free agency, to choose to be great, and earn their place in our hearts, without a prophecy telling us (or them) how special they are.

As James Kennedy pointed out in a guest post on my blog: "Aunt Beru says, 'Luke's not a farmer, Owen. He has too much of his father in him,' and Uncle Owen responds, 'That's what I'm afraid of.' Now we're truly intrigued by Luke—there's more to Luke than even Luke knows, and the key to it all is his father! So we're subtly prepped for when Ben Kenobi starts talking about Luke's father: Whatever Ben says about Luke's father (great star pilot, Jedi knight, cunning warrior) is something that is potentially true about Luke. Aunt Beru has promised it in this scene! She's planted the seed here!"

All the way from *Oedipus* to *Wonder Woman*, the secret of the hidden birth has been a beloved third-quarter twist. Of course, the even bigger reveal in *The Empire Strikes Back* will up the stakes for Luke, but even this first movie has a smaller version of the revelation: Luke finds out that his dad was a great Jedi.

A belatedly revealed legacy is the smart version of a prophecy. On the one hand, if you believe in nature over nurture, then you'll feel that you can inherit the qualities and/or abilities of your dad, even if you've never met him . . . but even if you believe strictly in nurture, a secret-dad reveal can still have a powerful psychological effect on a person, because we all have limiters in our head saying "A person like me can't aim that high." Finding out about great accomplishments in your family makes you think, "Hey, why shouldn't I be able to do the same thing?"

Luke just scoffs when Threepio calls him "Sir Luke," but once he finds out more about his father from Obi-Wan, he begins to change his way of thinking: "Hey, maybe a guy like me can be a knight . . ."

Sometimes, a hero has two conflicting legacies. In *The Hobbit*, Bilbo's mother was from the adventurous Took family, but his father was one of the unadventurous Bagginses. When Gandalf comes to Bilbo offering an adventure, he rejects it like a good Baggins, but then he finds that Gandalf has had an unexpected effect on him:

> *Then something Tookish woke up inside him, and he wished to go and see the great mountains, and hear the pine-trees and the waterfalls, and explore the caves, and wear a sword instead of a walking-stick.*

There is no prophecy saying that Bilbo will help the dwarves recover their kingdom, but there is the legacy of the Tooks prodding him toward this adventure.

Sometimes their legacy conflicts with their life goals, and the hero must choose between them. Dean in the *Supernatural* pilot is about to have his big law school interview when he reluctantly gets sucked back into the family demon-hunting business. By the end of the pilot, he's permanently abandoned his personal goals in favor of fulfilling his legacy.

And sometimes, the hero's challenge is to defy his legacy. James Baldwin's *Go Tell It on the Mountain* begins the morning that John decides to break free: "Everyone had always said that John would be a preacher when he grew up, just like his father. It had been said so often that John, without ever thinking about it, had come to believe it himself. Not until the morning of his fourteenth birthday did he really begin to think about it."

He fears it's too late, but he finds the inner strength he needs to stand up for himself: "The darkness of his sin was in the hardheartedness with which he resisted God's power; in the scorn that was often his while he listened to the crying, breaking voices, and watched the black skin glisten while they lifted up their arms and fell on their faces before the Lord. For he had made his decision. He would not be like his father, or his father's fathers. He would have another life."

This next section is one that I had under Care in my last book, but I've decided it's really part of Believe:

## Flaw

Once again, we'll start with some tools that may be familiar, but they'll include new examples.

### Give them a great flaw

The idea that a hero needs a great flaw is as old as Aristotle, and probably much older. Often the hero will begin a story aware of a longstanding external personal problem, but they'll be unaware of the internal flaw that is the real issue. The events of the story eventually force the hero to admit the truth: They can't make real progress as a person until they admit that the real source of their trouble is their own flaw, and they must overcome it in order to triumph.

As I've said before, the great flaw is often the ironic flip side of a great strength. You don't want a situation where abandoning a flaw is a no-brainer. It's better to give them a flaw that's hard to abandon, without losing a little something.

Harriet the Spy's big flaw is her cruelty, but that's the ironic flip side of her strength, which is her incisiveness. We want her to be less cruel, and we can see how it's ruining her life, but we love her sharp eye for the hidden realities of the world around her. We want her to find a way to become a writer without being so hurtful to others.

Riggan in *Birdman* is crippled with doubts, but his perfectionism is also his strength. He cares about the quality of his play, but he's willing to harm others to perfect it, which goes too far. We admire his tenacity, but we can see that it's out of control.

In *Toy Story*, Woody's strength is that he's an effective leader, but his flaw is that he's selfish about holding on to power. Eventually, as it gradually becomes obvious that he will do anything to keep his place, even harming Buzz Lightyear, his followers turn on him. Getting Buzz out of the way clears away the competition, but Woody loses everyone's respect along the way.

### Give them a shortsighted goal and philosophy

Some gurus say a hero should give a correct statement of philosophy on page five, but I say that, if a hero has a statement of philosophy at that point, it should almost always be false, and accompanied by a false goal.

Jeff in *Community* is a manipulative cheater who's coasted on his lies and can't cope with real adversity. For the time being he doesn't intend to change: "If I'd wanted to learn something, I wouldn't have come to community college." As it will turn out, he will learn quite a lot in the years he spends there.

George Bailey in *It's a Wonderful Life* says, "I'm going out exploring someday. You watch. And I'm gonna have a couple harems, and maybe three or four wives! Wait and see!" It will turn out he's needed at home, both as a town father and a good husband (to just one wife).

Let's look at cases where the hero has two statements of philosophy to choose between.

Thor announces his philosophy early: "When I'm king, I'll hunt the giants down and slay them all." But then at his coronation, he's forced to vow otherwise: "Do you swear to cast aside all selfish ambition?" The movie becomes a contest between the two visions.

Max in *Rushmore* also has two statements of philosophy to choose between. At the beginning, he's told that he'll be expelled from his beloved private school if he doesn't make better grades. Max reports this to his friend Mason, who asks, "What are you going to do?" Max responds, "The only thing I *can* do: try to pull some strings with the administration." If you define that as his philosophy then it's clearly false, and gets totally replaced with an ethic of hard work by the movie's end.

But along the way, Max gets another statement of philosophy, which also describes his life so far, but this is a version of his personal philosophy that he *doesn't* abandon. Max finds a mysterious notation in a library book: "When one man, for whatever reason, has the opportunity to lead an extraordinary life, he has no right to keep it to himself." He will come to realize that it's wrong to try to pull some strings with the administration. His goals will greatly change, but one thing won't change: He'll still feel that extraordinary people have no right to keep it to themselves. At his new school, he will mount a play just as ludicrously overambitious as the ones he mounted at Rushmore.

## Make them tone-deaf

In real life, tone-deafness is somewhat annoying, but we like it in stories, because it shows that our heroes are defiantly who they are. Their personality is too strong to be overwhelmed by the tone of the room. Who they are always shines through.

Peter Parker in *Spider-Man* is dropping science facts while on a school field trip, but his friend Harry is unimpressed. Harry rolls his eyes and asks, "Peter, what would make you think I would want to know that?" Peter perkily responds, "Who wouldn't?"

In the *Master of None* pilot, Dev attends the first birthday party of his friend Grant's son. Grant tells Dev how wonderful it is being a parent. But after the party, Dev returns to the house and asks to use the bathroom. While Grant shows him where to go, Dev ends up getting the full story he didn't get at the party. He presses Grant to tell him more about being a father:

Dev: *How do you do it? What's your secret?*

Grant: *My secret is, I'm getting a divorce.*

Dev: *What? Are you serious?*

Grant: *We've just been dealing with some issues lately. We tried to figure it out. I don't think it's gonna work.*

Dev: *I thought everything was going really well. What about all that stuff you said earlier?*

Grant: *Oh, come on, man. That's bullshit you say at a party. What am I supposed to say? I don't sleep. I haven't fucked in a year. I never see my friends. I hate my wife. God.*

Dev: *Yeah, I guess that's not really good party . . . What's the word? Party . . . fodder.*

Grant: *Fodder, yeah. It's tough, man. We'd only been dating six months. Brenda got pregnant, and we really thought we could pull it off. It started off okay, but then things got a little rocky. It was just too soon. And then you throw a kid in the mix . . . And Zach's awesome. We couldn't love him any more, but it just wasn't enough to keep us together. Anyway, here's the bathroom.*

Dev: *All right. [sighs] Man, it smells really nice in there. You got to hit me with the deets on that candle. [Off his depressed look] Sorry.*

Grant: *[Sighs, but must admit] It is a great candle.*

Dev is an aesthete. He cares more about sensory input than human emotions. At the end of the episode, he chooses to eat a gourmet sandwich instead of the adorable ketchup sandwich a child has made for him. Here, he can't resist complimenting a good-smelling candle even though it's not exactly an appropriate time.

Dev's personality is irrepressible, even when he really should repress it. That makes for a well-characterized hero.

### Give them odd logic

Every character should not just *speak* in a unique way, but *think* in a unique way. We like to see their brain firing, but occasionally, if they're going to seem alive to us, we want to see it *mis*firing.

*The God of Small Things* seems utterly real to us because of the way it intimately captures the crazy logic of childhood. Our own childhoods may not have been as traumatic as Rahel's, but Roy captures with startling intimacy the way a seven-year-old thinks. To read the book is to feel like a child again, not in an aw-shucks kind of way, but in an "Oh, right, childhood was *weird*" kind of way.

Rahel is convinced of odd things by her twin brother Estha:

> *According to Estha, if they'd been born on the bus, they'd have got free bus rides for the rest of their lives. It wasn't clear where he'd got this information from, or how he knew these things, but for years the twins harbored a faint resentment against their parents for having diddled them out of a lifetime of free bus rides.*

She's also convinced that the government pays for your funeral if you die in a crosswalk. That's harmless enough . . . but then we find out she's sure that her dead friend Sophie is still alive in her coffin when it gets buried, which is less so:

> *Inside the earth Sophie Mol screamed, and shredded satin with her teeth. But you can't hear screams through earth and stone. Sophie Mol died because she couldn't breathe.*

Likewise, in *Born a Crime*, Noah remembers his child logic:

> *At black church I would sit there for what felt like an eternity, trying to figure out why time moved so slowly. Is it possible for time to actually stop? If so, why does it stop at black church and not at white*

*church? I eventually decided black people needed more time with Jesus because we suffered more.*

But of course it's not just kids that have odd logic. Tony in *The Sopranos* must deal with the fact that his mother, Livia, won't answer the phone when it's dark outside.

Livia: *Somebody called here last night. After dark!*

Tony: *Who?*

Livia: *You think I'd answer?? It was dark out!*

Tony tries to explain why that makes no sense, but she just says, "Oh listen to him, he knows everything."

Esperanza in *The House on Mango Street* has odd child logic ("If you count the white flecks on your fingernails you can know how many boys are thinking of you"), but some of the adults she knows have even more extreme beliefs: "She's a witch woman and knows many things. If you got a headache, rub a cold egg across your face. Need to forget an old romance? Take a chicken's foot, tie it with red string, spin it over your head three times, then burn it. Bad spirits keeping you awake? Sleep next to a holy candle for seven days, then on the eighth day, spit. And lots of other stuff."

### Let their brains get away from them

We like to hear things go off the rails. Sometimes our brains veer in certain directions on the slightest bidding, even if we don't want them to . . . even if it's essential to the task at hand that we *not* do this.

Ted in the *How I Met Your Mother* pilot is trying to pick up a girl in a bar, so the last thing he should do is talk about how desperate he is to get married, but he can't help himself.

Before long, the girl he's hitting on is asking, "So do you think you'll ever get married?" Ted replies, "Well maybe eventually . . . some fall day, possibly in Central Park, a simple ceremony, we'll write our own vows, band, no DJ, people will dance, I'm not going to worry about it . . ."

Needless to say, he doesn't get her number.

Claire in the *Modern Family* pilot has to deal with the fact that her fifteen-year-old daughter has a boy over for the first time, and wants to keep her door closed. Claire decides this is a good time to take some laundry into the room, and finds them sitting on a bed together, watching TV. In cautioning them, she accidentally reveals too much about her own backstory: "I have, uh, seen this little show before: Lying on the bed with a tall senior. One minute you're just friends, watching *Falcon Crest*, and the next you're lying underneath the air hockey table with your bra in your pocket." She's revealed a little too much.

Of course, this is a great time to use subtext: As their mouth runs away with them, we realize they're talking about something else entirely. Issa in the *Insecure* pilot works at a nonprofit that helps Black kids, but one of the many reasons she feels insecure is that she's the only Black person who works there. Even worse, her tumultuous personal life is intruding on her job. These both come to a head when she tries to speak up for the children, and ends up revealing too much about herself: "I think these kids need permission to explore on their own. Nothing's gonna change for these kids if they're stuck in the same shitty place. They need to know that there's more out there for them." She then realizes she's actually confessing her own needs.

That brings us to the next part of Personality we'll look at . . .

## Secrets

There are lots of types of secrets a hero can keep, and the more the better. Let's start with some classics . . .

### Give them a public identity and a private self

Our public identity is how the world sees us. Our private self is how we see ourselves.

The world defines us one way, and we define ourselves differently. These are two essential aspects of character, and the bigger the gap between the two, the more meaningful the story will be.

When Joe in *Soul* is given a full-time teaching job, everybody is really happy for him, but we can see that this is the last thing in the world he wants. He doesn't want to be in an "inspirational teacher" story, he wants to be in a "jazz virtuoso in a smoky club" story.

Sometimes we live in fear of our private self coming out: In Don DeLillo's absurd *White Noise*, Jack Gladney has carved out his own little piece of fame: "I am chairman of the department of Hitler studies at the College-on-the-Hill. I invented Hitler studies in North America in March of 1968. It was a cold bright day with intermittent winds out of the east. When I suggested to the chancellor that we might build a whole department around Hitler's life and work, he was quick to see the possibilities. It was an immediate and electrifying success." But we later find out Jack's got a big secret: He's secretly taking, and failing, German classes. "I had long tried to conceal the fact that I did not know German. I could not speak or read it, could not understand the spoken word or begin to put the simplest sentence on paper. The least of my Hitler colleagues knew some German; others were either fluent in the language or reasonably conversant. No one could major in Hitler studies at the College-on-the-Hill without a minimum of one year of German. I was living, in short, on the edge of a landscape of vast shame."

In the opening chapter of *The Firm*, Mitch McDeere is walking a tightrope. He's trying to convince the partners of a ridiculously high-paying law firm that he'll fit in there. For the most part, he's been unable to keep his dirt-poor past a secret. They already know that his father died in a mining accident, that his mother married again and found herself in an abusive marriage, and that one of his brothers died in Vietnam. But he's determined to keep one last secret: that his other brother is in prison. In the end, when he comes to realize his new bosses are the real crooks, his brother will become an ally and he'll be glad he kept that secret.

Sometimes, heroes get to prove how brave they are by allowing their long-suppressed private self to come out. Sixty-nine-year-old Maura in the *Transparent* pilot is absolutely terrified of telling the world she's transgender, but she's begun to overcome her fear. She tells an LGBT support group:

> *"I went to Target, and I just, I 'took her out,' you know what I mean, and I got into, y'know, the checkout line, and the girl at the cash register said, 'I need to see some ID with that credit card of yours,' and um, you know what that's like, right, and I just knew, 'this is gonna not be good, this is gonna get ugly,' and so she just kept looking at me . . . and then she said, '. . . oh.' Like that, y'know? And she rung up the um, batteries or something. That was . . . That was a big victory. And I was like 'do not cry in front of this woman, do not cry in front of this woman.'"*

### Give them an open fear and a hidden fear

This is another way to contrast the face they show to the world and their private self. When asked, we'll tell the world about certain fears and anxieties, but we also have deeper fears and anxieties we keep to ourselves. Sometimes, we won't even admit them to ourselves, but they're always waiting there.

Jason Bourne's open fear is that he'll be killed or captured. His private fear is that he'll discover he's not a good person. All he wants at first is to find out who he is, but after he begins to figure it out, he says to his love interest: "I don't want to know who I am anymore."

Miles in *Sideways* openly fears that no one will read his novel. (He asks Jack if he's read his latest draft and Jack says he has. Miles then asks, "Did you like the new ending?" and Jack says yes. Miles snorts, "Everything after page 750 is exactly the same.") He privately fears that his novel isn't any good.

Brody in *Jaws* has an open fear of being disrespected by his new town, but he also has a private fear that might cost him his job if anybody found out: He's afraid of the water.

### Let them play their cards close to the chest

Frequently I'll watch or read something and think, "Why didn't this character come alive for me?" Then I'll realize the answer: The character had no *secrets*. We *all* have secrets. The more secrets a character has, the more compelling they will be.

In *Casablanca*, Vichy-France police chief Renault asks café owner Rick:

Renault: *Why did you come to Casablanca, Rick?*

Rick: *I came for the waters.*

Renault: *But we're in the middle of a desert.*

Rick: *I was misinformed.*

Sometimes, when the story starts, we find out the hero is keeping a secret from the other characters *and* from us. Gradually, *we* learn the secret, but the other characters don't for a while longer. We will eventually find out Rick's past, but Renault never will, despite the fact that they "end up" together. Rick plays his cards close to the chest.

In *Harriet the Spy*, we gradually realize that Harriet has a secret life, and we get glimpses of it. By the end of the first ten pages, we're mostly up to speed, and now *only* we are in on Harriet's secret. Only later does it get revealed to the world, in a disastrous fashion.

In *Silence of the Lambs*, Clarice is ashamed of her poor, unsophisticated, small-town past and she's hiding it from everybody. We just get glimpses of it as we jump into her head for little enigmatic flashbacks. Eventually, Lecter will force the whole story out of her.

Sometimes, heroes feel they must nobly keep secrets to help their community. Nobody is sitting on a bigger secret than T'Challa in *Black Panther*: He's keeping a whole space-age kingdom a secret behind a holographic forest. His secret makes it possible for his people to have a wonderful standard of living, but eventually he realizes that it's time to drop the hologram and share their prosperity with the world.

Sometimes our first-person narrator is keeping secrets from us, in a way that makes us eager to read the rest of the novel. The hero of Ralph Ellison's *Invisible Man* is coyly hiding secrets from us that he promises to reveal later: "I live rent-free in a building rented strictly to whites, in a section of the basement that was shut off and forgotten during the nineteenth century, which I discovered when I was trying to escape in the night from Ras the Destroyer. But that's getting too far ahead of the story." We are propelled forward into this fascinating novel by the tease of what's to come.

Okay, the next aspect of personality is . . .

## Assertiveness

We've looked at ways in which a hero's individuality can assert itself unintentionally, but eventually the hero must *choose* to reveal some piece of themselves to the world. We like heroes who let others know that they're different, whether boldly or mildly.

### Give them bursts of personality (or just flashes)

Some heroes have big personalities, and we love that. One of Bart's first lines in the *Simpsons* pilot is "I'm Bart Simpson, who the hell are you?" Levee begins *Ma Rainey's Black Bottom* by checking out two girls walking by and saying "Hey, hey! Good morning, Chicago!" It's easy to love a character with a lot of character.

But heroes with small personalities can work, too, as long as they offer *flashes* of personality.

In *The Babadook*, the heroine gives selflessly to her son and the patients at the nursing home where she works. But of course, the danger with selfless characters is that they can also be self-less, lacking enough personality to make them come alive for us. Thankfully she does have little flashes of personality that break through her self-sacrificing façade. When she's running a bingo game for the residents, she realizes that nobody is really paying attention. To amuse herself, she starts calling out absurd numbers: "Five billion, anyone got five billion?" She only stops when her supervisor gives her a disapproving look.

Without that flash of personality, we couldn't identify with this self-less character. She's got to get a bit of a chance to make fun of the residents, though she clearly loves them.

## Let them be odd

We've already talked a lot about oddness, but let's get to the heart of it. Characters can be oddly specific in lots of ways, but they can also just be *odd*. Deep down we all have the same secret: that we are so much weirder on the inside than we appear on the outside.

We'll look at an example in Part II from *Blue Velvet*. For now, let's look at an example with the same actor and director, but a very different character: Agent Cooper in *Twin Peaks* has the strength of being a gung-ho FBI agent, but he's got the flaw of being overenthusiastic about *everything*, in a disturbing way. He and the local sheriff are discussing a dead girl, when suddenly he gets a big smile on his face and asks, "Sheriff, what kind of fantastic *trees* have you got growing around here?"

## Give them stubbornness

There will be tremendous forces trying to budge your hero, but ultimately they will find a place from which they cannot be moved, and that will define them.

Moana's grandmother sings, "You are your father's daughter / Stubbornness and pride / Mind what he says, but remember / You may hear a voice inside / And if the voice starts to whisper / To follow the farthest star / Moana that voice inside is *who you are*." To a certain extent, that should be true of every hero.

Make your heroes reluctant to change. The challenge they'll face in this story will ultimately transform them, but they should resist that change as much as possible.

In *Manchester by the Sea*, Patrick is dealing with the recent death of his father. With no one to look after him, his father's hapless estranged brother Lee is brought in, but finds that taking care of a teenager is a hard job. Patrick isn't as reckless as some teenagers, but he does have his stubbornness. Lee is horrified to realize that Patrick has two girlfriends who don't know about each other. He assumed that Patrick would want to get his life together in the wake of this tragedy, but Patrick has no such intention. He's not going to dump one of his two girlfriends just because his dad died. He's stubborn.

## Let them relabel themselves

People like to relabel themselves. You see your characters as types, but they see themselves as individuals. *Nobody* wants to be seen as a type. In film school, when talking to visiting directors I sometimes made the mistake of mentioning what type of film-maker I considered them to be. They always bristled, and I had to remind myself to never do that. They wanted their new work to be unburdened by previous expectations.

On one level, *Do the Right Thing* is all *about* types, as in, "These are the types of people you see on an average Brooklyn street on an average summer day." That's a fine way to write. It's okay for *you* to see them as types, as long as you allow *them* to reject those labels in the dialogue.

On the excellent Criterion Collection DVD, there's a lot of video of writer/director Spike Lee's extensive rehearsal/workshop process and you can see him adjust the script to address the concerns of the actors, who were all invited to personalize their roles.

This leads to a wonderfully ironic moment, when Lee is rehearsing a scene with actors Danny Aiello (Sal) and Giancarlo Esposito (Buggin' Out). Sal is refusing to put any pictures of Black people on the walls of his pizzeria. Lee notices something: In the script, Sal insists, "Only Italian-Americans on the wall," but Aiello has changed it to "Only American-Italians on the wall."

Lee instantly sees that this is better, and points out to Esposito that his mocking response should also change to mirror Aiello. They change Buggin' Out's line to: "Well, I don't see any 'American-Italians' eating here!"

As Esposito is making the change in his script, Aiello explains that that's the way he says it, because he visited Italy and decided that he was more proud of being American than Italian. At this point, Esposito gingerly points out that he himself is in fact, unlike Aiello, Italian-born. Aiello is of course totally embarrassed, but Esposito chuckles and says it's no big deal.

Let your characters relabel themselves. Let them describe themselves in unique ways, so that their language will come alive. Let almost everything they say be specific to them and their particular worldview. Give them a chance to punch through the boxes you put them in.

Esperanza in *The House on Mango Street* talks about her desire to rename herself: "In English my name means hope. In Spanish it means too many letters. It means sadness, it means waiting. It is like the number nine. A muddy color. It is the Mexican records my father plays on Sunday mornings when he is shaving, songs like sobbing." Her solution? "I would like to baptize myself under a new name, a name more like the real me, the one nobody sees. Esperanza as Lisandra or Maritza or Zeze the X. Yes. Something like Zeze the X will do."

### Show who they are through whom and what they compliment

Heroes that feel realistic have specific *values*. Most of us are humble enough not to brag about our own values, but we reveal them in various ways. One way to reveal a hero's self-image is to have them compliment others.

We've already seen this in *The Hunger Games* when Katniss begrudgingly compliments her mangy cat as a "born mouser," which is the highest compliment she can give. How can she bring herself to kill a cat that earns her respect in that way?

Private investigator Kinsey Millhone in Sue Grafton's *A Is for Alibi* reluctantly praises the cop she has to work with: "His powers of concentration are profound and his memory clear and pitiless." "Pitiless" is such a strange adjective to describe memory. It tells us more about her than him.

In *American Hustle*, Irving is a self-sufficient con man, but then he meets his match, a fellow hustler named Sydney. We know he's falling for her because he describes her in the way he would describe himself: "She was smart, she saw through people and situations. She knew how to live with passion and style. She *understood* Duke Ellington."

Compliments toward objects can show a hero's odd values. In Colson Whitehead's *The Intuitionist*, Lila Mae belongs to a school of elevator inspectors that use almost super-human powers of "intuitionism" to do their evaluations. The traditional "empiricists" hate this new mystical faction. An empiricist named Chancre seeks to remain in control of the Guild, and bribes all of the inspectors with new screwdrivers. Lila Mae sees through this cheap ploy to curry her favor, but she has values that can't be denied. She does love a good screwdriver:

> *When a memo circulating soon after the raises announced that the new screwdrivers were on their way, few cared that the Guild Chair was so naked in his attempt to score points with the electorate. For the new screwdrivers were quite beautiful. Ever since the city granted license to the Department, bulky and ungainly screwdrivers had poked and bulged in the jacket pockets of the elevator inspectors, completely ruining any attempts at dapperness and savoir faire. It's difficult to look official and imposing while listing to one side. The new screwdrivers have mother-of-pearl handles and heads the exact width of an inspection-plate screw. They fold out like jackknives and lend themselves to baroque fantasies about spies and secret missions. And who can argue with that?*

Lila Mae still isn't going to be won over, but Chancre has come up with the perfect temptation for a woman of her unique values.

## Don't let them be saintly

There are certain types of characters that writers are tempted to portray as saintly, including old people and disabled people, so writers should defy that temptation in order to instantly seem more realistic.

The first thing Peter Parker's Aunt May says in *Spider-Man* is "Don't fall on your ass." We've never heard her talk like that in the comics, so we think, "Oh, this Aunt May is a more realistic person than we're used to."

Walter White's son in *Breaking Bad* has cerebral palsy, but the writers don't handle him with kid gloves. He's a smartass, and his parents are smartasses right back to him. We're a little shocked to see them giving him crap like that, but of course he can take it.

Skyler: *You're late . . . again.*

Walt Jr.: *There was no hot water . . . again.*

Skyler: *I have an easy fix for that. You wake up early, and then you get to be the first person in the shower.*

Walt Jr.: *I have an idea. How about buy a new hot water heater? How's that idea? For the millionth and billionth time. [Looks at plate] . . . What the hell is this?*

Walt: *It's veggie bacon. We're watching our cholesterol, I guess.*

*[. . .]*

Walt Jr., to Walt: *So, how's it feel to be old?*

Walt: *How does it feel to be a smartass?*

Walt Jr.: *[big grin] Good!*

Walt: *Eat your veggie bacon.*

The next subset of personality we'll look at is . . .

## Beliefs

We'll believe in your character more if they have things they believe in. Once again, we'll start with a classic with new examples . . .

### Give them three rules they live by

The idea here is that heroes should have a self-image. Things they believe. Rules to live by. For most heroes, these rules will be implied rather than stated. It's helpful for you as the writer to list them out, but you don't necessarily need to have the hero declare them. (Indeed, sometimes they're not really aware of them, and would have a hard time listing them.)

But heroes *do* sometimes list them. In *Selma*, Martin Luther King counts them off on his fingers: "We negotiate, we demonstrate, we resist." Once you know the hero's three rules, you can put them in situations where they have to choose between those rules.

Right around three-quarters of the way into many stories, the hero has a "spiritual crisis." In *Selma*, that crisis is quite literal. King is leading the second march across the Edmund Pettus Bridge, when he suddenly halts the crowd and decides to pray. Getting his answer from God, he decides to turn the march back and send everybody home. He explains later that he was worried they were going to be attacked, as the first set of marchers who crossed the bridge had been. Instead of crossing it in defiance again, he has decided to negotiate a solution with the White House and get permission for the march.

He must choose between his first two rules, and decides that, in this case, negotiating was a better choice than demonstrating. Eventually, however, he resumes demonstrating and his three rules are back in equilibrium.

### Give them a motto

This is similar, but it's less about self-image and more about the face they show to the world. Let's look at some mottos.

Sometimes mottos stand the hero in good stead for the whole movie: Micky in *The Fighter* says, "Boxing's a chess game, I'm gonna pick my punches to take him down." Bruce Wayne in *Batman Begins* says, "I seek the means to fight injustice. To turn fear against those who prey on the fearful." In each case, these turn out to be good mottos throughout the movie.

Malcolm X in his autobiography is fired up as a child by the motto of Marcus Garvey: "Up, you mighty race, you can accomplish what you will!" This phrase will come to mean very different things to Malcolm as he passes through the many phases of his life.

The title character in *House* has some rather misanthropic mottos, but they ironically help him do good in the world. He discusses his new case with his team members:

Foreman: *Shouldn't we be speaking to the patient before we start diagnosing?*

House: *Is she a doctor?*

Foreman: *No, but* . . .

House: *Everybody lies.*

Cameron: *Dr. House doesn't like dealing with patients.*

Foreman: *Isn't treating patients why we became doctors?*

House: *No, treating illnesses is why we became doctors, treating patients is what makes most doctors miserable.*

Foreman: *So you're trying to eliminate the humanity from the practice of medicine.*

House: *If we don't talk to them, they can't lie to us, and we can't lie to them. Humanity is overrated.*

Riggan in *Birdman* keeps a note with a handwritten motto stuck on the bottom of his mirror: "A thing is a thing, not what is said of that thing." But when he sends his assistant out for flowers, she can't find what he wants (and doesn't care), so she leaves a different bouquet on his desk, with a note that says, "They didn't have whatever you wanted." He unconsciously lays that note next to his motto, and it looks like an alternate motto that is intruding into his life.

### Give them theories

People interpret the data of their lives through certain lenses. These help establish their personalities. Once again, once established, this is a way you can test your hero. Theories are all well and good, until life upends them.

Ted in the *How I Met Your Mother* pilot has a theory, based on his friends Marshall and Lily: In each relationship, you should have one person who loves olives and one person who hates them, so one partner can always pass the olives to the other. When he meets Robin in the pilot, and discovers that she doesn't like olives, his theory helps convince him that he's found his soul mate. Unfortunately, he gets so enthused that he tells her he loves her shortly thereafter, scaring her off.

Later, Marshall and Lily console him after this disaster and Marshall gives him new information that upsets his theory: Marshall and Lily *both* like olives. It turns out that, on their first date all those years ago, Lily asked Marshall for his olive and he claimed not to like them to encourage her to take it. He's had to give up his olives ever since to maintain the lie, despite the fact that he'd love to eat them himself. Ted's belief in "soul mates" is tested, as he begins to discover what he must learn over the course of the show: to be open to the universe.

### Give them rituals

As we live our lives, we accumulate daily rituals, as surely as ships gather barnacles. We use them to soothe ourselves. Without realizing it, they come to define us.

*American Hustle* begins with the elaborate ritual whereby Irving installs his toupee every morning. We linger on it for a full three minutes of screen time. The character thinks this hides his shameful secret from the world, but it actually defines him in the eyes of others, as we'll see in the Care and Invest sections.

Young George Bailey in *It's a Wonderful Life* has an odd little ritual: Every time he enters the drug store where he works, he stops off at the counter to use some sort of bizarre cigarette lighter contraption, which presumably fails a lot, so he says, "I wish I had a million dollars," and tries to light it. When it lights, he says: "Hot dog!" As you can tell from my confused summation, the whole thing is unexplained and delightfully odd. It feels so vividly like real life.

Sometimes rituals are fun, like the Rube Goldberg–esque morning rituals in the *Wallace & Gromit* shorts and *Back to the Future*. We see the amazing minds of these inventors made manifest as they try to make their lives easier, though it never quite works out the way it's supposed to.

Sometimes rituals are the only thing keeping the hero going: In *All That Jazz*, an aging and exhausted Joe Gideon drags himself out of bed every morning, washes up, takes some pills, puts some eye drops in, then makes jazz hands at the mirror and says, "It's showtime, folks!"

Okay, the final element of personality is . . .

## Specific Tastes and Possessions

You should always look for as many chances as possible to define your hero as a specific individual. Let's start with . . .

### Give them specific tastes, often including brand names

In America, for good or ill, we let our purchases define us, so it's a great way to give your hero extra personality. Listing specific products places a story firmly in the real world.

Sometimes, our tastes reveal more than we think they do. Don Draper in *Mad Men* doesn't just smoke and drink, he drinks old-fashioneds and smokes Luckies. As it will turn out over the course of the show, "old-fashioned" and "lucky" will be two good ways of describing Don.

Postmodern novelists like Don DeLillo always have lots of lists of brand-name objects to make everything specific. In *White Noise*, Jack watches the students at his school arriving for the new semester and lists their stuff with an anthropologist's eye:

*As cars slowed to a crawl and stopped, students sprang out and raced to the rear doors to begin removing the objects inside; the stereo sets, radios, personal computers; small refrigerators and table ranges; the cartons of phonograph records and cassettes; the hairdryers and styling irons; the tennis rackets, soccer balls, hockey and lacrosse sticks, bows and arrows; the controlled substances, the birth control pills and devices; the junk food still in shopping bags—onion-and-garlic chips, nacho thins, peanut creme patties, Waffelos and Kabooms, fruit chews and toffee popcorn; the Dum-Dum pops, the Mystic mints.*

(Of course, such a style has its limits, and some writers are proud of the fact that they *don't* do it. Adichie can't resist skewering authors like DeLillo in *Americanah*. Her Nigerian American main character Ifemelu has just broken up with her overbearing Princeton boyfriend, and complains about his taste in modern literature:

*He was sure that she, with a little more time and a little more wisdom, would come to accept that the novels he liked were superior, novels written by young and youngish men and packed with things, a fascinating, confounding accumulation of brands and music and comic books and icons, with emotions skimmed over, and each sentence stylishly aware of its own stylishness.*

She doesn't name names, but who does that remind you of?)

## Give them a distinctive wardrobe

Superhero movies do this most slavishly, of course. We love "colorful characters," so why not give your character an eye-popping unitard? That said, there's always a slight costume change from movie to movie, sometimes because the character is evolving, but sometimes simply because the producers want to sell a new action figure.

But lots of non-superheroes do this as well. Max in *Rushmore* has a distinctive red beret. Hi in *Raising Arizona* has his Hawaiian shirts. Joe in *Soul* has his porkpie hat that follows him even into the afterlife.

Often the distinctive wardrobe helps to market the final product. Walt in *Breaking Bad* takes off his slacks when he cooks meth in his RV, so when drug dealers attack, he ends up confronting them in his tighty-whitey underwear. The image ended up summing up the whole series in the advertising: This is someone comically unprepared for a life of crime, going semi-naked out into the world.

### Give them a talisman or other signature object

Here we are back at objects! Sometimes we let ourselves get defined by a signature object we never go without. Others may rib us for it, but they don't understand how much comfort these things give us.

Harriet in *Harriet the Spy* would never dream of leaving the house without her notebooks:

> *"Wait, wait, I can't find my notebook."*

> *"Oh, whadya need that for?" Sport yelled from the steps.*

> *"I never go anywhere without it," came the muffled answer.*

When they are exposed to the world, she feels totally violated.

Peter Quill in *Guardians of the Galaxy* never wants to be separated from his eighties Walkman. It's a gift from his mother, with wonderful songs she selected for him. He listens to it all the time and it provides the kickass soundtrack to his life. (So of course when it's destroyed in the second movie, that's his breaking point.)

Investor Michael Burry in *The Big Short* also listens to headphones as he cracks the secrets of the real estate market, and he takes it further by having drumsticks in his hands so he can pound out the beat of the metal music he prefers.

Levee in *Ma Rainey's Black Bottom* has just purchased some flashy eleven-dollar shoes, and he's eager to show them off to everyone. As it turns out, he's gotten a little too attached to them, with tragic consequences.

Two other 2020 movies, *Onward* and *Nomadland*, feature characters that love their vans so much that they name them. This, of course, makes it inevitable that they will have to say goodbye to them, and feel like they've lost a lover.

### Let them quantify their life in lists, maps, and written plans

We also love it when heroes turn their thoughts *into* objects. We want to *see* what they're thinking.

Wendy in *Wendy and Lucy* is leading a tenuous life, living out of her car on a peripatetic journey to Alaska. She has almost none of the possessions that would usually define a character, but she is turning her thoughts *into* objects. We see the list of expenses she keeps, complete with elaborate doodles on every page. We see the map she traces a line on to track her trip. This detritus makes us believe in her and her journey.

In many stories, the heroes will find ways to externalize their dreams and wishes. Joe in *Soul* has a wall of great performers to visually remind himself of his ambitions.

In *Rushmore*, Max's "I understand you" moment with his love interest is when he sees that she's made an elaborate diagram for her model plane route, similar to the kind he would make. Holding the object in his hand, he can't deny he's found the one.

Rob in the novel *High Fidelity* turns his whole life into top five lists, including "Rob's desert island, all time, top five most memorable breakups" and "The top five things Rob misses about Laura." This speaks to something juvenile about him, and this is especially true if we look at one of the lists in detail. He knows he can't work at a record store forever, so he makes a list of "Rob's top five dream jobs":

1. *journalist for* Rolling Stone *magazine, 1976–1979*

2. *producer for Atlantic Records, 1964–1971*

3. *any kind of musician (besides classical or rap)*

4. *film director (any kind except German or silent)*

5. *architect.*

Some of those jobs are rather hard to get.

### Give them scars or tattoos

Of course, the most permanent physical reminders of a hero's life experience are scars and tattoos.

Every hero has a few scars on the inside, but some also have them on the outside. James Bond has a facial scar in the books, but not the movies. Hi has one in *Raising Arizona*.

In *Pirates of the Caribbean: The Curse of the Black Pearl*, Commodore Norrington offers to shake Jack Sparrow's hand, supposedly to thank him for rescuing his would-be fiancée, but then he seizes Jack's arm and lifts his sleeve to reveal that Jack has been branded with a "P." "Had a brush with the East India Trading Company, have we, pirate?"

Of course the most notable example is Harry Potter. The first thing anyone does when they meet him is look for his famous scar. Harry's scar causes us to Believe, Care, and Invest, all at the same time: We Believe because it makes him look unique, we Care because it proves he's been brutally attacked, and we Invest because it looks badass.

There are lots of villains with tattoos, but sometimes heroes have them, too. Aang in *Avatar: The Last Airbender* is just a ten-year-old boy, but his ceremonial tattoos give him a striking look.

**SO THAT'S LOTS** of ways to get us to Believe in a character's existence. Again, please don't toss every one into your story, or else your first ten pages will be fifty pages long! Choose just the ones that are right for *your* hero.

Put a few of the above together and your hero will have *individuality*. They will have *substance*. They will have *reality*. Your reader will forget that this is all a lie.

Okay, feeling exhausted yet? Well, sorry, but we're just getting started! Now that I've given you dozens of ways to Believe in a character, I have another huge question to ask you . . .

# CHAPTER 3

# CAN YOU MAKE YOUR READER CARE ABOUT YOUR HERO'S CIRCUMSTANCES?

THINK I GAVE THIS ASPECT OF HERO CREATION SHORT shrift in my last book because I was afraid writers overused it. It may seem like the easiest way to get us to connect with a character is to drown them in a sea of troubles, but too much of that will just make a reader weary and wary. Caring is impossible without Believing and Investing.

Nevertheless, Caring *is* essential. Our heart has to go out to your hero. We have to feel for them. Their circumstances have to *wound* them in some way, and the audience should feel wounded as well. Nothing bonds us to a character as surely as that.

So let's start by talking about the very best kind of wounding:

## The First Rule of Caring: Harm Them in a Way that Reveals Their Flaw

In *Raiders of the Lost Ark*, we first meet Indiana Jones as he sneaks into an ancient temple to get a shining golden idol, but there's one problem: The idol he seeks sits on a pressure plate, ready to trigger terrible consequences if it's disturbed.

But never fear: Indy apparently knew about this in advance and brought a bag of sand. He gauges the weight of the idol then lets some sand out of the bag until he's sure they weigh the same. He figures that if he lifts the idol off as he puts the bag down, the pressure plate won't be triggered.

And it seems to work perfectly. He switches them out smoothly, taking the idol and leaving the bag of sand behind. But somehow, something goes wrong. The pressure plate with the sandbag sinks into its pedestal and the machinery of the temple swings into action. The walls begin to crumble, darts shoot at him from all sides, and soon a huge boulder is bearing down on him.

So why didn't his clever plan work? We're never sure from a technical perspective, but Indy's thematic journey has been foreshadowed. Indy can't tell the fundamental difference between a religious idol and a bag of sand: They weigh the same, so what's the big deal?

Indy's flaw is his lack of faith, and that will get him into more and more trouble until he learns to "let go and let God" in the final moments of the film, saving his life. Ultimately, the difference between the idol and the bag of sand is its religious value. The gods of the temple can tell the difference. Not believing in God, Indy didn't count on that.

As we go through these examples, we'll see lots of instances of this. When your story begins, your hero will usually be unaware of their flaw. They will have to go through the events of this story in order to learn the truth, but if they paid more attention to how they were harmed in the beginning of the story, they might be able to guess it.

## The Second Rule of Caring: The Opening Harm Should Be Deserved but Outsized

This gets at another idea that may be familiar: The humiliation should usually be *somewhat* deserved, but *outsized*. It will not be meaningful if it is not deserved, but it will not feel unfair if it is not outsized.

In *Star Wars*, Luke is being selfish when he says that he doesn't want to help with the new droids, but his uncle is overly harsh when he says, "You can waste time with your friends later." Did he have to put it like that?

Likewise, the title character in *Lady Bird* is being self-centered in her opening argument with her mom, but she doesn't deserve to be told, "You're not even worth state tuition. Just go to city college, with your work ethic. Just go to city college, and then to jail, and then back to city college."

This will be true of almost all of the calamities that we're going to drop on our poor heroes' heads in this chapter: They will deserve a comeuppance, but they will get walloped with a lot more than they had coming.

## The Third Rule of Caring: Hurt Your Hero in a Way that Would Only Hurt Your Hero

Of course, we've already seen some examples of moments that cause you to Believe, Care, and Invest at the same time. One great way to get us to Believe and Care at the same time is to hurt your hero in a way that would only hurt this individual hero.

Most stories begin with a big harm visiting the hero. Occasionally you get stories in which the hero doesn't suffer *that* much, but nonetheless gets hit hard, because the harm they suffer affects them more than it would affect other people.

In the *Black-ish* pilot, Dre leads a blessed life, with a perfect family and a lucrative job at an advertising firm. And now things look like they're only going to get better because he's up for promotion to senior vice president. He's so overconfident that he's going to get it, the viewer is sure that he won't, because that's what usually happens to overconfident characters.

But then, to our surprise, he *does* get it: Specifically, his boss announces that he will be the "senior vice president of our new urban division." We're happy for him, but we're surprised to see that Dre feels horribly *wounded*. He says in his voiceover: "Wait, did they just put me in charge of *Black* stuff?" He doesn't want to be walled off in his own ghetto.

This is a specific individual, and he has his peculiar sensitivities. When one of those is violated, even though it seems like a great thing to us, he feels bitterly upset.

I mentioned in the previous chapter that when we come to believe in Irving in *American Hustle* is when we see his elaborate three-minute combover-and-toupee ritual. As it turns out, only spending that much time on it could set us up for his humiliation.

In the next scene, he goes into another room and walks into a tough situation: He's working for the FBI, seemingly against his will, helping them run an entrapment scheme. He's sick of his handler for screwing it up, and tells him so. They get in a shouting match. Then his handler decides to hit Irving where it hurts; he reaches over and musses Irving's meticulously sculpted coif. Irving is of course incensed, but it slaps us in the face, too, because we spent so much screen time watching him sculpt it. We feel Irving's humiliation.

In *The Hobbit*, nothing especially terrible happens to Bilbo Baggins at the beginning of the story. But he does suffer mightily in the first chapter. When Gandalf visits him and invites him on an adventure, Bilbo scoffs and sends him away, but as he does so he can't help but blurt out that Gandalf should come back to tea the next day. He doesn't really want to invite him back, but hospitality is so ingrained in him that he can't help himself.

Well, as it turns out, Gandalf does indeed come back, and he brings twelve hungry dwarves with him, who quickly make themselves at home, wrecking the place and consuming all the food and drink in Bilbo's house. Bilbo is exasperated the whole time.

So Bilbo *does* suffer some abuse: His *hospitality* is abused. That only hurts because it's been well established that his hospitality is especially important to him. He's been hurt in a way that would only hurt this particular hero. Knowing him like we do, we feel his suffering, so we bond to him.

## The Fourth Rule of Caring: Some Things Are Painfully Ironic Based on What We Know

Irony is any meaningful gap between expectation and outcome, and it's the source of all meaning in storytelling. The bigger the gap for the hero, the harder things will hit him, and hit the reader. We will care more if we know that his heart was set on the opposite outcome.

Here are the first four sentences of the novel *Holes*:

> *There is no lake at Camp Green Lake. There once was a very large lake here, the largest lake in Texas. That was over a hundred years ago. Now it is just a dry, flat wasteland.*

We then meet a fourteen-year-old boy who has been convicted of a crime, and sentenced by a judge to hard labor at Camp Green Lake. We find out that he comes from a poor background:

> *Stanley and his parents had tried to pretend that he was just going away to camp for a while, just like rich kids do. When Stanley was*

*younger he used to play with stuffed animals, and pretend the ani-*
*mals were at camp. Camp Fun and Games he called it. Sometimes*
*he'd have them play soccer with a marble. Other times they'd run an*
*obstacle course, or go bungee jumping off a table, tied to broken rub-*
*ber bands. Now Stanley tried to pretend he was going to Camp Fun*
*and Games. Maybe he'd make some friends, he thought. At least*
*he'd get to swim in the lake.*

We don't know yet that Stanley has been falsely accused, but
we don't care: *This poor bastard thinks he's going to get to swim!* Even
if he's killed sixty people, that's heartbreaking. We will soon find
out that our hero is there because of a crime he didn't commit,
but only after the book has established that *no one* deserves this
punishment.

Our feeling for Stanley is greatly magnified because we know
what he does not: There is no lake at Camp Green Lake.

Okay, so let's get down to specifics . . .

## Five Aspects of Caring

This chapter is even more à la carte than the last chapter. Do *not*
do *all* of these things to your hero! Audiences have little patience
for heroes whose lives are hopelessly abject. Do one or two of
these things, and have them hit as hard as possible.

When writers try to get us to care, they usually use some
combination of the following:

• Suffering

• Lack

• Embarrassment

• Humiliation

• Worry

Each of these will have several subcategories, too many to list here.

Let's start with everybody's favorite . . .

# Suffering

The most obvious way to get us to care is to have something terrible happen to your hero. Not every story needs to start with a gut punch, but it's the easiest way to get us on their side quickly. We're horrified, but we're also fascinated: We get to vicariously experience the worst things that can happen, without them happening to us.

Our first subcategory of suffering will be . . .

## A Death in the Family

Not all of us has experienced it, but we've all dreaded it, so the pain resonates with everyone. We'll naturally start with . . .

### Kill their parents

Why do so many stories kill off the hero's parents? It does double duty: It gives them horrible pain in their past that makes us care for them, but, more important, it also leaves the child on their own.

Anna in *Frozen* can't call her parents when things get tough. If she wants to save her sister, she has to hike up a mountain by herself in two feet of snow. It's all up to her. Likewise with Harry Potter, Tarzan, and Captain America.

In some cases, the child feels they're to blame for their parent's death. We often find ways to blame ourselves for terrible events that happened to us, even when we shouldn't. This multiplies the pain, and bonds us intensely to a character.

We've had to sit through Batman's tragic origin many times at this point, but undoubtedly the one that did it best was *Batman Begins*, because it added a few layers of irony. Young Bruce, while playing on the grounds of Wayne Manor, falls into a well and discovers the Batcave in the scariest manner possible. He's still shaken up later that day when his parents take him to the opera, where they're showing Strauss's *Die Fledermaus*, which involves a man dressed as a bat. Bruce becomes terrified and insists that they all leave immediately. His parents see how distraught he is and agree to slip out the back exit, which puts them out in an alleyway. There they run into a criminal who mugs them, killing the parents.

This is the only version of the origin in which Bruce has a reason to be guilt-wracked. He later tells his butler, Alfred, "It was my fault, Alfred, I made them leave the theater, if I hadn't gotten scared . . ." It's always emotional watching a hero's parents get killed, but this version really twists the knife. (And it's the only version that explains why a rich couple was in a back alley!)

Peter in *Guardians of the Galaxy* not only has to deal with the painful memory of watching his mother die, he has to remember that, when she plaintively asked him to hold her hand, he was too scared of her condition and wouldn't do it. Instead, he ran outside, where he was promptly sucked up into a spaceship and put to work as an intergalactic bounty hunter. We can tell he's never forgiven himself because he's never opened the final gift she gave him, which he still had in his hand. Finally, at the end of the first film, he forgives himself and opens the gift: a second mixtape for his Walkman. The music helps her come back alive for him.

Of course, one way you can heap even more misfortune on the hero is if the people who end up raising them turn out to be abusive. Harry Potter is of course an example, but it's not hard to imagine it was inspired by *Jane Eyre*. Here, too, the hero is raised by an aunt who prefers her own children and treats the hero as a menial servant; and here, too, the aunt hides evidence of an inheritance. Jane wonders, "Why was I always suffering, always brow-beaten, always accused, forever condemned?" Her cousin tells her, "You have no business to take our books; you are a dependent, mamma says; you have no money; your father left you none; you ought to beg, and not to live here with gentlemen's children like us, and eat the same meals we do, and wear clothes at our mamma's expense."

Here, too, Jane finds a way to blame herself. She says of her aunt: "She really must exclude me from privileges intended only for contented, happy little children." As we'll see later this chapter, she is internalizing her abuse in horrific ways.

### Kill their spouse

Killing the spouse also does double duty: You have something to mourn and you often have a kid or kids to raise on your own, like Amelia in *The Babadook* or Nancy on *Weeds*. The horror of Nancy's situation really sinks in when we hear the other PTA moms unkindly gossiping about her:

Mom #1: *I think she got a little botie between the eyes.*

Mom #2: *She probably treated herself, poor thing. If my husband dropped dead, I'd suck out, lift up, and inject anything that moves.*

Mom #1 (eyeing Nancy's purse): *She's got the big bag. I guess he left her pretty well fixed, huh?*

Mom #3: *I heard there was nothing. They spent all that money on the new kitchen. Have you seen it? It turned out gorgeous.*

We then cut to a scene that reveals Nancy's real source of income: She's dealing pot. She brags to her suppliers that people envy her bag, even though it's fake. Of course, as soon as she leaves them, they *also* start gossiping about her: "Can you imagine, though? Boy out, jogging with his daddy, having a *good* time. And boom! Daddy drops." Everybody's a gawker into Nancy's tragic situation.

Like most things in this chapter, there should be a sense of being *aggrieved*: Life wasn't *supposed* to be like this. They were promised a spouse until they were old and gray.

Okay, let's move on to another subcategory of suffering. It's always good to put your hero in . . .

## A Trap

There are lots of ways to clamp a steel cage around your hero, literally or figuratively. The most extreme version of this is to . . .

### Have them be falsely arrested

The ultimate unfair situation is false arrest.

It's not just the prospect of imprisonment, it's the sudden loss of certainty that the world works a certain way. The hero realizes that he's spent his whole life assuming that the good guys were on the outside of the prison and the bad guys were on the inside. Suddenly, he's not so sure. Maybe the whole world is an absurd, Kafkaesque nightmare.

Some heroes take their false arrest stoically like Stanley in *Holes* or Jack Reacher in *Killing Floor*. Jack even gives the cops tips to help them do a better job.

On the other hand, some heroes sputter and rage against the dying of the light, like Richard Kimble in *The Fugitive*. "Are you suggesting that I killed my wife? Are you saying that I crushed her skull and that I shot her? How *dare* you? When I came home, there was a *man* in my house! I *fought* with this man! He had a

mechanical arm! You find this man! You find this man! He took
everything from me! Oh Jesus, God!"

If they're stoic, that helps us Invest, because it's pretty badass. If they react with righteous indignation, it helps us Believe,
because we're pretty sure that's what we'd do.

In *Pirates of the Caribbean*, the arrest is somewhat deserved
(Jack is, after all, a pirate) but deeply ironic. Jack is in the process
of stealing a ship when he sees Elizabeth, the governor's daughter, faint and fall into the ocean. He realizes that he's the only one
who can save her, and reluctantly dives off the ship he was trying
to steal. When he pulls her out, he finds that Elizabeth's loved
ones now want him hanged to death, despite his heroic deed.

### Give them abusive parents

This is the scariest cage of all. Has there ever been any hero as
ingeniously trapped as Tara Westover in her memoir, *Educated*?
She can leave at any time. In fact, her grandparents offer to take
her off the mountain forever in the first chapter. But she couldn't
be more trapped.

She's never been to school. She hasn't even been homeschooled, just put to work in her father's deadly-dangerous junk-
yard. Worse yet, she's never been to a doctor. She has no birth
certificate. As far as the federal government is concerned, she
doesn't exist. How can she ever hope to start life again away
from the mountain?

As always, parental abuse is more powerful if it's ironic. In
another memoir, *The Autobiography of Malcolm X*, Malcolm has a
Black father and a biracial mother. By chance, Malcolm ends up
being much lighter skinned than his siblings. His dad is a fierce
advocate for Black nationalism and preaches the gospel of Marcus Garvey, but at home he unconsciously prefers his lighter-
skinned children, so he beats every child but Malcolm. His mother,

however, hates being reminded of her rapist father, so she beats Malcolm the worst.

Roald Dahl's Matilda may have the worst parents in fiction: "The parents looked upon Matilda in particular as nothing more than a scab. A scab is something you have to put up with until the time comes when you can pick it off and flick it away. Mr. and Mrs. Wormwood looked forward enormously to the time when they could pick their little daughter off and flick her away, preferably into the next county or even further than that."

We've all felt underappreciated and underprotected by our parents, but her case is extreme. Dahl says, "To tell the truth, I doubt they would have noticed had she crawled into the house with a broken leg."

### Give them an abusive spouse

The ultimate betrayal is getting hit by someone you've chosen to partner with. It can (and should be) hard to watch, but it can be a powerful storytelling tool if a writer handles it sensitively.

Of course, one delicate issue to deal with is that audiences are not always as sympathetic to abuse as they should be. Looking in from the outside, it's easy to say, "Why don't you just leave?" We all know that power dynamics are complicated, but it can be hard to capture that in a story, especially in a screen story, where we have no access to their heads.

*I, Tonya*, the story of Tonya Harding, does a great job capturing the horror of spousal abuse and showing why people *stay*. Tonya's spouse is charming and disarming, to the extent that every time he hits her, it comes as a fresh surprise. Each time, we think, "Well, maybe that was an aberration, he probably won't do it again." But of course he does. We come to understand the mindset of someone like Tonya (who grew up being abused by her mother), who keeps giving their abusive spouse another chance.

## Gaslight them

Of course, there's one movie that flags in the title the question of "Why doesn't he just get out of there?": *Get Out.* Why does Chris stay at his girlfriend's house, long after the world is literally screaming at him to get out? Because his girlfriend is so good at gaslighting him. Every time he starts to suspect he's in a horrible situation, she skillfully convinces him he's just imagining things.

Any discussion of gaslighting naturally has to include the story that gave the phenomenon its name. In the 1938 play (and 1944 movie) *Gaslight,* a wicked husband decides to slowly drive his wife crazy to get her money. He does so by messing with the gaslights, causing them to flicker, then, when his wife points this out, claims that she's imagining things. She starts to wonder if she really is going mad.

But I think the new champion for gaslighting movies has to be the wonderful 2020 version of *The Invisible Man*: Cecilia's boyfriend invents an invisibility suit, fakes his death, and then follows her everywhere. Once horrific things start to happen, she tries to explain her fears to his brother Tom, but she sounds totally crazy:

> *One night, I was sitting and I was thinking about how to leave Adrian. I was planning the whole thing, in my mind. And he was staring at me. Studying me. And without me saying a single word, he said that I could never leave him. That wherever I went, he would find me. He would find me. That he would walk right up to me, and I wouldn't be able to see him . . . He's not dead, Tom. He's not dead. I just can't see him. Please tell him to stop . . .*

Nobody believes a word of it, and soon she ends up arrested for murder and institutionalized. She thought she would finally be free of him, but she's more trapped than ever.

## Have the government or other institutions abuse them

The ultimate trap is the one that surrounds us at all times, even when we get out of the house: abusive governments and institutions.

Every dystopian novel, whether *The Hunger Games, 1984*, or *The Handmaid's Tale*, is about living under an oppressive government of some kind, but unfortunately, you don't have to go into the future to find unfair institutions. You can also find them in both the present and the past. *When They See Us* and *If Beale Street Could Talk* show us the realities of a racist legal system. *Beloved* captures the horror of slavery, as we'll see in Part II.

Sometimes, the hero's trap is rather ironic. Yossarian in *Catch-22* could not be engaged in a more heroic action: He's fighting the Nazis in World War II. But for him, it's turned into a nightmare. He was originally promised he could go home after twenty-five harrowing missions under enemy fire, which is good, because that's how many it took for Yossarian to crack, but his glory-seeking commanding officer keeps raising the number of missions exponentially. Yossarian knows that fear and death have driven him insane, but he's run afoul of the titular catch: You can get out of the army if you're crazy, but if you're trying to get out of the army, that proves you're sane. The longer he stays, the more he realizes that everyone around him is now equally deranged, and they're killing each other more often than they're killing any Nazis.

## Foreshadow doom

Sometimes a trap is being laid for the hero that *they* don't see, but *we* do, so it causes us to care about the hero, before they've become concerned for themselves.

*Aladdin* begins with Jafar sending a victim into the Cave of Wonders, with dire results. Jafar vows to find a better stooge, and the cut makes us realize he's talking about Aladdin, so we know to be worried, though Aladdin doesn't. Obviously, this happens all the time in horror movies. We see a young Black man kidnapped off the street in *Get Out*, and when we meet our hero we're afraid the same thing will happen to him.

In some cases, the hero might subconsciously notice something amiss, but they don't put it together at the time and only later realize that they heard or saw something scary. When Mitch is interviewing in the opening scene of *The Firm*, the partners tell him, "It is a rare, extremely rare occasion when a lawyer leaves our firm. It is simply unheard of." Mitch's alarm bells don't immediately go off. We are not sure we've heard something evil yet, but we have more information than Mitch does: We know he's in a thriller, so we know to be suspicious.

The final aspect of suffering is to simply have them get hit by . . .

## A Disaster

Sometimes, the hurt that hits the hero arrives on a much larger scale. No need for subcategories on this one, as the list would be endless: Fires, explosions, crashes, and so on.

Some disasters are so big that you need to go to considerable lengths to make the audience feel them. In the beginning of *The Hitchhiker's Guide to the Galaxy*, Arthur Dent suffers a personal disaster when his house is torn down to make room for a highway. While he's trying to process this, his entire planet is destroyed by aliens making a *galactic* bypass. Losing your planet is too absurd to process, but losing your house really hurts.

This is as good a time as any to bring up that the harm that causes us to care sometimes only exists in a flash-forward. In Part II, we'll look at how essential it is to have a flash-forward to a comeuppance in *Little Fires Everywhere*, because otherwise we wouldn't care.

*Iron Man* is another example of this. The movie begins with a flash-forward to a scene in which Tony Stark gets blown up and kidnapped in Afghanistan, then flashes back to show us his obnoxious tech bro life in the previous weeks. Director Jon Favreau explains why it was structured that way in his commentary on the sequel: "We had tried the first film, which, if you'll recall, starts with a flashback: He's driving around, he gets taken hostage, and then we flash back to six weeks earlier, and so that allowed us to play Tony Stark in a much different way than if we'd done it linear. We'd actually done linear cuts. Everybody who saw the movie said, 'Why are you doing flashbacks, could we see it linear?' And so we put it together and what happens is Tony Stark would just not be a very likable guy. Everything he was doing, he was forgiven much more because you knew that he was gonna end up in a really compromised position and probably the worst position that you could think of, basically in a hostage video."

Okay, moving on from suffering, we get to our next big category of Care:

# Lack

Sometimes you don't have to smack your heroes down, you just have to show that they lack something essential that others around them have. We've all felt disadvantaged and our hearts go out to people feeling the same, especially if their suffering is a little bit bigger than the version of it we've experienced.

This one will have five subcategories, starting with . . .

## Social Lack

We've all looked around us and felt like others had social supports we didn't have (even those of us who are actually rather privileged). There are lots of types of social lack. Let's start with a big one:

### Give them single parents

Sometimes, the parent has been missing since the beginning, sometimes they leave relatively peacefully, or sometimes the father or mother abandons the family.

We feel deeply for single moms moving heaven and earth to take care of their kids, such as the moms in *Boyhood* and *Stranger Things*.

It's painfully ironic when Frank gets abandoned by his father in *Angela's Ashes*. There are good jobs available in England during World War II. Frank's father initially wants to stay with his family in Ireland, but his son convinces him to go take one of the jobs, because the family needs the money. Little does Frank suspect that his father will fall completely into alcoholism once he's away from his family, never send any money home, and soon abandon them for good, plunging them even further into desperate poverty.

Ted in *Kramer vs. Kramer* doesn't really feel the pain of his wife's departure until he tries to make his son eggs and realizes he has no idea how to do it. At the end of the movie we see how much he's changed through reversible behavior, as he easily cracks a few eggs for breakfast.

Of course, once you've got one parent, then you're especially desperate to hold on to what you have: The boys in *Supernatural* are determined to face whatever demons they have to face in order to save their father, because he's all they've got.

### Isolate them

In the Believe section, I talked about how a great way to get us to Believe in a character is to give them friends, but of course, I also said that section was *à la carte*. Some great heroes don't have friends. Lacking friends takes away one thing that helps us Believe, but it gives us another big reason to Care. We'll see this a lot in Part II: Writers must balance Believe, Care, and Invest delicately, knowing that increasing one can decrease another.

Of course, one story can incorporate both at different points. When the first Harry Potter book begins, the narration tells us, "At school, Harry had no one." When we're first getting to know him, we don't get to see him interacting with peers in a way that would have helped humanize him, so Rowling has to humanize him in other ways. Later, however, she will give him excellent friends that will make him a strong enough character to sustain seven books.

Even the most social among us has had points in our lives where we found ourselves with no friends, at least temporarily, and we painfully identify with that ache in stories.

Cady in *Mean Girls* will also make friends soon enough, but first we get a brutal Care moment: She attends real school for the first time and it's pretty dreadful. She can't find anyone to sit with in the cafeteria, and so she ends up eating lunch in a bathroom stall, looking horribly pitiful and alone.

Joel in *Eternal Sunshine of the Spotless Mind* doesn't realize that the reason his life is so empty is because he's wiped the memories of his recent two-year relationship; he just knows he feels a tremendous lack. Ironically, after they've *both* wiped their minds, they meet again and begin their relationship all over.

The next subcategory of lack is . . .

## Emotional Lack

Sometimes we look fine from the outside, but we feel like we're missing some vital parts on the inside. Stories allow us to get to know a hero intimately, including their inner anguish. Let's start with a big one . . .

## Give them unrequited love

Unrequited love is one of the most universal and emotional experiences of all. Everyone past puberty has felt it, from time to time. Once I was pitching a teen story about a nuclear apocalypse. The person I was pitching to asked, "And who does the girl like that she can't get?" I thought surely nuclear apocalypse would provide *enough* drama in her life, but it's hard to really identify with that problem, whereas everyone can identify with unrequited love, so that will frequently be your way into a story.

Sometimes it's unrequited because only one side feels it. The kids of *Peanuts* seem to be rather young, but apparently they're old enough for unrequited love to spring up all over, whether Lucy for Schroeder, Peppermint Patty for Charlie Brown, or Charlie Brown for the Little Red-Haired Girl. Charles Schulz gets great comic and emotional mileage out of their various forms of frustrated longings.

Sometimes two characters both like each other, but other things keep them apart. In *Pirates of the Caribbean*, both Elizabeth and Will have unrequited love for the other, but they are kept apart because he is too aware of the difference in their social stations.

> Elizabeth: *Will, it's so good to see you! I had a dream about you last night.*

> Will: *About me?*

> Her father: *Is that entirely proper for you . . .*

> Elizabeth: *About the day we met, do you remember?*

Will: *How could I forget, Miss Swann?*

Elizabeth: *Will, how many times must I ask you to call me Elizabeth?*

Will (embarrassed smile): *At least once more, Miss Swann. As always.*

Her father: *There, you see? At least the boy has a sense of propriety. Now, we really must be going.*

Elizabeth (hurt): *Good day, Mr. Turner.*

Her father sweeps her out the front door, leaving Will alone. Will chases after her and says in response "Good day . . ." and then, only once she's gone does he add, in a voice overflowing with love and longing, ". . . Elizabeth."

Why do we swoon every time at something like this (especially if they're dressed in eighteenth-century garb)? It's familiar but outsized: We've been in situations where we've encountered obstacles to our love, but not like the kinds that used to be erected when society was more structured. As Hercules Mulligan says in *Hamilton*, "It's hard to have intercourse over four sets of corsets."

Even modern-day couples sometimes have big social stigmas standing in their way. In *Arrested Development*, George Michael's unrequited love for Maeby is forbidden because they're cousins. (They do eventually hook up after they discover they're not blood relations.)

It's always good to take universal emotions and project them onto a bigger canvas. We've all felt that we can't get over an ex, but in the *Scandal* pilot, that ex is the president of the United States. Everyone secretly wishes their ex was doing poorly in life, but Olivia has to watch her ex living out the *ultimate* success story.

## Make them lose friends

Sometimes the lack hasn't arrived yet, but it's looming on the horizon.

Back in the world of corsets, the hero of *Emma* is naturally hard to identify with. The opening lines of the novel are, "Emma Woodhouse, handsome, clever, and rich, with a comfortable home and happy disposition, seemed to unite some of the best blessings of existence; and had lived nearly twenty-one years in the world with very little to distress or vex her."

So why do we care about her? Well, it turns out that she has engaged in her favorite activity, playing matchmaker for her governess, but she only realizes on the morning of the wedding that a trap is snapping shut around her, because her governess was also her best friend. "Sorrow came—a gentle sorrow—but not at all in the shape of any disagreeable consciousness.—Miss Taylor married. It was Miss Taylor's loss which first brought grief. It was on the wedding-day of this beloved friend that Emma first sat in mournful thought of any continuance." Even worse she's stuck with her beloved but dim-witted father, who only ever wants to play backgammon: "she was now in great danger of suffering from intellectual solitude. She dearly loved her father, but he was no companion for her. He could not meet her in conversation, rational or playful."

*Bridesmaids* begins with a delightful scene in which Annie and her friend Lillian hang out together having breakfast, cracking each other up by pretending to have food stuck in their teeth. Then disaster strikes: Lillian invites Annie over and shows her a surprise. Her boyfriend, who lives in another city, has given Lillian an engagement ring.

Annie: *What is that??*

Lillian: *I got engaged! He asked me last night!*

Annie (overwhelmed with emotion, both positive and negative): *What? What??*

Lillian: *I know. That's why he's been acting so weird, because he's a terrible liar and he thought he was going to blow it, and he was ignoring me, and I thought he was going to break up with me and . . .*

Annie: *. . . Oh my gosh! [They hug] Oh my gosh! Lil!*

Lillian: *I'm shocked, still, but I'm happy.*

Annie: *Oh my— [Suddenly Annie starts overheating. She pulls at her shirt to try to cool down] Oh my god—I just got hot.*

Lillian: *You did? Are you okay?*

Annie (still feigning utter happiness, but can't stop talking): *Yes, my pits are sweating, my stomach hurts, I don't know. I'm hot, OH MY GOD, LIL! HAH! WHY IS THIS HAPPENING?*

Then Lillian's fiancé calls. Annie yells "YAY!" into the phone. Lillian explains, "It's Annie, I just told her, yeah, she's so happy!" Then Annie, supposedly joking, yells into the phone "NO, I'M NOT!," but it's instantly obvious to both of them that maybe she meant it. Lillian scoots away to take the call. As soon as she leaves Annie behind, Annie's face begins to fall.

All of the toys in *Toy Story* are worried they might be replaced if Andy gets a new toy at his birthday party. One of them says, "Yes, sir, we're next summer's garage sale fodder for sure." Woody reassures them that they'll all be fine, but then ironically he is the one who gets knocked out of his place: Andy runs upstairs with his new Buzz Lightyear action figure and puts it in Woody's place on his bed, not noticing that Woody has fallen onto the floor. Woody will spend the rest of the movie going to increasingly desperate steps to restore his place in Andy's affections.

## Give them a collapse of confidence

This is tricky, because, as we'll see in the Invest section, we generally like confident heroes, and we have a hard time identifying with heroes who lack confidence. Nevertheless, it can work, if the level of confidence is *shifting*.

If a hero lacks confidence, we are *conditionally* sympathetic to that, on the condition that they gain some soon. Peter Parker is a total sad sack in *Spider-Man*. We feel for him, but we'd get exasperated pretty quickly if he didn't get a chance to turn his life around thirty minutes in.

In fact, when a hero's confidence level is shifting, we like watching it go either way. "We Are Never Getting Back Together" is an okay song title. "We Are Never Ever Getting Back Together" is a great song title, because we don't believe it for a second. That "ever" implies her confidence is collapsing as she's saying it, and we're always sympathetic to a collapse of confidence. "Call Me Maybe" is another great example of confidence collapse in a song title.

In *Rushmore*, Max is bluffly dismissive when the dean threatens to kick him out of the titular school if he fails another class:

Max: *Dr. Guggenheim, I don't want to tell you how to do your job, but the fact is no matter how hard I try, I still might flunk another class. If that means I have to stay on for a postgraduate year then so be it.*

Dr. Guggenheim: *We don't offer a postgraduate year.*

Max: *Well, we don't offer it yet.*

Then it gradually begins to sink in that he won't be able to bluff his way out of it this time. Finally he shrinks down and says out of weakness, "Couldn't . . . Couldn't we just let me float by? For old times' sake?" Our heart goes out to that collapse. Dr. Guggenheim feels a pang of sympathy but says, "Can't do it, Max."

In the first chapter of *Americanah* we find out that Ifemelu had a blog where she commented on race, and we enjoy listening to her mentally skewer the Americans she sees on the train, so we know her blog would have been fun to read, but we also feel for her when she reveals that her confidence is collapsing:

*She began, over time, to feel like a vulture hacking into the carcasses of people's stories for something she could use. Sometimes making fragile links to race. Sometimes not believing herself. The more she wrote, the less sure she became. Each post scraped off yet one more scale of self until she felt naked and false.*

We've all felt naked and false, and we feel for any hero who feels the same.

Another category of lack is, of course, when a hero has . . .

## Money Trouble

If we have unrequited love or confidence problems, we can just tell ourselves to get over it, but it's much harder to wake up one day and simply wish away your economic troubles. Obviously, we'll be starting with . . .

## Make them poor

We've all *felt* poor at one time or another, but hopefully we won't find out what real, crushing poverty is until we read about it or see it onscreen.

Sometimes poverty tears us apart as readers, such as the desperately poor family in *Angela's Ashes* that watches three children die of preventable diseases. Every page of that book has a new permutation of extreme poverty. When the father, too proud to ask for shoes from the St. Vincent de Paul charity house, insists on clumsily repairing the boys' shoes with old tires, and then they get relentlessly mocked by their schoolmates, we feel new depths of sympathy we didn't know we had.

Sometimes, the story begins when a child becomes aware for the first time of how humiliating their situation is: Esperanza describes moving to her new house on Mango Street, which is nicely personified as having "windows so small you'd think they were holding their breath." She has to go through the humiliating ritual of asking kids to be her friend: "You want a friend, she says. Okay, I'll be your friend. But only till next Tuesday. That's when we move away. Got to. Then as if she forgot I just moved in, she says the neighborhood is getting bad." Later, a teacher walks her home: "You live there? There. I had to look to where she pointed—the third floor, the paint peeling, wooden bars Papa had nailed on the windows so we wouldn't fall out. You live there? The way she said it made me feel like nothing. There. I lived there. I nodded."

In some stories, there's a poignant irony to pluckiness in the face of crushing poverty. Mr. Micawber's motto in *David Copperfield* is "Something will turn up." Yes, Mr. Micawber, you will turn up in Australia.

We feel especially for poor people when they have to deal with rich people. Woody on *Cheers* tries to explain to his rich girlfriend, Kelly, why he can't give her a chain for the locket he's given her.

Woody: *I . . . don't have any money.*

Kelly: *Oh, we can just stop by your automatic teller on the way.*

Woody: *Kelly, when I say I don't have any money, I don't have any money. Nothing in my shoe, nothing under my mattress. Nothing. [She clearly doesn't understand, so he tries another way of explaining it] You take all the money in all the world, and get rid of it, and that's how much money I have.*

Kelly: *Wait a minute. You can't afford this, can you? That's why you've been so upset. Now I understand. It's like when Daddy wanted to buy Shell Oil and couldn't.*

But poverty doesn't have to be so extreme. Sometimes you can just . . .

### Give them any inequality

Even in a wonderful situation, inequality always creeps in. It's universal.

Eleanor Shellstrop in the *Good Place* pilot has it pretty sweet. She's gotten into heaven! And every aspect of her new life has been custom made to match her preferences and tastes! Michael, the angel who created this paradise, knows that she prefers her architecture "in the Icelandic primitive style," so he's given her a very modest (and bizarre) house to match it. (He also knows that she loves clown paintings, so he's filled the house with those.)

But Eleanor has two problems. One problem is that, like most of us, she has imposter syndrome. She knows she doesn't deserve any of this. She's actually a terrible person, and she's been accidentally mistaken for a *different* Eleanor Shellstrop. The other problem is that she doesn't actually like some of the things she's supposed to love, starting with her house.

She looks at her tiny house, then looks at her next-door neighbor Tahani, who lives in a ridiculously huge mansion. Even though Eleanor is literally living in paradise, we can't help but feel for her. Any sort of extreme inequality triggers our sympathy.

There have been several articles written recently about how the standard of living on *The Simpsons* is actually impossibly high compared to today's working people. On the show, one man without a college degree is able to support a family of five with one nine-to-five job, and his wife doesn't have to work at all. But the family, at least in the 1989 pilot, *feels* financially challenged, because their neighbor lives so much better. Homer tries to do his Christmas shopping at the dollar store and runs smack into Ned and his son on the sidewalk outside carrying a huge stack of beautifully wrapped presents. Ned tries to figure out which ones are his but Homer grumbles, "They're *all* yours!"

The last subcategory of lack is:

## Medical Problems

Of course, one way to hurt your heroes is to *really* hurt your heroes. Let's start with a big one . . .

### Take away a body part

Every hero has a hole in their life, of one sort or another. Of course, one old trick of writers is to make the figurative literal.

Michael Burry in *The Big Short* has a literal hole in his life: "I've always been more comfortable alone. Maybe it's because of my glass eye. I lost the eye to a childhood illness. Separates me from people." In a flashback, we see his glass eye pop out in a football game, disgusting his teammates and the cheerleaders.

In the book, he eventually realizes that a lot of the isolation (and lack of eye contact) he attributes to his glass eye is actually the result of undiagnosed Asperger's syndrome. The movie oddly doesn't have that realization, but Christian Bale has clearly read the book and his performance makes it pretty clear.

There's a big irony here: Burry and his fellow investors are introduced to us by the narrator saying, "While the whole world was having a big old party, a few outsiders and weirdos saw what no one else could. . . . These outsiders saw the giant lie at the heart of the economy and they saw it by doing something the rest of the suckers never thought to do. They looked." In this case it's actually true that in the kingdom of the blind, the one-eyed man is king.

Of course, missing eyes can have an ironic twist: We spend twenty movies imagining all the badass ways Nick Fury could have lost an eye, only to find out in *Captain Marvel* that it was a literal case of cat-scratch fever.

As with everything in this chapter, we like it when heroes meet this lack with pluck. In a great Humans of New York photo story, a one-armed man is taking out a huge bag of trash on the street by holding it above him on his back, but he's got a happy smile on his face. Stanton asks him, "What's your greatest struggle right now?" He gamely responds, "No struggles." We're totally on his side now.

## Have them be physically disadvantaged

We've all felt relatively disadvantaged at some point in our lives, surrounded by people who have some quality we lack. We may not all have been picked last in PE, but we've all been worried we would, which means we'll identify with anybody in that position.

This can be as simple as being shorter than those around us, such as when Clarice gets on the elevator in *The Silence of the Lambs* and she's shorter than all of the other FBI trainees. She gamely shoulders her way in and pretends she's not intimidated.

Chiron in *Moonlight* is relentlessly stalked for beatings by the other boys just because he's small. They've given him the nickname Little. We've all been smaller at some time in our lives, and intensely identify with him as he flees. When he finds a protector in the character of Juan, we share his overwhelming gratitude. When he finds out Juan is selling drugs to his mom, we share his torn feelings.

In the original animated *Mulan*, it's made clear that Mulan doesn't have as much arm strength as her fellow soldiers, so what chance does she have when faced with a task that even they can't do? Their commander, Shang, shoots an arrow into the top of a tall post, then asks his trainees to shimmy up and retrieve it. They scramble to do so, but then he adds a twist: They have to tie heavy weights to their arms using sashes. That makes it impossible. Eventually, however, Mulan figures out a trick: She whips the sashes around the post until the weights form a natural knot. She uses that to pull herself up the post.

In the 2020 live-action remake, the trainees were given a similar task, involving buckets of water and a mountain, but in that version, she simply showed more arm strength than the male soldiers. Two different, and equally valid, ideas of what it means to be a strong female protagonist.

## Make them sick or injured

Once again, these can range from mild to major. We feel for Ryan in the opening minutes of *Gravity* primarily because zero gravity is making her nauseous. (Of course, we'll soon care much more when she suffers a huge disaster.) Sometimes it can be much bigger, such as the two cancers afflicting Hazel in *The Fault in Our Stars* (physically embodied by the oxygen tank she drags behind her).

Jeff in *Rear Window* has gotten hurt taking a picture of a race car accident, and now his leg is in a huge cast and he can't leave: "Six weeks sitting in a two-room apartment with nothing to do but look out the window at the neighbors." As it turns out, there's a lot to see out there, and he eventually figures out that one neighbor is a murderer.

They've made five gazillion *Spider-Man* movies now, but I'm always surprised they've never used one trick that the comics have used many times over the years: Giving him a cold. It helps give Spider-Man his trademark humbling circumstances, and, of course, it's delightfully gross when he sneezes inside his mask.

Dr. House is disabled and self-conscious about it. He complains to his friend Wilson:

House: *They all assume that I'm a patient because of this cane.*

Wilson: *So put on a white coat like the rest of us.*

House: *I don't want them to think I'm a doctor!*

Wilson: *You can see where the administration might have a problem with that attitude.*

House (self-pitying): *People don't want a sick doctor.*

Sometimes an injury is especially grievous. Joe in *Soul* says of a local jazz great, "I would die a happy man if I could perform with Dorothea Williams." Sure enough, he gets the chance to play with her, then, walking home in a daze, falls into a manhole and gets so injured that his soul goes to the afterlife. Eventually, he will find out that, back on Earth, he's been taken to the hospital, still barely alive.

Sometimes an illness is the *only* reason we care about a terrible person, as we'll see in Part II when we look at Tony Soprano.

## Make them depressed

This is another one that's very tricky. We don't automatically care about depressed characters. Unsympathetic audiences can just end up yelling at characters to get over it. Nevertheless, we can intensely care for depressed characters, if they're written well. The most important thing is that they not be passively mopey. We'll root for them more if they're trying to do something about it.

For my money, the most delightfully depressed character in literature is Ishmael in *Moby-Dick*. Don't worry, though, he's got a plan to tackle it. (Like Abraham Lincoln, he refers to his depression as a "hypo.") "Whenever my hypos get such an upper hand of me, that it requires a strong moral principle to prevent me from deliberately stepping into the street, and methodically knocking people's hats off—then, I account it high time to get to sea as soon as I can."

Of course, we love any chance for irony. Jack in *Sideways* tells Miles, "You have been officially depressed for two years now. You still seeing that shrink?" Miles replies, "I saw him on Monday. I spent most of the time helping him with his computer."

There are a million permutations of depression, such as

post-traumatic stress disorder. This naturally shows up in a lot of sequels, such as *Iron Man 3*. You can also see it in some of the abuse stories I mentioned before, such as the recent movie *The Invisible Man*. When Cecilia gets away from her abusive boyfriend, she is terrified to leave her safe house, and considers it a great triumph to finally make it as far as the mailbox (though she quickly flees inside.)

### Put a monkey on their back

Of course, one of the most tragic permutations of depression is that it often leads to addiction. Again, just as in real life, we're not automatically inclined to sympathize with addiction. It's a flaw with no flip-side strength: It doesn't give you any superpowers, and there's no good reason not to abandon it.

If we're going to sympathize with it, it's good to put them in a world where their addiction is all around them, and they would have to give up their life in order to get away from it. The title characters of *House* and *Nurse Jackie* are both addicted to pills, but they work in hospitals, and do good work there, so we'd hate to see them quit their jobs. Likewise Sam on *Cheers* is a great barkeep, but we're aware that this probably isn't the best job for a recovering alcoholic to have. In the pilot, Diane finds out Sam was a legendary baseball pitcher:

Diane: *If you were so good, why aren't you still playing?*

Sam: *I developed an elbow problem. I bent it too much.*

Diane: *You were a drunk? Are you kidding? Are you drunk now?*

Sam: *I haven't had a drink in three years.*

Diane: *Why do you own a* bar?

Sam: *I bought it when I was a drunk. I held on to it for sentimental
reasons.*

Sometimes, the job doesn't directly supply them with the object of their addiction, but the two still seem to go together. The
cops of *Hill Street Blues* and *NYPD Blue* find that policing and
drinking are closely entwined. In a macho culture, it's the only
type of self-medication that's allowed.

There's no shortage of great novels about alcoholics, possibly
because there's no shortage of great alcoholic novelists. In some
cases we can look back and see why they're drinking maybe more
than they can. We can look at Frederick Exley's semiautobio-
graphical masterpiece *A Fan's Notes* and say, "Uh, that's bipolar
disorder," but to him his crisis seemed more existential.

Sometimes, it's intentionally ironic that characters can't see
the reason a person is really drinking. Every ad man in *Mad Men*
is an alcoholic to some degree, but by far the worst is Freddy
Rumsen. After one embarrassing incident too many, his bosses
have to fire him. They imply it's ironic that he's come to such an
ignoble end, since he was such a hero in World War II: "Turns
out, he was in charge of killing people, and by people, I mean
Germans. What was it, like fifteen of them?" Gee, I wonder why
he has to drink so much?

Okay, let's get to the next big category . . .

## Embarrassment

Not every hero needs to suffer greatly. Sometimes we can feel for
them just as much from watching them feel acute *embarrassment*.

As with everything else in this chapter it's tricky for a writer to maintain our sympathy here. You don't want the reader to join the world in laughing *at* the hero, you want us to intensely identify with the hero, and cringe *for* them. Place us in their shoes, and remind us what it feels like to be on the receiving end.

Let's start with . . .

## Sexual

Is there any type of embarrassment that stings more than this?

### Do the old "thought they were waving at you" trick

Let's start with the most basic embarrassment any story can deliver. You think someone you're attracted to is waving at you, so you start waving back, then you realize they were waving to someone behind you.

When it happens to you, don't feel bad. Apparently, it's quite common. There's an entire Facebook Community group entitled, "Waving at someone when you think they're waving at you and you feel stupid."

In *Spider-Man* it goes a step further: his crush notices his half-wave, and when the girls she was actually waving to catch up to her, they giggle about what Peter did. I don't think you're going to find any other tip in this book that creates as much immediate, blush-all-over, easy-to-identify-with embarrassment as that.

### Make them admit their attraction accidentally

This is another classic that always makes the audience blush and chuckle with shared embarrassment. Most of us will stifle our crushes as long as possible until it comes out against our will.

In *Frozen*, Anna's first meeting with Hans could not be more embarrassing. She blathers: "This is awkward. Not 'You're awkward.' But just 'cause we're . . . *I'm* awkward. You're gorgeous." She realizes what she just said. "Wait, what?"

Speaking of being frozen, Austin Powers has just woken up from cryogenic sleep and doesn't realize he's now saying out loud what he used to say in internal monologue, causing him to inadvertently blurt out his attraction to Vanessa.

Austin: *My God, Vanessa's got a smashing body. I bet she shags like a minx. How do I tell them that because of the unfreezing process, I have no inner monologue? [Pause] I hope I didn't say that out loud just now.*

He has, and Vanessa looks rather embarrassed.

Sometimes we accidentally indicate our interest in other ways: Back in the Friends section, we already covered the fact that T'Challa freezes up around Nakia in *Black Panther*. This is particularly embarrassing when he finds out that he's well known for doing this. He's mortified.

## Make them have bad sex

Of course, sometimes you score and it still doesn't go well.

Annie's hookup in *Bridesmaids* is played by one of the most attractive actors of all time, Jon Hamm, but he's terrible at sex, which just makes her feel awkward and self-conscious.

In a typically disappointed postcoital cuddle, she reluctantly asks him to be her date to her friend's wedding. He says no, so she lies and says she'll go with someone else. He says, "Really? Who?" She makes up the name George Glass. Now feeling jealous he says, "Well let me ask you this, can George Glass do *this* to you?" Then he just grabs her breast and moves it around a little bit. She awkwardly responds, "Probably?"

We totally identify with her cringing.

### Have them get hit on uncomfortably

Watching a person get uncomfortably hit on is reliably infuriating, embarrassing us just as much as it does them.

This is of course a persistent problem for women in any type of setting, no matter how professional. In *Silence of the Lambs*, the asylum director, Chilton, is warning Clarice about the serial killer she's about to face, when suddenly he says, "Will you be in Baltimore overnight . . . ? Because this can be quite a fun town if you have the right guide." She already finds him repellent, but this is just icing on the cake.

But sometimes it goes the other way. Poor Dr. Jones is trying to teach his students in *Raiders of the Lost Ark* when he discovers that one has written "Love" and "You" on her eyelids. He becomes rather flustered.

The next subcategory of embarrassment . . .

### Social

There's a whole subgenre of "cringe comedy," which perhaps reached its apotheosis in *Curb Your Enthusiasm*. Some people can't get enough of it, while others react with revulsion. But everyone is fine with cringing a little if only to get us to intensely bond with the character's embarrassment.

One reliable classic is to . . .

### Have them get caught lying (or almost get caught)

You can base a whole story on an embarrassing fact coming out, such as the titular secret in *The 40-Year-Old Virgin*.

Andy tries to hide his condition from his new work friends but doesn't do it too well. At a late-night poker game, the other guys are talking about different types of breasts they've encountered over the years. Andy grows increasingly uncomfortable, afraid that they'll notice he's not contributing to the conversation. Finally, he feels he must say something:

Andy: *You know, when you, like, you grab a woman's breast and it's . . . And you feel it and . . . it feels like a bag of sand when you're touching it.*

David: *Bag of sand?*

Andy: *You know what I mean. [Realizing they don't] Why don't we just play? Why don't you just deal the cards?*

David: *What are you talking about?*

Cal: *Have you ever felt a breast before, man?*

They keep pressing until the full story comes out.

Sometimes the hero gets away with a lie, but we feel for their worry that they won't.

In *Lady Bird*, the title character runs into her crush at a supermarket. He says that in an upcoming musical they're starring in, he wants to look like Jim Morrison. She has to pretend she agrees, then quickly runs to ask someone who that is. We've all been in that embarrassing situation.

## Make them wear clothing they find embarrassing

We like stories about people going to glamorous parties, of course, so that we can feel lifted out of our own modest circumstances.

But if we're going to identify with the heroes in these situations, we're going to want them to feel just as out-of-place as we would feel.

Richard Kimble in *The Fugitive* is uncomfortable when we first meet him, because he's been forced to attend a gala in a tux. He admits to his wife with some embarrassment, "I always feel like a waiter in one of these things."

Martin Luther King, when we first meet him in *Selma*, is uncomfortably trying to tie an ascot and suspects that it looks a little ridiculous. "Wait till the brothers back home see me like this, they'll have a good laugh." His wife, Coretta, has to step in and tie it for him.

As we mentioned before, Elizabeth Swann in *Pirates of the Caribbean* finds it profoundly humiliating that she's expected to wear a corset with her new dress. Her father says, "I'm told it's the latest fashion in London." Elizabeth responds, "Well, women in London must have learned not to breathe." Ultimately, she will pass out from lack of breath and almost fall to her death.

### Put them in an uncomfortable situation

Some heroes suffer more than others. Some struggle with miserable poverty, which makes them instantly sympathetic, but others live in comfort, which means that the writer has a trickier job. When a writer chooses to write about a hero leading a comfortable life, they have to quickly pluck that hero out and put them in an upsetting situation, even if it's just social embarrassment.

Harriet in *Harriet the Spy* lives happily ensconced in her life of privilege on the Upper East Side of Manhattan with her cook and her nanny, Ole Golly, whom she's had since she was born. Then one day Ole Golly suddenly gets the idea to take Harriet to visit Golly's mother, who lives in a degraded condition far out at the end of the subway line. Harriet is deeply embarrassed to be in the new and uncomfortable situation, seeing how the other half lives for the first time, and finding out that this nanny, whom she thought she knew so well, had been hiding this painful secret from her this whole time. We all remember those little moments, around this age, when we realized that authority figures were human beings with their own struggles and perspectives.

George Bailey in *It's a Wonderful Life* gets thrust into a very uncomfortable situation. He needs advice in a life-or-death situation, so he insists on seeing his father, even though his father is in the process of trying to get a loan extension from the town banker, Mr. Potter. He walks in on his father saying:

George's dad: *I'm not crying, Mr. Potter.*

Potter: *Well, you're begging, and that's a whole lot worse.*

George's dad: *All I'm asking for is thirty days more . . .*

George (interrupting): *Pop!*

George's dad: *Just a minute, son. [To Potter] Just thirty short days. I'll dig up that five thousand somehow . . .*

After some back and forth, George's father finally asks:

George's dad: *What makes you such a hard-skulled character? You have no family—no children. You can't begin to spend all the money you've got.*

Potter: *So I suppose I should give it to miserable failures like you and that idiot brother of yours to spend for me?*

George: *He's not a failure! You can't say that about my father!*

George's dad: *George, George, quiet. George, George . . .*

George: *You're not! You're the biggest man in town!*

Seeing your father get called a miserable failure would be a formative experience for any child, and it's painful for the audience to watch.

Marty in *Back to the Future* has just been telling his girlfriend how much he's looking forward to taking her on a camping trip the next day. Then he comes home and finds the family car totaled in the driveway. He comes inside and finds that his father's asshole boss has borrowed it and wrecked it: "I can't believe you loaned me your car without telling me it had a blind spot!" Marty is deeply embarrassed at watching his father take abuse.

## Make them feel exasperation

We quickly bond with heroes if we identify with exasperation they're feeling. Nothing is more exasperating than dealing with parents, grandparents, or coworkers and their outdated assumptions or prejudices.

Billi in *The Farewell* dearly loves her grandma, Nai Nai. Billi lives in New York City, but keeps in phone contact with Nai Nai back in China, despite the fact that they live twelve hours apart. Of course, she must deal with Nai Nai's assumptions.

Nai Nai: *Is it cold there? Are you wearing enough? Cold travels through the head! Are you wearing a hat?*

Billi (lies): *I am. Stop worrying about me!*

Nai Nai: *You have to be careful. I read that in New York there are men who steal your earrings. They rip them out! And then you have to go to the hospital to get your ears stitched up!*

Billi: *I'm not wearing earrings, Nai Nai!*

Nai Nai: *Ah. So you heard, too.*

We can see how it's both exasperating and endearing to hear these things.

Nicole in *Marriage Story* has left her cheating husband and has taken their son to live with her mother, Sandra, until she can find a new home. Her mother is not on board with the divorce:

Sandra: *Even though I'm sixty-four and have a dead gay husband, I manage to get up every day and live my life and feel pretty good about myself, so maybe your mom knows a thing or two. You know what I would do?*

Nicole (no idea): *About what?*

Sandra: *When Charlie gets here, I would whisk him off to Palm Springs! That's what your father and I did whenever we hit a speed bump—*

Nicole: *Didn't you walk in on Dad blowing the porter in Palm Springs?*

Sandra: *And I always regretted getting so upset about it.*

Nicole: *Charlie and I are getting a divorce, Mom. There's nothing for us in Palm Springs.*

Sandra (suddenly yelling over Nicole at her grandson, to avoid yelling at her daughter): *YOU NEED TO WASH YOUR FACE BEFORE YOU GO TO SLEEP!*

We're still not sure we're taking Nicole's side in the divorce yet, but the exasperation we feel in this scene helps bond us to her.

But your hero doesn't have to be exasperated with family members. It can be anyone pestering them, such as Ned Ryerson pestering Phil to buy more insurance in *Groundhog Day*.

Ned: *I sell insurance!*

Phil: *What a shock.*

Ned: *Do you have life insurance? You could always use a little more. Am I right or am I right or am I right? Right?*

Phil: *I would love to stand here and talk with you, but I'm not going to.*

This brings us to the final subcategory of embarrassment:

## Self-Consciousness

Anytime a hero becomes uncomfortably aware of themselves, suddenly forgetting what to do with their arms and legs, a reader will identify.

### Have them not know what to do with themselves

A classic literary invocation of this feeling is the first paragraph from *The Phantom Tollbooth*:

*There was once a boy named Milo who didn't know what to do with himself—not just sometimes, but always. When he was in school he longed to be out, and when he was out he longed to be in. On the way he thought about coming home, and coming home he thought about going. Wherever he was he wished he were some-where else, and when he got there he wondered why he'd bothered. Nothing really interested him—least of all the things that should have.*

Hazel in *The Fault in Our Stars* encounters something she never thought she'd see again: A cute boy staring at her. Now she's aware of things she hasn't thought about in a long time:

*I looked away, suddenly conscious of my myriad insufficiencies. I was wearing old jeans, which had once been tight but now sagged in weird places, and a yellow T-shirt advertising a band I didn't even like anymore. Also my hair: I had this pageboy haircut, and I hadn't even bothered to, like, brush it. Furthermore, I had ridicu-lously fat chipmunked cheeks, a side effect of treatment. I looked like a normally proportioned person with a balloon for a head. This was not even to mention the cankle situation. And yet—I cut a glance to him, and his eyes were still on me.*

*It occurred to me why they call it eye contact.*

We've all been in that position, but our pitifulness was prob-ably less abject than poor, dying Hazel's. Seeing her endure an extreme version of a common emotion creates a strong bond.

The second paragraph of *The Intuitionist* begins:

*She doesn't know what to do with her eyes. The front door of the building is too scarred and gouged to look at, and the street behind her is improbably empty, as if the city had been evacuated and she's the only one who didn't hear about it.*

We're plunged right into her self-conscious head, describing her unease in a way we've never heard but instantly recognize as similar to our own self-consciousness in such situations.

The unnamed title character of the novel *Invisible Man* feels that he's been almost totally eradicated by racism.

> *I am invisible, understand, simply because people refuse to see me . . . Invisibility, let me explain, gives one a slightly different sense of time, you're never quite on the beat. Sometimes you're ahead and sometimes behind. Instead of the swift and imperceptible flowing of time, you are aware of its nodes, those points where time stands still or from which it leaps ahead. And you slip into the breaks and look around.*

## Surround them with smarter / more witty / more sophisticated people

Amy in *Gone Girl*, like many of us, finds herself at parties where she doesn't feel like she's up to snuff.

> *Now, I like a writer party, I like writers, I am the child of writers, I am a writer. I still love scribbling that word—WRITER—any time a form, questionnaire, document asks for my occupation. Fine, I write personality quizzes, I don't write about the Great Issues of the Day, but I think it's fair to say I am a writer. I'm using this journal to get better: to hone my skills, to collect details and observations. To show don't tell and all that other writery crap. (Adopted-orphan smile, I mean, that's not bad, come on.) But really, I do think my quizzes alone qualify me on at least an honorary basis. Right?*

At a party you find yourself surrounded by genuine talented writers, employed at high-profile, respected newspapers and magazines.

You merely write quizzes for women's rags. When someone asks what you do for a living, you:

*Get embarrassed and say, "I'm just a quiz writer, it's silly stuff!"*

*Go on the offense: "I'm a writer now, but I'm considering something more challenging and worthwhile—why, what do you do?"*

*Take pride in your accomplishments: "I write personality quizzes using the knowledge gleaned from my master's degree in psychology— oh, and fun fact: I am the inspiration for a beloved children's-book series, I'm sure you know it,* Amazing Amy? *Yeah, so suck it, snobdouche!"*

*Answer: C, totally C*

Of course, her situation is nothing compared to Eleanor in the *Good Place* pilot. Eleanor realizes that she's in heaven and doesn't belong there. She finds herself at an afterlife party and says to her newly assigned soul mate, Chidi:

Eleanor: *All I'm saying is these people might be "good," but are they really that much better than me?*

Jump cut to one partygoer saying: *Well, I spent half my life in North Korea fighting for women's rights and the other half in Saudi Arabia fighting for gay rights.*

Cut to another one: *So we said, "If the U.N. won't remove those land mines, we will." And we dug up over a thousand unexploded mines from the area surrounding the orphanage.*

Cut to another one: *Well, then he said, "You can't give me both your kidneys; you'll die." And I said, "But you will live." And I know we just met on this bus ten minutes ago, but he seemed nice.*

*Eleanor groans to Chidi: Oh, forget it. Heading to the bar!*

## Make them clumsy

For some reason, romantic comedies love this trope. I think there's more of an expectation that women will be graceful, and audiences feel a pang of sympathy when this standard is upended.

Romantic comedy is more squarely targeted at an audience of women than any other genre, so they zero in on this trope like a hornet, but you can see it everywhere . . .

Anna in *Frozen* is of course clumsy, as are many Disney heroines. Tonks from the Harry Potter books certainly counts. We've already seen Jo's clumsiness in *Little Women*. ("Jo brought wood and set chairs, dropping, over-turning, and clattering everything she touched.") Evy in *The Mummy* adorably destroys an entire library, as each shelf keeps knocking over another.

Male characters are clumsy far less often. It was more common in the silent era when characters played by Charlie Chaplin, Buster Keaton, and Harold Lloyd frequently made a mess of things, then abruptly had to cover for what they'd done when someone else walked into the room. Christopher Reeve's Clark Kent from the classic *Superman* movies is a more modern male example.

## Have them emerge from a reverie to find humbler circumstances

We like heroes who dream big, but we also like to identify when they suddenly get yanked back down to earth.

As *Rushmore* begins, a classroom of math students asks about an extra credit question on the sideboard. The teacher responds, "Well, considering I've never seen anyone get it right, including my mentor Dr. Leaky at MIT, I guess if anyone here can solve that problem, I'd see to it that none of you ever have to open another math book again for the rest of your lives." They all turn expectantly to Max, who confidently goes up and solves it. He's carried out of the classroom on the shoulders of his cheering classmates. He then wakes up to find that he's actually fallen asleep in a class assembly. We quickly realize he's nowhere near as accomplished or acclaimed as he is in his dreams.

*A Christmas Story* goes back to this well many times, as Ralphie imagines more and more heroic ways he can save the day with his "official Red Ryder carbine action two hundred shot range model air rifle."

When we first see Jack Sparrow in *Pirates of the Caribbean* he's standing atop a crow's nest sailing into a harbor, looking like a majestic pirate captain, then we pan down and see that he is the only person on a tiny, leaky boat that is in the process of sinking. He finally bows to reality, scrambles down and bails out some of the water. Once he's bailed out just enough, he once again climbs atop the mast and blithely steps off it onto the port just as his boat goes under.

Okay, that's enough embarrassment. Let's move on to . . .

## Humiliation

The goal with a good humiliation is to make your audience burn with indignation. The hotter they burn, the more they'll identify with your hero.

Let's start with the gentlest type of humiliation and get more intense from there:

### Have them overhear criticism they weren't supposed to hear

I must confess that I'm overly fond of this plot turn in my own screenplays. It's always good to have conflict in every scene, but it can't always be *open* conflict. Your characters won't choose to openly humiliate each other until things have reached a boiling point. But having characters *overhear* themselves being frankly discussed is a great way to humiliate them without anyone boiling over.

When Buddy in *Elf* turns out to be terrible at making Etch-a-Sketches, his boss, Ming Ming, assures him that he's "special in other ways." They switch him to play-testing jack-in-the-boxes, even though the boxes terrify him every time they pop. Then he hears Ming Ming talking to Foom Foom on the other side of the bookshelf behind him:

Ming Ming: *I hate to do this to you, but you think you could help me pick up the slack on those Etch-a-Sketches?*

Foom Foom: *No problem.*

Ming Ming: *I appreciate it. Buddy's killing me. I already got Lum Lum and Choo Choo working doubles.*

Foom Foom: *That was quick thinking yesterday with that "special talents" thing.*

Ming Ming: *I feel bad for the guy. I just hope he doesn't get wise.*

Foom Foom: *Well, if he hasn't figured out he's a human by now, I don't think he ever will.*

Buddy's world is destroyed in an instant, without any confrontation at all.

That's a classic example of "overhearing on the other side of a barrier." On the other hand, sometimes a character overhears because someone is called into the room to give their opinion on the hero, and doesn't realize the hero is there, such as in *Sunset Boulevard.*

Screenwriter Joe Gillis is pitching a screenplay called *Bases Loaded* to a producer named Sheldrake. Sheldrake calls in his reader Betty to give him the studio's coverage on the script. She enters and doesn't see that Joe is in the room. She hands over her coverage and says:

Betty: *I covered it with a two-page synopsis. But I wouldn't bother.*

Sheldrake: *What's wrong with it?*

Betty: *It's from hunger. It's just a rehash of something that wasn't very good to begin with.*

Sheldrake: *I'm sure you'll be glad to meet Mr. Gillis. He wrote it.*

In this case, it's equally humiliating for both Joe and Betty, who will eventually become his love interest. She never would have said that to his face. Once she realizes he was in the room, she says, "Right now I wish I could crawl into a hole and pull it in after me." But Joe has gotten a gift: He's the only Hollywood screenwriter who's ever heard the honest truth at a studio.

Of course, it's always a bit of a contrivance to put the hero in earshot of someone criticizing them, but they don't have to be there to hear something they weren't supposed to hear. The wonderful podcast Dead Eyes tells of the lifelong struggle of host Connor Ratliff to recover from a traumatic event: He was hired to act in an episode of *Band of Brothers* directed by Tom Hanks, then he got dropped at the last moment. Connor's agent unkindly passed on the reason why: Tom told someone Connor had "dead eyes." Connor never got over the humiliation. Sometimes agents are supposed to lie!

## Have no one listen to them

We've all felt unheard at times, no matter how much we howl for attention. It's one of the most universal emotions, so it's great for getting us to bond with a hero.

Evil Miss Gulch is trying to kill Dorothy's dog in *The Wizard of Oz* film, but no one will listen to Dorothy until it's too late. She finds her Auntie Em and Uncle Henry counting chicks:

> Dorothy: *Aunt Em! Aunt Em! Just listen what Miss Gulch did to Toto.*

> Auntie Em: *Dorothy, please, we're trying to count.*

> Dorothy: *Oh, but Aunt Em, she hit him.*

> Uncle Henry: *Don't bother us, honey. This old incubator's gone bad and we're likely to lose some of our chicks.*

> Dorothy (sees the chick, concerned, and picks it up): *Oh, the poor little things. [Gets back on subject] Oh, but Aunt Em. Miss Gulch hit Toto right over with the back of a rake. Just because he gets in her garden, he chases her nasty old cat away.*

> Auntie Em (continues counting): *Seventy, Dorothy please!*

Dorothy: *Oh, but he doesn't do it every day. Just once or twice a week. He can't catch her old cat anyway. And now she's gonna get the sheriff.*

Auntie Em: *Dorothy, Dorothy, we're busy.*

Dorothy (understands and walks away): *Oh, all right.*

Poor Bilbo Baggins tries to make a dozen objections to the demands and schemes of the dwarves in *The Hobbit*, but everybody just ignores him. We burn with indignation for him.

Dr. Stone in *Gravity* could not be more out of her element (surrounded by a vacuum with no elements at all, in fact) but she's been brought out there because she's an expert in her field . . . not that anybody listens to her. The folks back home finally have to say, "Engineering admits that you warned us that this could happen, but that's as close to an apology as you're going to get from 'em. We should have listened to you, doc."

How many people eventually die in the Alien franchise because of one bad decision in the first movie? Ripley and Ash have stayed behind on the ship while Dallas, Kane, and others leave the ship to investigate a sign of life. Kane discovers a creepy egg-type thing, and a creature bursts out of it and attaches itself to his face. Dallas and the others drag Kane back to the ship and demand to be let in. They speak over the radio:

Dallas: *Something has attached itself to him, we have to get him to the infirmary right away!*

Ripley: *What kind of thing, I need a clear definition.*

Dallas: *An organism! Open the hatch!*

Ripley: *Wait a minute, if we let it in, the ship could be infected, you know the quarantine procedure. Twenty-four hours for decontamination.*

Dallas: *He could die in twenty-four hours. Open the hatch!*

Ripley: *Listen to me, if we break quarantine, we could all die.*

Ash overrules Ripley and opens the hatch. Ripley can only grumble: "Since when is that standard procedure?" Soon, everybody will wish they'd listened to her.

That brings us to a major subcategory . . .

## Disrespect
Starting with . . .

### Have them be disrespected at work
Whenever some story guru gets going about all the things a hero has to do, there's always a joker jumping in to cut them down with, "Yeah? What about Sean Connery's James Bond? He doesn't change! He doesn't have any flaws! He's unflappable!" Well, I can't speak to change or flaws, but I would say he was certainly capable of being flapped. Let's look at a flappening in the first ten minutes of his first movie.

We first meet Bond in *Dr. No* in a tuxedo at a casino, famously telling a beautiful woman that his name is "Bond, James Bond." He wins the game and then, of course, scores a sex-date with the girl he defeated, making plans to see her the next day. But then he gets called in to work at three a.m. by his boss, M. He gets an emergency assignment that will require him to leave right away, so he's already having his sexual rendezvous canceled, but then he gets a further humiliation.

Before going out the door on his assignment, M contemptuously says to Bond, "Take off your jacket, give me your gun." When Bond reluctantly does so, M says, "Yes, I thought so, this damn Beretta again, I've told you about this before." He then calls in an armorer (Q wouldn't appear until the next movie) and hands the gun over to him. The armorer weighs it in his hand, then says, "It's nice and light . . . in a lady's handbag. No stopping power." Ouch!

Bond is then given a different type of gun because "the American CIA swears by it." Bond doesn't like taking his cues from the CIA. His sexuality has been emasculated, and his British pride has been offended. He's going on this mission with something to prove.

Liz in *30 Rock* goes with her coworker Pete to meet their new boss, Jack. Jack quickly sizes her up: "New York, third-wave feminist, college-educated, single and pretending to be happy about it. Overscheduled, undersexed, you buy any magazine that says 'healthy body image' on the cover, and every two years you take up knitting for . . . a week." Liz is embarrassed but Pete is amazed: "That is dead-on!"

House's boss, Cuddy, keeps humiliating him:

Cuddy: *I was expecting you in my office twenty minutes ago.*

House: *That's odd, because I had no intention of being in your office twenty minutes ago.*

Cuddy: *Your billings are practically nonexistent.*

House: *Rough year.*

Cuddy: *You ignore requests for consults.*

House: *I call back. Sometimes I misdial.*

Cuddy: *You're six years behind on your obligations to this clinic.*

House: *See, I was right: This doesn't interest me. It's five o'clock, I'm going home.*

Cuddy: *To what?*

He has no snappy answer to that last one. Later, his ability to do tests is taken away, and she's humiliating him more effectively, going after his disability:

House: *You showed me disrespect. You embarrassed me, and as long as I work here—*

Cuddy: *Is yelling designed to scare me, because I'm not sure what it is I'm supposed to be scared of. More yelling? That's not scary. That you're going to hurt me? That's scary, but I'm pretty sure I can outrun you.*

The hero doesn't have to be insulted by a boss. A coworker will do. Levee in *Ma Rainey's Black Bottom* wants to change the set list of his band, but he's quickly cut down to size by one of his bandmates. "Look, you want to be one of them, uh, what you call it, virtuosos or something, you in the wrong place. You ain't no King Oliver or Buddy Bolden. Just an old trumpet player, come a dime a dozen." We've seen how good Levee is and we feel the sting of those words.

Of course, independent contractors can get insulted, too: Peter Quill in *Guardians of the Galaxy* thinks he's going to impress Korath when he says, "You may know me by a different name: Star Lord!"

Korath responds, "Who?" which wounds Peter more than a laser blast would. Later, this gets a callback when they run into each other again, and Korath exclaims, "Star Lord!," pleasing Peter.

## Have them fail at work

Those heroes got disrespected out of nowhere, but obviously humiliations sting much more if you've actually screwed up.

Anthony Bourdain in *Kitchen Confidential* fails to pass his literal trial by fire: He gets his first chance to cook in a high-pressure kitchen at a restaurant called the Dreadnaught, assisting a broiler man named Tyrone, and finds himself totally overwhelmed, which pisses off everyone around him. Things come to a head:

> *I struggled and sweated and hurried to keep up the best I could, Tyrone slinging sizzle-platters under the broiler, and me, ostensibly helping out, getting deeper and deeper into the weeds with every order. On the rare occasions when I could look up at the board, the dupes now looked like cuneiform or Sanskrit—indecipherable.*

> *I was losing it. Tyrone, finally, had to help the helper.*

> *Then, grabbing a sauté pan, I burned myself.*

> *I yelped out loud, dropped the pan, an order of osso bucco milanese hitting the floor, and as a small red blister raised itself on my palm, I foolishly—oh, so foolishly—asked the beleaguered Tyrone if he had some burn cream and maybe a Band-Aid.*

> *This was quite enough for Tyrone. It went suddenly very quiet in the Mario kitchen, all eyes on the big broiler man and his hopelessly inept assistant. Orders, as if by some terrible and poetically just*

*magic, stopped coming in for a long, horrible moment. Tyrone turned slowly to me, looked down through bloodshot eyes, the sweat dripping off his nose, and said, "Whachoo want, white boy? Burn cream? A Band-Aid?"*

*Then he raised his own enormous palms to me, brought them up real close so I could see them properly: the hideous constellation of water-filled blisters, angry red welts from grill marks, the old scars, the raw flesh where steam or hot fat had made the skin simply roll off. They looked like the claws of some monstrous science-fiction crustacean, knobby and calloused under wounds old and new. I watched, transfixed, as Tyrone—his eyes never leaving mine—reached slowly under the broiler and, with one naked hand, picked up a glowing-hot sizzle-platter, moved it over to the cutting board, and set it down in front of me.*

*He never flinched.*

*The other cooks cheered, hooted and roared at my utter humiliation. Orders began to come in again and everyone went back to work, giggling occasionally. But I knew. I was not going to be the Dreadnaught's broiler man this year—that was for damn sure.*

As with all the best humiliations, it's not undeserved, but it's outsized. He really is ruining it for everyone, but they don't have to "hoot and roar at [his] utter humiliation."

## Thwart their process

This returns to the concept of "hurt your hero in a way that would only hurt your hero": If they're particularly proud of how well they do something, and that's not respected, it hits especially hard.

When I think about the recent humiliations I've seen on-screen that have made me burn with indignation, *La La Land* is one of the first to come to mind.

Mia is leading the typical life of an out-of-work actress in LA, auditioning every chance she can get for producers who seem to go out of their way to make the process as humiliating as possible. This culminates when she's doing an audition that requires her to summon real tears. This is the ultimate test of an actor, and you can tell she has to reach deep within her. Finally, she achieves her goal . . .

. . . but then the producer's assistant comes into the room to ask her about something and the producer starts talking to the assistant. Mia sits there, perched on the edge of fake tears, and also, presumably, perched on the edge of real tears. Finally, the producer notices that Mia is still there and says, "Oh, you know what? I think we're good, thanks for coming in."

It's particularly painful for me to see, because I was once upon a time an amateur film director in my early twenties, dealing with professional actors, and not mature enough to be properly respectful of their process. It hurts to have to identify with what it feels like to be on the receiving end of that.

### Give them a humiliating work task

There's nothing inherently humiliating about having to work hard for a living, but there are all sorts of ways for it to suddenly feel horrible. Whenever you stick a knife into your heroes, it's always good to give it a little twist.

Walter White in *Breaking Bad* is a great teacher, as we'll see later, and he should be able to make a living doing that. When the show was shown in other countries, viewers were confused: Why would a teacher need a second job? (And can the American healthcare system really be that bad?) But this show was set in

America, where teachers get paid a pittance, so Walt works after school at a car wash.

It's inherently undignified for a science teacher (who, according to a plaque in his house, once contributed research toward work that won a Nobel Prize) to have to kneel down and suds up people's rims, but then things get particularly humiliating: A student who already disrespected him in class early in the day drives up in a sports car and mocks Walt while he's on his hands and knees scrubbing, saying, "Hey, Mr. White! Make those tires shine, huh?"

Walt will take a tremendous amount of motivation if we're going to believe that he "breaks bad," snapping and turning into a meth dealer, but the script heaps on enough humiliation to make it believable.

### Have them be disrespected by a spouse or potential romantic partner

We are never more vulnerable than we are in romantic situations. We gingerly lay our necks on the chopping block, and hope the cleaver doesn't come down.

When Sam the bartender first meets Diane the literature graduate student in the pilot for *Cheers*, he asks her some friendly questions. She responds, "I'm sorry, but I'm not in the habit of talking to bartenders." He replies, "I know what you mean. One's trying to move into my neighborhood."

Sam eventually won Diane over, and they would get close to marrying many times over the next five years, before she finally left forever. One can't imagine that their marriage would ever have the bedrock of respect a good marriage needs, but it would have to be better than Tony Soprano's marriage.

Tony is a psychopathic mob boss, but we care about him because he's having crippling panic attacks that have humiliated him. Finally Tony ends up in a place I know something about: lying on a tray about to be sucked into a PET scan machine. His wife visits him there, but she has no solace to offer. He tries to elicit some sympathy from her, but she ends up snapping, "What's different between you and me is you're going to hell when you die." That's what he's left with as he is sucked into that terrifying tunnel.

Micky in *The Fighter* has trouble with *both* his potential romantic partner *and* his ex-wife. The girl he's trying to pick up is unimpressed by him and cuts him down to size: "I heard you were a stepping stone, the guy they use against the other fighters to move the other fighters up." Then when he tells his daughter he's going to win his upcoming fight, his ex-wife says, "It's cruel to mislead your child, Micky."

### Have them be disrespected by their child

Is there any more thankless task than parenting? Kids have to carve out two special days of the year when they are grudgingly reminded to be grateful for everything. The other 363 are fair game.

Of course, few fathers get more disrespected by their son than Homer Simpson. Bart even refuses to call him Dad and just calls him Homer. His daughter's a lot nicer, but still condescends to him, not regarding him as her intellectual equal.

Both Dre on *Black-ish* and Walt on *Breaking Bad* named their sons after themselves, and they both get a humiliation when their son decides to change that name. On *Black-ish*, Dre finds out that his son Andre Jr. has been letting his white friends call him Andy, and he's horrified. His son says, "I think it says I'm edgy but approachable." Dre responds, "I think it says 'I hate my father and I play field hockey.'"

In the *Transparent* pilot, we see how terrible Maura's kids are to her before we've even met her. In a nice pun, her deadname was Mort and, indeed, they see her as walking death. She's been asking them to meet with her to tell them her big news, but they assume it's something else:

Ali: *Have you talked to Daddy?*

Josh: *Yes.*

Ali: *And?*

Josh: *You think he has cancer?*

Ali: *Kind of.*

Josh: *Well, if he's really sick, he should start gifting us twelve thou a year now.*

Ali: *Why?*

Josh: *Tax purposes.*

When Maura does get together with her three grown children, she tries to tell them that she's transgender, but they're too busy infantilizing her and criticizing her parenting:

Sarah (to Maura): *You have sauce right here. [Touches her own chin]*

Ali: *Oh my god, leave him alone, he's mid-meal. This is the golden rule, let him be as messy as he wants, we'll hose him down at the end.*

Sarah: *No! You clean up as you go along!*

Josh (to Maura): *You guys never taught us how to eat. You realize that, right?*

Finally, Sarah leans over and wipes the sauce off Maura's face: Maura says, "Oh, that's cold!" Sarah replies, "I'm sorry," but keeps wiping. Maura will later say to her LGBT group, "They are so selfish. I do not know how it is I raised three people who cannot see beyond themselves."

Any movie can be a horror movie if it taps into our deepest fears, even if just in a domestic setting. *Marriage Story* really shook me. It captures a fear that I think every parent has felt from time to time: That our kids really don't care much about us. Charlie wasn't a very good husband, but he's always been a good father, and he tries his best to remain in his son's life after his wife and son move across the country, but ultimately he's confronted with a horrible truth: His son just doesn't really miss him. This movie really tore me up with the deep-seated fear that, if everything went disastrously wrong, I could lose my kids in more ways than one.

## Have them get needlessly insulted

Sometimes life smacks us in the face, other times it just kicks us in the shins.

When Joe in *Soul* gets the chance to audition for one of his favorite musicians, she just gives him a withering look and says, "So, we're down to middle school band teachers now?" That's exactly what he's most afraid to hear.

In *In a Lonely Place*, kids hang around a Hollywood nightclub asking everyone for autographs. One approaches screenwriter Dix Steele: "Have your autograph, mister?" He smiles and asks,

"Who am I?" The kid replies, "I dunno." A girl rolls her eyes and says, "Don't bother, he's nobody." Dix says, "She's right," but signs it anyway. Just because you cheerily absorb the blow doesn't mean it doesn't hurt. And the audience feels it, too.

There's a Believe-and-Care moment from the beginning of *Holes*. Stanley is about to be hauled to jail for a crime he didn't commit, but he's already suffered other indignities:

> *On his last day of school, his math teacher, Mrs. Bell, taught ratios. As an example, she chose the heaviest kid in the class and the lightest kid in the class, and had them weigh themselves. Stanley weighed three times as much as the other boy. Mrs. Bell wrote the ratio on the board, 3:1, unaware of how much embarrassment she had caused both of them.*

It deeply touches our sympathy, but it's also a Believe moment, because you read this and subconsciously think, "The author didn't make that up out of whole cloth. I *know* that really happened to him or somebody he knew."

Sometimes we realize the deck has been stacked against us before we even joined the game. Marty in *Back to the Future* is late to school, so he tries to sneak in, but he's caught by the principal, Strickland:

> Strickland: *You got a real attitude problem, McFly. You're a slacker. You remind me of your father when he went here. He was a slacker, too.*

> Marty: *Can I go now, Mr. Strickland?*

> Strickland: *I noticed your band is on the roster for dance auditions after school today. Why even bother, McFly, you don't have a chance,*

*you're too much like your old man. No McFly ever amounted to anything in the history of Hill Valley.*

Marty: *Yeah, well, history is gonna change.*

Marty doesn't know how right he is.

The last subcategory of Humiliation is . . .

## Loss of Power or Reputation

It's one of the essential paradoxes of trying to please an audience: On the one hand, readers like to feel sympathy with underdog heroes, but, on the other hand, they like to root for powerful heroes, so which should you give them? This whole book, to a certain extent, is about ways to split the difference. Of course one way to do it is to give them some power just long enough to get us to root for them, then yank it away just when they need it most.

Let's start with . . .

## Have power taken away from them

Everyone loses their mojo from time to time. We've all had our status kicked out from under us, even it's just going from senior back to freshman. In stories, of course, the scale tends to be much bigger.

Thor's father says to him, "You've forgotten everything I've taught you about a warrior's patience. You're a vain, greedy, cruel boy. I was a fool to think you were ready. You have betrayed the express command of your king through your arrogance and stupidity. You are unworthy. I cast you out." He then robs Thor of his super-strength, rips off his cape, takes his hammer away from him, and kicks him into a portal going to a notoriously awful place: Earth.

But not all stripping of power is so dynamic. Olivia Pope in the *Scandal* pilot used to work for the White House, and now just runs a law firm. Several people in the pilot remind her that she no longer wields the power she used to have. The DA says to her, "You don't have the muscle of the White House behind you anymore. You're just a private citizen who is, by the way, annoying."

Jeff in the *Community* pilot has had his license to practice law taken away, which makes him realize that he's coasted through his life until this point. He realizes that he'll actually have to study in community college, but: "Well, the funny thing about being smart is you can get through most of life without having to do work. So I'm not really sure how to *do* that."

## Fire them

We've talked a lot about jobs. We've talked about the value of economic activity to make us Believe, and we've talked about the various indignities heroes may have to suffer on the job. But now let's get to the biggest indignity of all: Getting fired.

*Gone Girl* is a good example because it speaks to real-life national pain, which all great stories should do: "Blame the economy, blame bad luck, blame my parents, blame your parents, blame the Internet, blame people who use the Internet. I used to be a writer. I was a writer who wrote about TV and movies and books. Back when people read things on paper, back when anyone cared about what I thought. . . . I had a job for eleven years and then I didn't, it was that fast. All around the country, magazines began shuttering, succumbing to a sudden infection brought on by the busted economy."

Nick's creator, Gillian Flynn, used to write reviews for *Entertainment Weekly* and explored thriller writing after she lost that job, so she's mining her real-life experience for pain she went through and gifting that pain to her character so that he will be more sympathetic to us.

*Ghostbusters* shows how to make it particularly humiliating. We begin with the three paranormal investigators getting fired en masse from Columbia University:

> Dean: *You are being moved off-campus. The board of regents has decided to terminate your grant. You are to vacate these premises immediately.*

> Venkman: *This is preposterous. I demand an explanation.*

> Dean: *Fine. This university will no longer continue any funding of any kind for your group's activities.*

> Venkman: *But the kids love us.*

> Dean: *"Doctor" Venkman, we believe that the purpose of science is to serve mankind. You, however, seem to regard science as some kind of dodge, or hustle. Your theories are the worst kind of popular tripe, your methods are sloppy, and your conclusions are highly questionable. You are a poor scientist, Dr. Venkman.*

Of course, this will only give the three men the kick in the pants they need to start their own business.

There's no shortage of great firing scenes. My favorite comes well outside the first ten minutes of *The Simpsons*, but I couldn't resist including it. Kirk Van Houten, the father of Bart's friend Milhouse, gets divorced, then unexpectedly gets fired from his job as a result:

> Kirk: *You're letting me go?*

Cracker Factory Executive: *Kirk, crackers are a family food. Happy families. Maybe single people eat crackers, we don't know. Frankly, we don't want to know. It's a market we can do without.*

Kirk: *So, that's it after twenty years? "So long, good luck?"*

Cracker Factory Executive: *I don't recall saying "good luck."*

Okay, let's move on to one last category of Care . . .

## Worry

It could be that nothing terrible has happened to your hero . . . *yet*. It's always good to put a Sword of Damocles dangling over their heads.

### Give them an impending deadline

Deadlines are always good for giving structure to a story. The establishment of a deadline automatically gives you two dramatic questions: Will they succeed, and will they do it in time? The more crucial the goal, the higher the stakes, and the more insistent the urgency, the more your story will be propelled forward.

Deadlines are also good at helping us care. We've all felt that sweat. There's a reason that perhaps the most universal anxiety dream of all is the one where we're back in high school and have to cram for a test we can't possibly pass.

Obviously lots of action movies are deadline-driven. In the opening minutes of the first *Mission: Impossible* movie, the team seemingly kills one of their own as part of an elaborate con. Once they have what they want, they have to act lightning fast to revive her before it's too late. The movie almost convinces us for a moment that they won't make it.

But not all deadlines are action-based. Don Draper in the *Mad Men* pilot is supposed to make a presentation to a tobacco company, but he can't come up with anything when the episode begins. He confesses to his mistress, "I have nothing. I am over, and they're finally gonna know it. Next time you see me, there'll be a lot of young executives picking meat off my ribs."

When we first meet Sam in the *Supernatural* pilot, he's preparing for a big deadline: his law school interview in three days. Sam says, "It's my whole future on a plate." But then his brother shows up: Their demon-hunting father has gone missing. Can they find him and get Sam back in time? That deadline hangs over the whole pilot.

## Have them worry that they're a bad person

Of course, you don't have to be worried about what someone else will do to you. You can be worried about something much larger: what you're becoming.

The greatest sketch show of all time, and I'll fight you over this, is *That Mitchell and Webb Look*. Five of their sketches rank in my top ten. One that's gotten a lot of internet exposure shows two Nazis on the Russian front:

> Nazi #1: *Have you noticed that our caps have actually got little pictures of skulls on them?*
>
> Nazi #2: *I—I don't . . . er—*
>
> Nazi #1: *Hans . . . Are we the baddies?*

We use that phrase a lot in my house, whenever we suspect we're doing something we shouldn't.

Harriet in *Harriet the Spy* is used to unleashing her venom upon the world without reserve, both in her diaries and in person, but she's begun to realize this may be a problem. At one point, when she is teasing her friend Sport, she has a sudden apprehension: "Harriet felt very ugly all of a sudden." Or, to put it another way: "Am I the baddie?"

Sometimes the hero gets confronted about it. Brody in *Jaws* tries to close the beaches when he sees a girl who's been mauled by a shark, but the mayor convinces him to reopen them. A boy gets killed as a result. Later, Brody is talking to the mayor again when the boy's mother comes up to Brody and suddenly slaps him:

> Mrs. Kintner: *I just found out that a girl got killed here last week, and you knew it! You knew there was a shark out there! You knew it was dangerous! But you let people go swimming anyway? You knew all those things! But still my boy is dead now. And there's nothing you can do about it. My boy is dead. I wanted you to know that. [Brody has no response and she walks away in disgust]*

> Mayor Vaughn: *I'm sorry, Martin. She's wrong.*

> Brody: *No, she's not.*

Brody is worried about what he's become. Now he commits to finding the shark, no matter what the mayor thinks.

It's always great when you can create irony, of course. The hero of the novel *Invisible Man* finds himself in a very ironic position: He spends most of his early years just trying to please those in power, but they always treat him like an enemy, and he secretly fears they are right: His grandfather told him on his deathbed to feign subservience and then betray the white man. Now, every time he tries to do what white people want him to do, he worries that he's just following his grandfather's dictum, without trying to, and he's secretly a traitor.

Perhaps the ultimate example: Jane Eyre very much fears she's the monster at the end of her own book. When she is sent to a creepy gothic bedroom to await punishment, her attention is drawn to a dusty mirror. "The strange little figure there gazing at me, with a white face and arms specking the gloom, and glittering eyes of fear moving where all else was still, had the effect of a real spirit. I thought it like one of the tiny phantoms, half fairy, half imp, Bessie's evening stories represented as coming up out of lone, ferny dells, in moors, and appearing before the eyes of belated travellers." She will spend years convincing herself she's not a monster.

OKAY, IT'S TEMPTING to simply keep maximizing pain until you're ready to launch your hero out into the world. We've all been told by our parents that suffering builds character, so more suffering = more character = more love you'll get from your audience, right?

But no, the audience ultimately has a limited tolerance for suffering. If we start to feel that the hero is hopelessly hapless, our emotions will flip. We'll go from caring more to caring less. In fact, it's time to balance out all that pain . . .

CHAPTER 4

# WILL WE INVEST OUR HOPES AND DREAMS IN THIS HERO?

O KAY, SO NOW WE BELIEVE THAT THIS IS A REAL PERSON in a real world, and we care deeply about them because we've felt their pain. But believing and caring are not enough.

We tell stories to show each other how to solve problems. Most great stories are ultimately about one primary hero solving one large problem. We want to be reassured that we can trust *this* hero to solve *this* problem, and we want a least a *few* clues early on that they have what it takes.

We want to feel that it's safe to invest our hopes and dreams in this hero. We don't want the story to abuse our emotions. We don't want a story in which we care more about this hero than they care about themselves.

It's a myth that readers love an everyman that goes from zero to hero. We want heroes to have particular strengths that are the ironic flip side of their flaws, and we want those strengths to be established early on. Then we want them to rely on those strengths throughout the story.

So how do you get us to invest in a hero? Let's start with . . .

## The First Rule of Getting Us to Invest in a Hero: Find the Ironies

We love heroes who lose by winning, and we also love heroes who win by losing. Every element of a story is more meaningful and interesting if it's ironic.

Martin Luther King in *Selma* arrives in the titular city, whereupon a white man walks up and says, "Let me shake your hand." King extends his hand but then the man coldcocks him in the face and bolts back into the crowd. King is knocked flat, and colleagues help him to his feet. As he gets up, he says to one of them, "This place is perfect."

Later, he walks into a room to find his people locked in a debate with the leaders of the Student Nonviolent Coordinating Committee, John Lewis and James Forman. He wades in and explains a bit about his tactics, contrasting the new Selma campaign with a failed campaign King just abandoned in Albany, Georgia:

> King: *We were in Albany for nine months, and we made a lot of mistakes. But their sheriff, Laurie Pritchett, he never made a mistake. Kept his cool, kept arresting us in a human way, carried people to jail wagons on stretchers. Day in, day out. There was no drama.*

> James Forman (rolls eyes): *You mean there was no cameras.*

> King: *Exactly. Now I know, we all understand, that you young people believe in working in the community long-term. Doing the*

*work to raise black consciousness. It's good grassroots work. I can't tell you how much we admire that. But what we do is negotiate, demonstrate, resist. And a big part of that is raising white consciousness. And in particular the conscience of whichever white man happens to be sitting in the Oval Office. Right now Johnson has other fish to fry and he'll ignore us if he can. The only way to stop him doing that is by being on the front page of the national press every morning and being on the TV news every night. And that requires drama. Now John . . . James . . . Answer me one question. I've been told the sheriff in this town isn't like Laurie Pritchett in Albany. He's a big ignorant bully like Bull Connor in Birmingham. Well, you tell me. You know Selma. You know Sheriff Jim Clark. Is he Laurie Pritchett? . . . or is he Bull Connor?*

John Lewis (thinks about it, admits): *He's Bull Connor.*

One of King's lieutenants yells out, "Bingo!" King smiles: "Good. That's good."

King is dedicated to running a nonviolent movement, but his tactics only work if they are met with violence in return. He has to go city to city seeking out violent sheriffs who will club his organizers, because that's the only way to move the nation. It's a deeply ironic strategy.

Here's a more lighthearted example. (It seems a little obscene to compare Ted Mosby to Martin Luther King, but this is just to show that very different types of heroes can use ironic tactics to very different purposes.)

In the *How I Met Your Mother* pilot, Ted meets Robin in a bar, falls in love at first sight, and tries to flirt with her. There's just one problem: She's in the bar with a group of friends, and she's supposed to be showing solidarity to one who just got dumped. Her friends are glaring at her for letting herself get hit on when she's supposed to be commiserating with them about all guys being jerks. Then Ted comes up with a brilliant solution:

> Ted: *You know, if it'll make your friend feel better, you can throw a drink in my face. I don't mind.*

> Robin: *She would* love *that! It does look fun in the movies.*

> Ted: *Hey, you wanna have dinner with me?*

They make the date, she slyly slides him her card, then, just when Ted has forgotten about it, she does indeed throw her martini in his face and loudly says, "You jerk!" Her friends are overjoyed. He's sopping wet, but doesn't mind because it got him her number.

By letting himself look like the ultimate loser, he's a winner. That's the sort of irony that gets us invested every time.

## The Second Rule of Getting Us to Invest in a Hero: Have Them Bridge Two Worlds

As we go through this chapter, many of these Invest examples will involve the ability to traverse two worlds, so let's look at what that means before we get started . . .

Ripley in *Alien* and Mookie in *Do the Right Thing* might not seem at first glance to be that similar, but they actually have a lot in common. Both spend the movie defending their bosses as everybody else turns against them. Finally, this culminates in a moment where each hero belatedly and definitively breaks with their boss, initiating the fiery destruction of their workplaces.

But you don't have to wait until the end of their movies to see their similarities. Right away, they're each the only one in their environment who can traverse two worlds. Only Ripley goes down into the bowels of the ship to visit the engine workers Parker and Brett, and only Mookie traverses the Black and white worlds.

In *Mean Girls*, only Cady is welcomed by both the art freaks and the plastics. Only Malcolm X is welcome with both the up-scale Black residents of Roxbury in Boston and the less preten-tious people who hang out at the Roseland Ballroom downtown. Harriet in *Harriet the Spy* leads a life of privilege, but she sneaks into the homes of the poor to see how they live.

This is one of the greatest strengths a hero can have: We want a hero who can see more angles than those around them. We want a hero who is more aware of the intricacies of their world.

## The Third Rule of Getting Us to Invest in a Hero: Sometimes Heroes' Root-For Moments Will Be Self-Destructive

Eventually, Lady Bird can't take her mother's abuse anymore and so she reacts. Does she stand up for herself? Does she cleverly defeat her mother's logic? Does she insist on her own dignity? Does she throw the abuse back in her mom's face? None of these. She opens the door and jumps out of the moving car onto the two-lane highway. That's not a wise problem-solving strat-egy, but nevertheless, we love it. It's certainly active, it's certainly badass, and ultimately effective, because it does momentarily end the abuse.

So this is something to keep in mind going forward: The action that gets us to invest in a hero can sometimes be self-destructive.

When we first meet Liz Lemon in the *30 Rock* pilot, she's waiting in line at a hot dog stand outside the titular building, when a businessman breaks in line. She gets a clever solution: "Yeah, I want all the hot dogs, please? I'm buying *all* the hot dogs. And I'm giving them to the *good* people!" She then walks the street happily handing out hot dogs to everyone, but most people angrily throw them out. Even a homeless man throws it back at her. We root for her because we can see that she's willing to act big to enforce her beliefs ("You know how I hate it when people cheat or break rules?"), even though the script is mocking her misguided efforts.

And of course, what's more badass than breaking into the dispensary with a stolen screwdriver in the pilot of *The Queen's Gambit* and swallowing a handful of pills all at once? She's solving her craving problem cleverly and proactively, but she's not exactly acting wisely. Still, we know not to mess with this girl.

## The Fourth Rule of Getting Us to Invest in a Hero: Have Them Grin with Defiance

Many of these crucial moments boil down to one thing: defiance. In *Kitchen Confidential*, Anthony Bourdain remembers the moment his family heads out on the boat of a friend named Monsieur Saint-Jour, to see what it's like picking oysters off the ocean floor at low tide. Then the monsieur unexpectedly makes them an offer:

> *Monsieur Saint-Jour [. . .]—as if challenging his American passengers—inquired in his thick Girondais accent, if any of us would care to try an oyster.*

> *My parents hesitated. I doubt they'd realized they might actually have to eat one of the raw, slimy things we were currently floating over. My little brother recoiled in horror.*

*But I, in the proudest moment of my young life, stood up smartly, grinning with defiance, and volunteered to be the first.*

"Grinning with defiance." Readers always love reading those words. They could be tacked on many of the examples we'll look at below. Try adding those three words to your manuscript right now.

At another point in that first chapter, Bourdain's crappy parents go to a fancy French restaurant and, wanting to enjoy it fully, just leave their young children sitting in the car in the parking lot for a few hours. "I remember it well, because it was such a slap in the face. It was a wake-up call that food could be important, a challenge to my natural belligerence. By being denied, a door opened." That's a central irony of many stories: When a door is shut in their face, it compels them forward all the more strongly.

Okay, we're going to look at . . .

# Four Aspects of Investing in a Hero

We'll look at many reasons to invest in a hero, but they'll all fit into four broad categories:

- Badassery

- Wish fulfillment

- Special skills

- Attitude

So let's start with . . .

# Badassery

Let me start off by insisting that not every hero needs to be a badass, neither on the surface nor deep down. We're eventually going to look at many different ways to get us to Invest. But let's start off with the most obvious reason.

The first subset of badassery is:

## Personal Qualities

There will be a lot of forces wearing your hero down, but after they've been whittled down mercilessly, what's left that can't be chipped away? What's at their core? Let's start with . . .

### Give them a great strength that's the flip side of their great flaw

We've looked at this from the flaw side, but now let's look at it from the strength side, by diving into one show in depth.

Let's look at a pilot with six coequal heroes: *Modern Family*. We'll examine them couple by couple.

• Claire: Strength (Responsible) / Flaw (Stick in the mud)

• Phil: Strength (Friendly) / Flaw (Irresponsible)

Phil and Claire are raising Haley, Alex, and Luke. In the pilot, Haley has a boy named Dylan coming over, and Luke just shot Alex with a BB gun. Claire orders Phil to shoot Luke in retaliation, as they had previously threatened. They figure out when to schedule it and Claire writes "Shoot Luke" on the day's schedule. Claire also urges Phil to intimidate Dylan, but he's too busy trying to be Haley's best friend and fails miserably. Ultimately, Phil tries to back out of shooting Luke, but ends up accidentally shooting Luke, Dylan, and himself.

Claire is clearly the responsible parent, though she knows that makes her no fun. Phil is the friendly parent, but that means he fails in most of his actual parenting duties.

The show is intercut with each couple being interviewed for a documentary, and Claire tells the interviewer: "If Haley never wakes up on a beach in Florida, half-naked, I've done my job." Phil smiles and says, "*Our* job." She says, "Right. I've done *our* job."

- Jay: Strength (Speaks truths) / Flaw (Ends up sounding mean)

- Gloria: Strength (Passionate) / Flaw (Inconsiderate of others' feelings, especially her husband's)

Next we meet Claire's father, Jay, and his much younger wife, Gloria, rooting for Gloria's son, Manny, at a soccer game. A man tries to hit on Gloria, and Jay wants to confront him but has trouble getting out of his chair. Manny wants to give a love poem to an older girl, and Jay tries to dissuade him ("I'm just trying to toughen him up a little bit"), but Gloria encourages Manny's romantic escapades.

Gloria tells the interviewer: "Manny's very passionate, just like his father. My first husband—he's very handsome but too crazy. It seemed like all we did was fight and make love, fight and make love, fight and make love. One time, I'm not kidding you, we fell out the window together!" Jay can only force a smile and ask, "Which one were you doing?"

- Cameron: Strength (Emotional openness) / Flaw (Melodramatic)

- Mitchell: Strength (Witty) / Flaw (Judgmental)

Finally, Mitchell and his husband, Cameron, have adopted a baby girl from Vietnam, and Mitchell refuses to tell his family. Cameron invites the family over on his own, then tells Mitchell he'll have to face them. When they arrive, Mitchell starts to slowly explain to his family what's going on, but when he says he and Cameron *considered* adopting a baby, Jay and Claire jump in to tell him that's a bad idea: "You're a little uptight, kids bring chaos, and you don't handle it well." Then Cameron comes out in an African robe with the *Lion King* music playing and presents them all with the baby. Speaking about the music, Mitchell says, "Just turn it off." Cameron responds, "I can't turn it off, it's who I am."

In the interview, Mitchell makes various witty snips at Cameron. Finally, Cameron is telling the interviewer that he's gained a little weight, but that's common for new mothers. Mitchell just purses his lips a little bit, but that's enough to wound Cameron. Mitchell says, "I'm not saying anything." Cameron says, "You're saying *everything.*"

For all six of them, their great strength is the flip side of their great flaw, and that ironic frisson powered eleven seasons of wildly successful TV.

### Give them secret honor

In our last chapter, we looked at lots of ways for our heroes to suffer, but one way you can instantly turn that on its head, and turn that suffering into strength, is to have them suffer in silence.

As soon as we meet Harry Potter, we see that he's treated horribly by his aunt, uncle, and cousin, but he takes it on the chin gamely. Later in the series, this quality reaches its apotheosis when his sadistic Defense Against the Dark Art professor, Dolores Umbridge, subjects him to horrific torture, forcing him to write "I will not tell lies" with a quill that cuts the words into his arm as he writes on the page. Night after night, when people ask him how detention's going, he tells them it's going fine. He has secret honor.

Homer in the *Simpsons* pilot finds out he won't be getting his Christmas bonus, but he doesn't want to make his wife and kids worry, so he doesn't tell them. Besides, they still have that jar of money they've saved up . . . but then he finds out Marge had to use all that money to remove Bart's tattoo. Now he decides he'll just have to take extra jobs and not tell them. He'll do anything to buy Christmas presents for his kids, but he's not going to tell anyone about the suffering he had to go through to get them. He's got secret honor.

### Have them walk into situations eagerly

You might think we would admire smart heroes who cleverly protect themselves from embarrassment and humiliation, but we actually prefer heedless heroes who fling themselves into situations unprepared. One of our favorite qualities is if a hero is *game*.

Two of the worst filmmakers of all time have both had biopics made about their misadventures. Ed Wood in *Ed Wood* and Tommy Wiseau in *The Disaster Artist* are totally incompetent, so they should be hard to root for, right? But we actually love these guys, because they're so *eager*. They're following their dreams and diving right in with gusto.

Ed sends out reels of his previous feature film and then calls up studios asking for funding for his new one. We just hear his side of the conversation: "Really? Worst film you ever saw? [undeterred] Well, my next one will be better! Hello? Hello?"

Later, he makes it onto a studio lot where he gets to see an editor screening stock footage.

Ed: *Why, if I had half a chance, I could make an entire movie using this stock footage! The story opens on these mysterious explosions. Nobody knows what's causing them, but it's upsetting all the buffalo. So, the military are called in to solve the mystery!*

Editor: *You forgot the octopus.*

Ed: *No, no, I'm saving that for my big underwater climax!*

We love this guy. He's hapless, but we can tell just from his attitude that somehow he'll come out all right.

## Make them uniquely brave

Bravery is great, but even better is bravery when it's contrasted with everyone around the hero, who fail this particular test.

I've talked before about the scene in *Captain America: The First Avenger* where the general in charge of boot camp tosses a grenade into a group of new recruits and falsely announces that it's live. Everybody dives for cover except our hero, who jumps onto the grenade to absorb its shrapnel. Guess who our hero is?

I've previously recommended against panning across a hero's wall to show their accomplishments, but I can think of one scene where it works, simply because what we're seeing is so badass: In *Rear Window*, we see the photo that Jeff took just as his leg got smashed up. He stepped out onto a racetrack to get a better shot, and a piece of the car hit him when it exploded.

Ariel in *The Little Mermaid* must choose between her love of objects and her personal safety: She's salvaged a fork and pipe from a shipwreck and put them in her bag, when suddenly she finds herself being attacked by a giant, ferocious shark. She tries to get away, but when she drops her bag, she bravely goes back to get it, though she has to put herself right in the shark's way to do so. That's how much your hero should love objects! (Indiana Jones going back for his hat would also count.)

### Give them confidence

In the Care section, we talked about the power of moments where the hero's confidence is collapsing, and how that makes us care acutely. But it can also work to have the hero bluff their way through the first section with confidence intact. It doesn't make us Care as much, but it certainly helps us Invest.

In the Believe section, we saw how Irving's elaborate combover ritual in *American Hustle* made him believable. In the Care section, we saw how his FBI handler then knew that he could mess up Irving's hair and hurt his hero in a way that would only hurt this hero. You would think, then, that this guy is the opposite of badass.

But, ironically, something that would seem to be proof of his insecurity winds up proving the opposite. His love interest says of him in a voiceover: "He wasn't necessarily in good shape and he had this combover that was rather . . . elaborate, but he had this air about him, and he had this confidence that drew me to him. He was who he was. He didn't care." Cocky confidence is a superpower that can turn any liability into an asset.

Jack Sparrow has nothing in the world when *Pirates of the Caribbean* begins, but he's got his confidence and that's enough to get on with. He just blithely walks onto the government boat he wants to steal. Guards named Mullroy and Murtogg try to belatedly stop him:

> Mullroy: *Hey! You! Get away from there! You don't have permission to be aboard there, mate!*

> Jack: *I'm sorry, it's just, it's such a pretty boat.*

Murtogg: *What's your name?*

Jack: *Smith. Or Smithie, if you like.*

Mullroy: *What's your purpose in Port Royal, Mr. Smith?*

Murtogg: *Yeah, and no lies.*

Jack: *All right then, I confess. It is my intention to commandeer one of these ships, pick up a crew in Tortuga, raid, pillage, plunder, and otherwise pilfer my weasel-y black guts out.*

Murtogg: *I said no lies.*

Mullroy: *I think he's telling the truth.*

Murtogg: *If he was telling the truth, he wouldn't have told us.*

Jack: *Unless of course, he knew you wouldn't believe the truth, even if he told it to you.*

We instantly love this guy.

## Make it clear they've been trained in badassery

Tara Westover's father in *Educated* is a doomsday prepper and totally divorced from reality, but, given that *our* world is becoming genuinely apocalyptic, we can't help but feel a little envy at the training she gets:

> *I had grown up preparing for the Days of Abomination, watching for the sun to darken, for the moon to drip as if with blood. I spent my summers bottling peaches and my winters rotating supplies.*

*When the World of Men failed, my family would continue on, unaffected.*

Again, it's a little obscene to compare a real person's suffering to a fictional character's, but I just do so to show that the same tools can be used by memoir writers and writers of more frivolous fiction: For instance, Sam in the *Supernatural* pilot complains to his brother, "When I told dad I was scared of the thing in my closet, he gave me a .45."

The next subcategory of badassery is . . .

## Badass Accomplishments

Of course, when we evaluate the people around us, deeds are always more impressive than words. Let's start with the big one . . .

### Have them flat out kill a dude

What could be more badass than that?

Of course, in real life, we prefer not to associate with murderers, but we have different standards for fictional characters than we do for real-world friends. We love heroes who set up explosions and then walk away without bothering to turn around. (But please don't write that scene anymore.)

This is where our reluctance to believe in the reality of your world pays off in your favor. If you don't grant humanity to a character, then the audience won't really care that you kill them off, they'll just think your hero is a badass for being willing to do it.

J. K. Rowling commits the cardinal sin of novel writing: She starts when the hero is a baby! Who can Believe/Care/Invest in a baby? But, amazingly, she manages to do all three: This baby has a scar, which gives him individuality. He has just watched his parents murdered in front of him, which makes us care about him. And, oh yeah, he's just killed the most evil wizard ever! (We're invited to assume for the first four books, as do all the adults in Harry's world, that Harry did this with some sort of inborn ability. It's only at the end of the fourth book that we find out it was really his mom's magic and Harry didn't really have anything to do with it.)

James Bond frequently begins movies by killing a guy. Sometimes this is jovial: A man tries to kill Bond in the opening moments of *Goldfinger* so Bond tosses him into a full bathtub and drops a fan in to electrocute him. As the man twitches and dies, Bond simply says, "Shocking." Sometimes it's deadly serious. In the prequel film *Casino Royale*, we begin with Bond's first kill: He has a brutal fight in another bathroom and eventually breaks away from grappling long enough to get his gun, and shoots the man in the head. M later asks how he died, and Bond responds, "Not well."

### Have them hunt and/or kill an animal

This is obviously even riskier. Readers have wildly different levels of sensitivity to the killing of animals. Some readers will be relieved that an animal died instead of a human, but many animal lovers will have the opposite reaction: "This isn't one of those filthy little humans, this is an innocent animal! *They* don't deserve to be killed off!"

So for some readers this will be an instant deal breaker. Others will say, "Damn, that's badass." But everyone will know that this is a hero who can take care of herself.

That poor lynx in *The Hunger Games* just wants to love Katniss, but it's pretty badass that she kills it for its pelt anyway. As I said before, if she wasn't desperately poor and living in a police state, we'd despise her, but as it is we see she had no choice.

We first meet Sokka in *Avatar: The Last Airbender* fishing with a big-bladed pike. That's pretty badass, even though he never catches anything. (When he's hunting in a future episode, he'll tell a land creature: "You're awfully cute, but unfortunately for you, you're made of meat.")

Of course, sometimes they kill an animal that's hunting *them*, which is *totally* justified. The most notable example would, of course, be when Luke takes out the Wampa in *The Empire Strikes Back*.

## Have them win or at least do okay in a fight

Of course, if you want to keep a death off their conscience, you can just have them do some knuckle-dusting.

Bruce isn't Batman yet at the beginning of *Batman Begins*, but he can already handle himself just fine in a fight in a foreign prison camp. He's eventually thrown into solitary confinement. He asks why and the guards tell him, "For protection." He responds, "I don't need protection." They shake their heads: "Not for you, for them."

When Sam finds an intruder in his dark apartment in the *Supernatural* pilot, he tries to wrestle the man to the floor. He quickly realizes it's his estranged brother, Dean, but they keep fighting. Each has their chance to flip the other over and pin him to the floor. We realize that each can handle himself in a fight, which will stand them in good stead for the next fifteen seasons of TV.

A hero doesn't have to have the fighting abilities of those three: We can't help but root for Ralphie to whale on the bully that's been plaguing him in *A Christmas Story*, though he doesn't exactly show much skill when he does it.

When you've got a broken-down hero, it's good to have them remember that they *used* to be able to handle themselves in a fight. The hero of the novel *Invisible Man* now lives in fear of the world, but that wasn't always the case: "One night I accidentally bumped into a man, and perhaps because of the near darkness he saw me and called me an insulting name. I sprang at him, seized his coat lapels and demanded that he apologize." The hero gets increasingly violent: "I kicked him repeatedly, in a frenzy because he still uttered insults." Eventually our hero whips out a knife and the man runs away. But the hero admits that this is not the personality he will display for most of the book: "Most of the time (although I do not choose as I once did to deny the violence of my days by ignoring it) I am not so overtly violent." It's common to get us to invest in a reader by giving a brief flash of their bravest moment, even if they won't be that way for the rest of the story.

We've looked at how mistreatment makes us care for a character. If they fight back, that will then make us invest: Jane Eyre eventually reaches a point where she can take no more: "I was conscious that a moment's mutiny had already rendered me liable to strange penalties, and, like any other rebel slave, I felt resolved, in my desperation, to go all lengths." Her relatives are impressed: "Hold her arms, Miss Abbot; she's like a mad cat."

Of course, this does not have to be a fight we approve of. In Part II, we'll look at a fight that the hero instantly regrets, and we agree that it was a bad idea, but it still helps us to invest.

### Have them stand up to a bully, or defy a corrupt person

There is no shortage of stories that begin with the hero standing up to a bully to defend a third party, like when Jim stands up for Plato in the beginning of *Rebel Without a Cause*. But of course, there are all sorts of ways to stand up to the Man.

Lila Mae in *The Intuitionist* inspects an elevator and tells the building superintendent that he needs to make a repair. He then stuffs sixty dollars in her jacket pocket and asks her to forget it. She refuses, but doesn't return the money. As he sputters, she tells him:

> *"You placed sixty dollars in my pocket. I don't think I implied by my behavior that I wanted you to bribe me, nor have I made any statement or gesture, such as an outstretched palm, for example, saying that I would change my report because you gave me money. If you want to give away your hard-earned money"*—Lila Mae waves her hand toward a concentration of graffiti—*"I see it as a curious, although in this case fortuitous, habit of yours that has nothing whatsoever to do with me. Or why I'm here."*

That's pretty badass.

### Have them get in a car chase

There's a reason that so many movie trailers focus on the movie's car chase. (And even if you're writing a novel instead of a screenplay, you can still ask yourself, "What's the 'trailer moment' here?")

The high-octane opening of *The Fast and the Furious* was thrilling enough to power us through at least ten more movies. (Want to feel old? They were stealing cutting-edge technology in that high-speed heist: DVD players.)

*Drive*, on the other hand, begins with a slower and more deliberate chase. The unnamed main character knows how to speed up just enough to hide himself on the streets of Los Angeles.

But your hero doesn't have to be a master driver: Joe in *Sunset Boulevard* sees repo men pull up behind him to repossess his car and floors it, leading them on a merry chase across town, until he ends up at Norma Desmond's mansion. That's enough to get us to root for him. Anyone who's ever been pulled over has imagined what might have happened if they'd dared to just peel out.

## Have them put themselves in harm's way

Arthur Dent in *The Hitchhiker's Guide to the Galaxy* will ultimately turn out to be a fairly passive protagonist for most of the series, but he starts out doing the most active and badass thing he does in any of the books. He realizes bulldozers are about to tear down his house, so he goes out in his robe and lies in the mud to block them, essentially daring them to kill him, and he even manages to effectively verbally spar with the foreman while he's there.

Pretty badass to "stand up" to someone when you're actually lying down in front of a bulldozer with mud seeping into your ears.

We've already looked at how one heroine flung herself out of a moving car just to escape emotional distress, but sometimes heroes must leap from a vehicle for more immediate reasons.

When Trevor Noah and his mother find themselves in an illegal cab driven by men of a rival ethnic group, they realize the men want to kill them. They have no choice: They must leap from the moving vehicle:

> *Sometimes in big Hollywood movies they'll have these crazy chase scenes where somebody jumps or gets thrown from a moving car. The person hits the ground and rolls for a bit. Then they come to a stop and pop up and dust themselves off, like it was no big deal. Whenever I see that I think, That's rubbish. Getting thrown out of a moving car hurts way worse than that.*

There's a reason that, out of all of the incidents from his eventful life, Noah begins the book with that moment.

Okay, the next subcategory of badassery:

## Showing Power

Let me just reiterate yet again that none of these things is true of every hero. There are lots of beloved heroes who have no decision-making authority or who wilt in the face of resistance, at least at first. My purpose here is not to say that any of these things are things the hero *must* do. I'm just trying to list things that you *might* have your hero do if your early readers aren't really rooting for them.

That said, let's start with . . .

## Give them decision-making authority

This is another one that's worth reiterating here. Writers love to write about rookies, but they often find that the bosses end up taking over the story, because all stories naturally gravitate in the direction of decision-makers.

Tony in *The Sopranos* says, "I'm the person who says how things go, that's who I think I am!" That's the person we want to see. In our personal lives, we sometimes hate our bosses, but we're drawn to them in fiction. We want to be with the one who can solve the problem.

This is often the flip side of having a dead parent. We feel bad for T'Challa in *Black Panther* and Elsa in *Frozen* because their fathers are dead, but we love that they're now monarchs with decision-making authority.

Moana is the rare Disney hero with living parents, but they're preparing her to take over. Her father tells her, "You are the next great chief of our people," and we see her making wise decisions about fisheries and tree groves, but in this case, it ultimately becomes a humiliating Care moment, because she keeps finding out that her role is limited. She knows that ultimately they will have to row out beyond the reef that surrounds their island, but her father still won't let her do that, even though he's telling her she's ready to be chief. "We have one rule, a rule that keeps us safe." "There's nothing beyond our reef but storms and rough seas." "Motunui is paradise, who would want to go anywhere else?" Ultimately, she will prove that she, not her father, is fit to be chief, because she will find the solution to her tribe's problems by sailing far beyond the reef.

Woody in *Toy Story* not only has a room full of toys that hang on his every word ("Woody has never steered us wrong before"), he's also got a special crack commando unit of army men to send out on special recon missions, such as spying on Andy's birthday party to see if he gets any new toys. That's a leader we want to invest in.

## Have them dominate a room or flex their power

Many writers falsely assume that we always identify with downtrodden heroes, but sometimes we prefer to gravitate toward the alpha in the room.

Jack Bauer begins the *24* pilot by taking flak from his family at home, but then he goes into work where he quickly establishes himself as top dog. An employee tries to give him some pushback, telling him that his actions may be interpreted the wrong way, but he responds, "I don't care how it's interpreted on the outside, I just gave you an order and I want you to follow it."

I said before that Olivia Pope in the *Scandal* pilot has less power than she used to, but she still has enough that when someone drops her name, the other person says, "THE Olivia Pope??" We always want to meet THE person. In fact, we find out that she can still say, when the president's people are trying to dodge her, "You tell the president to *make* time for me."

When we first meet Venkman in *Ghostbusters*, he seems like a typical Bill Murray slacker, but when he shows up at the library to investigate the paranormal activity, he suddenly takes charge. When he's questioned, he snaps, "Back off, man, I'm a scientist!"

We can see a hero dominate a room before we even meet them. In *Casablanca* we hear several people talk in awe about Rick's power before we actually meet him. Many ask to eat or drink with Rick, but the maître d' refuses them:

> Banker: *Perhaps if you told him I run the second largest banking house in Amsterdam?*

> Carl: *It wouldn't impress Rick, the leading banker in Amsterdam is now the pastry chef in our kitchen.*

We can't wait to meet this guy. We'll finally get a glimpse of him at nine minutes in, and we already love him.

### Have them keep their mouths shut

Sometimes the hero doesn't have a lot of power to flex, but they use the one type of defiance left to them: They simply refuse to speak.

There are few heroes more powerless than Chiron when he's a little kid in the first section of *Moonlight*, but he manages to hold his own simply by refusing to speak when spoken to. Sometimes silence is the only power you have.

Other times, heroes are less helpless, but still know better than to talk. When the police ask Jack Reacher questions in *Killing Floor*, he doesn't respond at all, not even to confirm that he understands English. He's been a military policeman, and he knows better:

> *Again I didn't respond. Long experience had taught me that absolute silence is the best way. Say something, and it can be misheard.*

*Misunderstood. Misinterpreted. It can get you convicted. It can get
you killed.*

Sometimes heroes are forced to respond, but keep it short,
and earn our admiration by doing so. By all rights, Billy Pilgrim
in *Slaughterhouse-Five* should be an overly frustrating hero: He's
stuck behind enemy lines in World War II and he proves to be
totally incompetent at surviving. Even worse, he's not even trying that hard, which is usually a deal breaker for audiences. In
fact, it's odd that the reader doesn't select a *different* hero. Billy
gets rescued by a badass Nazi-fighter named Roland Weary, who
has come to war ready to strike with his own personal arsenal,
and saves Billy's life a few times. Shouldn't we identify with *him*?

*"Saved your life again, you dumb bastard," Weary said to Billy in
the ditch. He had been saving Billy's life for days, cursing him,
kicking him, slapping him, making him move. It was absolutely
necessary that cruelty be used, because Billy wouldn't do anything to
save himself. Billy wanted to quit. He was cold, hungry, embarrassed, incompetent. He could scarcely distinguish between sleep and
wakefulness now, on the third day, found no important differences
either, between walking and standing still.*

*He wished everybody would leave him alone. "You guys go on with-
out me," he said again and again.*

But this is an antiwar book, and author Kurt Vonnegut gets
us to love Billy and totally despise Roland. Like Billy, we've come
unstuck in time, and as we jump around, we've begun to adopt
Billy's zen-like attitude toward life and war, and we find Roland's
belligerence to be repellent.

Billy finds it impossible to stay completely silent when

interrogated by Roland, but he manages to hold his own by being delightfully *terse*. Roland is horribly frustrated, but we love it. Sometimes all you need to do to hang your opponent is simply let them do the talking.

*"How'd you like to be hit with this—hm? Hmmmmmmmmmm?" he wanted to know.*

*"I wouldn't," said Billy.*

*"Know why the blade's triangular?"*

*"No."*

*"'Makes a wound that won't close up."*

*"Oh."*

*"Makes a three-sided hole in a guy. You stick an ordinary knife in a guy—makes a slit. Right? A slit closes right up. Right?"*

*"Right."*

*"Shit. What do you know?"*

So you have a totally non-badass character, but by refusing to engage, he holds his own and infuriates his repulsive tormentor, and we cheer him on for doing so.

Okay, so that's badassery. We love to watch people throw some power around. But now let's look at the sort of power flexing that we all can do, or at least long to do. The next category of Invest is . . .

# Wish Fulfillment
And of course the ultimate wish fulfillment is . . .

### Have them stand up to their boss and/or quit their job

At some point in our lives, we've all had a terrible boss, and we're eager to see heroes defy that situation. We long to see a hero say "Take this job and shove it," or at least stand up for themselves definitively.

Sometimes you can get a whole series out of watching a hero clash with her boss. Snarky feminist Liz Lemon turns out to be an effective sparring partner for her alpha male boss on *30 Rock*. When she skewers him upon first meeting her, he gets a little smile, then says "I like you. You have the boldness of a much younger woman."

Few people stand up to their boss as effectively as Bart in *Blazing Saddles*. When his railroad boss insists all the workers sing an old slave song, Bart instead leads a rousing rendition of "I Get No Kick from Champagne." Of course his boss, having been humiliated, seeks revenge. This eventually leads to a conflict where Bart swings a shovel to knock his boss out, which ends up with him on the gallows (only to be saved at the last second, which launches the plot of the movie).

Sometimes the hero has been planning for some time how to get out from under the yoke of his boss. Apprentice blacksmith Hiccup in *How to Train Your Dragon* is told to "Stay. Put. There." during the dragon attack, but as soon as his boss is gone, he grabs a dragon-catching device he's created and runs out to use it.

Sometimes, heroes stand up to their colleagues by abandoning their line of work entirely, turning a corner in their lives and embarking on a new path. The long opening montage of *Raising Arizona* takes Hi on quite a journey. At first he's committed to a

life of crime, like his friends Gale and Evelle. In a group coun-
selling session, they have this exchange:

Counselor: *Most men your age, Hi, are getting married and raising up a family.*

Hi: *Well, factually—*

Counselor: *They wouldn't accept prison as a substitute. Would
any of you men care to comment?*

Gale: *Well, sometimes your career's gotta come before family.*

Evelle: *Work's what's kept us happy.*

But by the end of the montage, Hi has decided to fly right
and settle down with a cop named Edwina. He honestly tells the
parole board, "That ain't me anymore."

### Have them stand up to their customers

On the other hand, if your hero *is* the boss, you can have them live
out the dream of every *boss*, and finally stand up to their *customers*.
Rick does this a lot in *Casablanca*:

• He refuses to let a Deutschbanker gamble in the casino:
"You're lucky the bar's open to you."

• He cuts off one of his bar customers: "You've had too
much to drink."

• He won't accept money to buy out Sam's contract: "I
don't buy or sell human beings."

Jake in *Chinatown* knows it's best by starting off trying to dissuade his private investigation clients: "You're better off not knowing."

Dix in *In a Lonely Place* is part of a new generation of 1950s screenwriters working as independent contractors instead of studio employees, which gives him the freedom to have this conversation:

Dix: *I won't work on something I don't like.*

Producer: *Are you in any position to be choosy?*

Dix (sneering back): *You know what you are, you're a popcorn salesman.*

We all wish we could lip off like that to the people buying our work.

## Have them live out a fantasy

Heroes don't necessarily have to quit their job to live out their fantasy. We gravitate toward heroes who do what they've always longed to do, even if it's somewhat foolish.

Miles in *Sideways* presumably doesn't quit his teaching job, but he does steal money from his mother to spend a week drinking in wine country on an extended bachelor party with his best friend. Stealing from his mother is unlikable, of course, but it's in service of going on a dream trip, which we've always wanted to do ourselves, so we're torn.

Riggan in *Birdman* follows his dreams. The critics ask him, "Why does somebody go from playing the lead in a comic book franchise to adapting Raymond Carver for the stage? . . . It's a big leap you've taken." "Well, absolutely." Later, his new costar asks him, dubiously, "You wrote this adaptation? . . . And you're *directing* the adaptation and *starring* . . . Ambitious." "Thank you," he says, deciding to take it as a compliment.

These are heroes who have put everything they have at risk to live their dream, if only for a brief moment, though there may be consequences later.

We looked before at Jane Eyre attacking her abusers like a wildcat, but abuse need not inspire physical violence. Matilda gets back at her terrible parents in her own clever way. "She decided that every time her father or her mother was beastly to her, she would get her own back in some way or another. A small victory or two would help her to tolerate their idiocies and would stop her from going crazy." She then begins to engage in a series of wicked pranks, such as permanently gluing her father's hat to his head. We've all dreamed of standing up for ourselves like that.

Okay let's get to the next big aspect of Invest . . .

## Special Skills

It's easier to invest in a hero if we know they have the know-how or training to get by. Before we get to subcategories of special skills, let's start with the three big ones:

### Make them great at their jobs

We love watching our heroes be great at their jobs. I can tell you from developing TV pilots that the number one note you get from development executives is that the hero excel at their jobs, no matter what.

John Watson meets his new roommate, "consulting detective" Sherlock Holmes, in *A Study in Scarlet* and quickly realizes how brilliant he is, as Sherlock can guess Watson's whole biography from a glance.

Agent Cooper in *Twin Peaks* is a total badass. He knows to examine a dead victim's fingers, then shoves his tweezers way up into the fingernail to pull out a typed letter *R* that was buried deep under the cuticle. This is a super-cop.

Walt in *Breaking Bad* is depressed and dispirited about his life, but he doesn't let that stop him from being a great chemistry teacher. We begin on the first day of class as he speaks about volatile reactions and turns on a Bunsen burner. He's brought spray bottles of various chemicals, and as he talks, he sprays them into the flame, causing the fire to flare up in different colors. Of course, it's ironic to see him teaching this lesson, because he will learn quite a bit about volatile reactions as the series progresses.

Jeff in *Community* is clearly a great lawyer: "I discovered at a very early age that if I talk long enough, I could make anything right or wrong, so either I'm God, or truth is relative, and in either case, boo-yah."

Even if the hero's work is dishonorable, we still want them to be good at it, such as in this exchange from *The Good Place*:

Chidi: *So your job was to defraud the elderly—sorry, the sick and elderly?*

Eleanor: *But I was very good at it. I was the top salesperson, five years running.*

Michael in *The Office* is terrible at his current job, managing the employees of a paper company, but we occasionally get reminded that he was an all-time-great *salesman*. He's the living embodiment of the Peter Principle: He was so good at sales that they felt they had to promote him to boss, which was the level of his incompetence.

## Make them resourceful

Private detective Jake Gittes in *Chinatown* is a wonderfully resourceful character.

He's been ordered by his client to follow around the water commissioner, Hollis Mulwray. Mulwray goes to the beach at night on a surveillance trip of his own, staking out a water pipe to see if fresh water gets pumped into the sea. Jake gets tired of watching Mulwray. He eventually realizes that all he really wants to know is what time Mulwray drives away. Luckily he has a resource: He keeps a collection of cheap fob watches in his glove compartment. He puts one underneath Mulwray's back tire and goes home. In the morning, he goes back and finds that Mulwray's car is gone. The smashed watch tells him what time Mulwray backed out of his spot.

Later, driving at night, Jake needs to tail a car. To make the job easier, he gets out, runs up to the other car, smashes out one of its taillights, then gets back in his own car. Now he can hang back and keep the car within sight easily, since it's the only one with one taillight.

Jake is a fairly unlikable guy in other ways, but resourcefulness goes a long way to get us to like a character, even if they're off-putting. We accept his flaws because he's so capable that we just can't help but invest in him.

Sometimes heroes have a lot less confidence than Jake, but still manage to use whatever resources they have. Cecilia in the movie *The Invisible Man* is in hiding, crippled by abject terror of her abusive boyfriend, suffering too much PTSD to go outside, but she's still doing what she can. We see her googling about ways her abuser may spy on her. When she reads about how stalkers can hack into webcams, she tries out her own webcam and determines that this is a potential danger. She considers what to do, then finds some nail polish and paints over her webcam. Even heroes in a supposedly powerless position can use whatever resources they have at hand to protect themselves, and we admire them for it.

### Show them exercising, running, lifting weights, or bicycling

We all know that heroes aren't supposed to be passive. What better way to keep them active than to get some exercise?

Put them on the track team, like Max in *Rushmore*. Put them on a cheap step machine, like Walt in *Breaking Bad*. Give them a weight set, like Donnie Brasco. Have them do some impromptu pull-ups on whatever's handy, as in *The Bourne Identity*. Have them do a full-on ropes course, like in *Silence of the Lambs*. (She passes signs that say HURT, AGONY, PAIN, and LOVE IT.)

In other words, get them up and moving. We're hardwired to root for characters who are exercising. They're preparing their bodies for whatever may come. (And, of course, preparing your body helps prepare your mind. The brain needs some oxygen, too.)

And exercise, like anything else, can be ironic. Don Draper in *Mad Men* uses one of those bizarre spring-loaded chest expander things in his office, but he's smoking a cigarette while he does so.

One particularly good form of exercise is to ride a bicycle. If you're on a bicycle, you're out in the world, exposed to the elements, propelling yourself with your own leg power.

Ten years before *The Imitation Game* came out, I wrote and *almost* sold my own biopic of Alan Turing. When I saw the film that *did* get made, I was shocked they didn't include Turing's beloved bicycle. In Turing's case, his bicycle riding also showed off his mental skills, because he knew his chain would pop off every 150 revolutions or so, so he would always count how many times he'd pedaled, then get off and cinch it back on just before it could pop off.

This brings up another reason bicycles are great: They often imply the hero is economically disadvantaged, but still gamely going about their lives. Andy in *The 40-Year-Old Virgin* gets mocked for not having a car in LA, but he doesn't let it keep him from getting around.

One subcategory of special skills is . . .

## Intellectual Skills

Starting with . . .

### Have them do mental math

We just discussed Turing's mental bicycle math, but now let's jump to a hero who is *not* generally known as a mathematician.

Lee Child's books aren't meticulous works of literature, but they do have some fans with literary pedigrees, including *New Yorker* editor David Remnick and one of his star writers, Malcolm Gladwell. Gladwell did a good job summing up the appeal of the Jack Reacher books: "Action, in a Reacher book, is nearly always a secondary matter. We know going in that Reacher will kill the bad guy through some combination of tactical brilliance and brute force. The pleasure is in Reacher's moment of introspection in the millisecond before the action occurs: his silent consideration of the variables of physics, geometry, and psychology that comprise a violent encounter."

Indeed, this is something novels are uniquely good at showing us, even novels that are primarily known for their action. If we're going to be in the hero's head, we want to see the unique angles that only they see.

In the original Arthur Conan Doyle novels, Sherlock Holmes was an accomplished boxer, but most screen versions have left that out. The Robert Downey Jr. version kept it in, and showed during each fight how Sherlock would mentally plan his moves in advance.

In *Captain America*, the army trainees are marched out to a flagpole and told that the first one who can get the flag down will get to ride home in a jeep with the female observer, Sharon Carter. The men instantly start climbing all over each other to try to make it to the top but nobody can make it. After they give up, however, scrawny Steve Rogers spots something: There's a way to undo the latch at the bottom and knock the flagpole over. He topples it to the ground, scoops up the flag (don't worry, it's not the American flag), and enjoys the car ride back, eventually finding love with Sharon.

## Make them wilier than those around them

Sometimes, it's not so much a matter of outsmarting as it just is of wiliness. Have them be attentive to any chance to press their advantage.

Luke Skywalker is notable for his openhearted idealism. There's a reason he dresses all in white: He's unambiguously good! But Luke is a big fan of tricks and traps. He actually uses a *lot* of indirect and manipulative dialogue, in an admirably crafty way:

- He tries to trap his Uncle Owen by talking up the usefulness of the new droids before slyly segueing to the idea they could take his place on the farm ("I think those new droids are going to work out fine. In fact, I, uh, was also thinking about our agreement . . .")

- He goads Han into accepting their offer in the cantina ("We could buy our own ship for that!") and into working harder on making the jump to light speed ("I thought you said this thing was *fast*?")

- He hammers away at Han when he won't help in rescuing Leia, circling around him looking for weak spots, until he finally figures it out ("She's *rich!*")

- Once he wins Han over, he's the one who comes up with the trick where they pretend Chewy is their captive.

We think of Han as the slick one, but he's actually transparent and plainspoken, while Luke is far more wily, and more likely to wrap Han around his finger. This culminates in the finale, when Luke finally convinces Han to totally betray his own self-interest by hitting him below the belt one last time: "Well, take care of yourself, Han . . . guess that's what you're best at, isn't it?"

Obi-Wan isn't the only one who knows how to play mind tricks!

### Have them show great enthusiasm

Mike in *Stranger Things* could not be a better Dungeons & Dragons dungeon master. He holds his friends Will, Dustin, and Lucas spellbound:

Mike: *Something is coming . . . Something hungry for blood . . . A shadow grows on the wall behind you, swallowing you in darkness. It is almost here . . .*

Will (worried): *What is it?*

Dustin: *What if it's the Demogorgon? Oh, Jesus, we're so screwed if it's the Demogorgon.*

Lucas: *It's not the Demogorgon.*

Mike: *An army of* troglodytes *charges into the chamber!*

Dustin: *Troglodytes?*

Lucas: *Told ya. [Chuckling]*

Mike (softly): *Wait a minute . . . Did you hear that? That . . . that sound? [Whispers] Boom . . . boom . . . [Yells] Boom! [Slams table] That didn't come from the troglodytes. No, that . . . that came from something else. The Demogorgon!*

Dustin: *We're in deep shit.*

Mike: *Will, your action??*

Will: *I don't know!*

Soon, Mike will show just as much enthusiasm for resolving a real-life monster problem.

Sometimes enthusiasm scenes can be fairly comic. Miles in *Sideways* is at a vineyard teaching his friend Jack how to drink a glass of fine wine. He shows him how to swish it around, then stick your nose into the glass and smell it. While Miles does so, he unconsciously puts his finger to his ear. No one is talking at the time, so there's no noise to distract him from his smelling, but his senses are simply overwhelmed by the wine and he has to cut down on sensory information somehow.

It's a ridiculous moment, it's a funny moment, but I think it's also an Invest moment. We wish we had so much expertise that our senses could be overwhelmed by our experiences.

Sometimes, we just like that a first-person narrator is showing a lot of enthusiasm in telling us this story. Ishmael in *Moby-Dick* is a fun storyteller to listen to: "But look! here come more crowds, pacing straight for the water, and seemingly bound for a dive. Strange! Nothing will content them but the extremest limit of the land." His enthusiasm is infectious and helps get us wrapped up in his story.

### Have them strategize

Some heroes have virtually no resources, but everyone has the ability to *plan*.

In *Snowpiercer*, we meet a group of desperate stragglers living in the back of a train that never stops. They stand at attention as troops from the front of the train come in for a bed check. One of the troops has a little clicker and orders them to sit down in rows. When he gets to the seventh row, one man doesn't sit down. This is Curtis. Does he intend to defy them? To get in a fight? His friend Edgar has sat down next to him and yanks on Curtis's leg. The guard barks:

Guard: *Hey you, sit down.*

Edgar: *Curtis, sit down.*

Guard: *Sit down! I said sit down!*

When the guards see that Curtis is defying them, they signal for doors behind them to be closed. First one closes, then the other. At this point, Curtis finally sits down. Edgar hisses in his ear:

Edgar: *What the fuck are you doing?*

Curtis: *Counting.*

Edgar: *Can't you sit and count? Do you want to get shot? You're crazy.*

Curtis: *Shut up, Edgar, I'm thinking.*

Edgar doesn't understand what Curtis means and just assumes that Curtis was showing defiance. Later, when they're ordered to sit down again, Curtis goes down but Edgar refuses. This time Curtis pulls Edgar down.

Curtis: *Now isn't the time.*

Edgar: *When is the time?*

Curtis: *Soon.*

A few scenes later, when he's talking to his mentor, Gilliam, we finally find out what Curtis was counting how long it takes each door to close when someone defies them: "Four seconds when all three gates are open at once."

Now he's almost ready to go. He just needs one more sign. When the evil ruler comes back, she says to one of her men at one point, "Put down that useless gun." This is the trigger he's been waiting for: He realizes that the bad guys are out of bullets. He's finally ready to begin the revolution.

On to another subcategory of special skills . . .

## Social Skills

We've seen that we sometimes Care more about heroes when they fall all over themselves, but the opposite can help us Invest. Watching heroes deftly handle social situations makes us worry about a character less, but it wins our admiration. Let's start with . . .

### Have them be good parents

Sometimes this is just a sympathetic portrait of things many parents do: With a benign smile on her face, Amelia in *The Babadook* goes through the elaborate ritual every night of checking under the bed and in each closet for monsters with her son.

But sometimes, the parent goes a little more above and beyond . . . *Breaking Bad* and *The Americans* both cheat to get you to commit to their heroes. Over the course of these shows, both dads will be pretty horrible to their kids, putting them in a tremendous amount of danger in furtherance of their own criminal schemes. But there are similar beats in both pilots: Each dad stands up to people picking on their kid (in a clothing store) in a way they would never really do again for the rest of the series.

On *Breaking Bad*, bullies are picking on Walt's disabled son in a jeans store. At first Walt leaves, but, emboldened by his titular psychotic break, he comes back, kicks one to the ground, then stands on his leg: "What's the matter chief, having a little trouble walking?" Finally, the bully mutters "Psycho" and leaves. We think, "Hey, it'll be *good* that Walt breaks bad!" In fact, he will rarely stick up for the little guy, but they knew that he had to do it in the pilot, just to get us on his side.

The pilot for *The Americans* basically stole that storyline, for similar purposes: Undercover Soviet spy Phil Jennings is clothes shopping with his thirteen-year-old daughter when an older man starts hitting on her. Once again, Phil backs down at first, but then he tracks the guy down and beats him into submission. As with Walt, Phil will rarely use his powers for good in the series, but he does so in the pilot just to get us on his side.

### Have them be good with other people's kids

Treating kids like adults is always likable. We've all been in awkward situations with other people's children and admire anyone who can navigate those treacherous waters.

Dev in *Master of None* masterfully bonds with his friend's little children, Lila and Grant, which also bonds him to us.

> Dev: *Hey, what's up, guys? Lila, what's going on? How are you? I heard you got married recently. How come I didn't get invited to the wedding?*

> Lila (not sure if he's kidding): *I didn't get married!*

> Dev: *That's not what I heard. I heard you have a husband. It was a small ceremony, just family and friends. Fine, whatever. I get it.*

> Lila (amused but exasperated): *I'm not married!*

> Dev: *Okay, well, I guess I'll just keep that blender for myself, then. [Turns to Grant] Grant, what's up, man?*

> Grant: *Farts!*

Dev (laughs, tries again): *All right, well, that's cool. Um, you want to arm wrestle?*

Grant: *Sure.*

Dev: *All right. [Arm wrestles, pretends to lose] Oh, God. Oh, my arm! Ooh!*

Grant (laughing): *You're so weak!*

In *Snowpiercer*, someone in the front of the train sends a message to the wretches in the back, hidden in one of the gelatinous protein cubes that provide their only sustenance. They're searching for which cube has it and find it belongs to a five-year-old boy, who won't give it up. Curtis gets down on the boy's level and does an elaborate high-five ritual to win him over.

## Have them be cool
Sometimes everyone around the hero finds them cool, as is the case with James Bond. The game that Bond wins at the beginning of *Dr. No* (chemin de fer) has no element of skill, you just have to be lucky, but he looks so cool doing it that the girl he defeats, Sylvia Trench, is very impressed:

Sylvia: *Too bad you have to go. Just as things were getting interesting.*

Bond: *Tell me, Miss Trench, do you play any other games? Besides chemin de fer.*

Sylvia: *Hmm . . . Golf . . . Amongst other things.*

Britta in the *Community* pilot tells Jeff she doesn't want to make small talk. Jeff asks, "What's your deal?" She asks, "Isn't that small talk?" He replies, "What's your deal and is God dead?" We and Britta are both amused. (But soon his coolness sours on those around him. Once he's revealed to be a jerk, his new friend Abed says, "I thought you were like Bill Murray in his films. But you're more like Michael Douglas in his films.")

Sometimes only *we* find the hero cool. Jenny in *An Education* leads a pretty empty life, but *we* certainly think she's cool, passing her high school years listening to awesome French pop records in her room.

Sometimes the hero knows she's cooler than she's generally perceived. The title character in *Juno* is mocked in a high school hallway by a bully named Steve Rendazo, but she assures us in a voiceover:

> *The funny thing is that Steve Rendazo secretly wants me. Jocks like him always want freaky girls. Girls with horn-rimmed glasses and vegan footwear and Goth makeup. Girls who play the cello and wear Converse All-Stars and want to be children's librarians when they grow up. Oh yeah, jocks eat that shit up.*

## Have them be witty

Not every hero has to be witty. You can even make comedies in which nobody cracks a joke, it's just the situations that are funny. *Airplane!* is a good example.

The Marvel Cinematic Universe relies on wit a bit too much. In the comics, both Dr. Strange and Shang-Chi are, each in their own way, deeply spiritual characters and not remotely quick with a quip, but Marvel's heroes all trend in the same direction. In order to fit in, they both had to become a lot more chuckleheaded.

Nevertheless, wittiness can be a great tool for winning us

over, especially in breezy movies. In the 2001 version of *Ocean's Eleven*, we know right away we'll like Danny:

> Parole Board Member: *Mr. Ocean, what we're trying to find out is: Was there a reason you chose to commit this crime, or was there a reason why you simply got caught this time?*

> Danny: *My wife left me. I was upset. I got into a self-destructive pattern.*

> Another Parole Board Member: *If released, is it likely you would fall back into a similar pattern?*

> Danny: *She already left me once. I don't think she'd do it again just for kicks.*

Will Smith in *Men in Black* jumps from a bridge onto the open top deck of a double-decker bus in pursuit of a suspect. When the tourists yelp in shock, he says, "It just be raining Black people in New York."

In the *Cheers* pilot, Sam has to endure Diane quoting a long poetry verse. She then smiles and says, "That's Donne." He smiles back and says, "I certainly hope so."

In *In a Lonely Place*, Dix may be a downer, but his personality nevertheless sparkles: The girl at the bar complains that he never picks up the phone when she calls: "Don't you like to talk anymore?" "Not to people who have my number." Later, she says, suggestively, "Remember how I used to read to you?" He responds, "Since then I've learned to read by myself."

Sometimes only *we* know it's funny: After seducing the reporter who was trying to write a damning profile of him, Tony in *Iron Man* explains to his friend Rhodey why he was late: "I was doing a piece for *Vanity Fair.*" Rhodey doesn't realize that this is a joke, so it's just between Tony and us.

Sometimes, the hero's humor can be self-deprecating and droll: Ishmael in *Moby-Dick* amuses us by humbly imagining where his sea voyage will be listed in the book of fate, hidden among more impressive events: *"Grand Contested Election for the Presidency of the United States.* WHALING VOYAGE BY ONE ISHMAEL. BLOODY BATTLE IN AFFGHANISTAN." (I read the book in 2002, when I was sandwiched between a grand contested election for the presidency of the United States and several bloody battles in Afghanistan, so it was a rather uncanny thing to read.)

### Have them be precocious

We first meet Lisa Simpson in a Christmas pageant portraying Towanga, the Santa Claus of the South Seas, doing a badass dance whirling torches around herself. We can tell she's pretty awesome.

Max in *Rushmore* says to his headmaster, "Do you remember how I got into this school?" The headmaster replies, "You wrote a play." Max says, "A little one-act about Watergate." We're bemused: What could a kid know or understand about Watergate? We're sure the play was awful, but we can't help but admire his gumption.

Jo in *Little Women* also fancies herself capable of writing elaborate plays about adult topics. The play she stages with her sisters starts off poorly, but then improves:

> *Then things went smoothly, for Don Pedro defied the world in a speech of two pages without a single break. Hagar, the witch, chanted an awful incantation over her kettleful of simmering toads, with weird effect. Roderigo rent his chains asunder manfully, and*

*Hugo died in agonies of remorse and arsenic, with a wild, "Ha! Ha!"*

*"It's the best we've had yet," said Meg, as the dead villain sat up and rubbed his elbows.*

*"I don't see how you can write and act such splendid things, Jo. You're a regular Shakespeare!" exclaimed Beth, who firmly believed that her sisters were gifted with wonderful genius in all things.*

*"Not quite," replied Jo modestly. "I do think The Witches Curse, an Operatic Tragedy is rather a nice thing, but I'd like to try Macbeth."*

Generations of girls (and boys) who have read this have longed to be Jo, collaborating with her sisters to create fun works of art at a young age.

But Matilda is more of a genuine genius than those two:

*It is bad enough when parents treat ordinary children as though they were scabs and bunions, but it becomes somehow a lot worse when the child in question is extra-ordinary, and by that I mean sensitive and brilliant. Matilda was both of these things, but above all she was brilliant. Her mind was so nimble and she was so quick to learn that her ability should have been obvious even to the most half-witted of parents.*

Many young readers have had their own experience of being precocious, and identify intensely with Matilda. No one, not even the sympathetic librarian, believes she's really reading all the books she checks out. Every precocious kid has had that experience.

The final subcategory of special skills is . . .

## Superpowers and Gadgets

Obviously beginning with . . .

### Just give them actual superpowers

This is tricky because most superhero movies get us to Believe, Care, and Invest *before* the hero has powers. If the hero's not going to get powers until the forty-minute mark, such as in *Spider-Man* or *Captain America: The First Avenger*, you can't wait until then to get us to Invest.

But in some stories, the heroes have powers from the beginning, and that certainly makes them easy to Invest in, such as with *Captain Marvel* and *Black Panther*.

It's not just superheroes who have superpowers. Lila Mae in *The Intuitionist* has a mystical ability to sense what's wrong with elevators without having to open a single panel.

Sometimes superpowers are unwanted. Danny certainly doesn't enjoy getting flashes of blood filling a lobby, but ultimately his titular psychic powers will come in handy in *The Shining*.

Riggan in Birdman *seemingly* has superpowers. We first meet him levitating in his apartment. Later, he seems to mentally make a light fall on his fellow actor, then he turns off a TV with his mind. Ultimately, we conclude that he's probably imagining things—he used to play a superhero on screen and it's twisted his mind a bit—but it helps us Invest in him at first.

Sometimes, in a world where superpowers are common, you have to make your hero stand out by giving them even *more* superpowers. In the *Avatar: The Last Airbender* pilot, we meet a firebender and a waterbender, but Aang can bend earth, air, fire, *and* water. We can see why he's the title hero.

Irony is always good, so it's good to turn your hero's disability into a superpower. This will certainly be the case with one of the comics we'll look at in Part Two, but there are lots of examples.

Percy Jackson finds that his ADHD can be turned to his advantage. Carrie in *Homeland* finds that the same bipolar disorder that makes her paranoid also gives her a unique ability to see conspiracies that everyone else fails to spot.

### Give them super tools or gadgets

Of course, Aang doesn't just have superpowers, he's also got a neat glider thing. We always like unique objects.

One great thing about Thor's hammer is that no other superhero has one. It makes him a unique individual. The other great thing about it, as opposed to a sword, is that it doesn't require bloodletting to work well. You can whack the hell out of superpowered bad guys without slicing them open, which makes for a good all-ages comic or movie.

Some heroes are positively gadget-dependent, such as James Bond or Batman. Other heroes are less defined by their gadgets, but still rely on them to win us over. Peter Quill in *Guardians of the Galaxy* has no powers, but he has awesome gadgets. When we first meet him, he uses special goggles to see what a ruined city used to look like. Then he uses boot jets to cross a fissure. Then he uses some sort of super-magnet to pull an orb out of a force field. We now Invest in this guy.

Sometimes a hero can turn a normal tool into a super-tool. Jeff has gotten himself laid up with his picture-taking in *Rear Window*, but now that he's turned into a full-time Peeping Tom, he finds that his telephoto lens has other uses.

Okay, let's look at the final category for Invest:

# Attitude

Sometimes, the hero has few skills, superpowers, or hammers, but they do have a good attitude, and that stands them well in life . . .

## Give them spirit

Heroes often have everything going against them, but we want them to brave that with good spirits.

Anna in *Frozen* lives a pretty bereft life. Yes, she's rich and has a palace and servants, but she's essentially been locked in for years, her parents died, and her only family member has stopped speaking to her with no explanation. But Anna has one thing going for her: She has pluck. She sings as she dances around the castle, leaping up to imitate the poses in the paintings on the wall.

The early versions of that song were too depressing, before they realized they needed to give her more spirit. Writer/director Jennifer Lee appeared on the Scriptnotes podcast, where she was interviewed by guest cohost Aline Brosh McKenna:

McKenna: *So you made it less sad by making her sort of an imp.*

Lee: *Yes. And saying this is the girl that you're going to go on the journey with. These are things about her that you can laugh in her loneliness, I mean, and that's very Anna. But that was the hardest, I mean, a lot of songs came and went, but that one was the one we all believed in and couldn't make work for the longest time. And it was because it was so much. It had to do so much.*

Buddy in *Elf* doesn't really have any special skills. He's totally incompetent at all elf tasks, and he doesn't really have other skills to compensate, but he does have one thing that makes all the difference.

Buddy finally finds out why he doesn't fit in: He's actually a human who crawled into Santa's bag one day at an orphanage. He decides to seek out his human dad, but Santa warns him that his dad's on the naughty list:

Santa: *Some people, they just lose sight of what's important in life, that doesn't mean they can't find their way again, huh? Maybe all they need is just a little Christmas spirit!*

Buddy: *Well, I'm—I'm good at that!*

Santa: *I know you are.*

So this is a classic story about an incompetent hero with just one valuable quality, put into a situation where that one quality is badly needed.

## Have them do the right thing

It's appropriate that we finish this section of the book with the closest we're going to get to saving cats.

I will now begrudgingly admit that, though it's not common, you do *sometimes* get actual "save the cat" moments and they *can* help us like the hero. Moana protects a baby turtle making his way to the ocean for the first time. Cecilia in the movie *The Invisible Man* takes the electronic shock collar off her abuser's dog, even though it puts her in more danger.

But it doesn't have to be animals. *It's a Wonderful Life* begins with George Bailey in present day considering suicide, but then we find that, ironically, he's led a wonderful life. Part of that wonderfulness is that he's been a great hero. We begin with a younger actor doing two heroic actions: First he dives into a freezing lake to rescue his brother (costing him his hearing in one ear), then we see him intervene when the pharmacist he works for almost makes a mistake that would kill people.

Sometimes, there's a hero who does the right thing when we least expect it. Katniss is no cat-saver, but she does ultimately do the right thing, signing up for the Hunger Games to save her sister. As I've said before, this is much more meaningful because she's been so focused on staying out of the games, and so it's ironic that she ends up signing up.

Nick in *Gone Girl* isn't a particularly noble person. He was living the frivolous life of a New York magazine writer when he got married, then got fired and started hanging out on the couch for months. But then he gets a call from his twin sister: Their mother is sick and she wants Nick to come home and take care of her. Nick knows it will probably ruin his marriage, but he also knows that it's the right thing to do, so he moves back home to take care of his mom.

OKAY, SO THAT'S Believe, Care, and Invest! Mix and match from all the advice above to make your hero pop vividly in the first ten pages. Make the reader say, "I *love* this hero, and I'll follow her *anywhere*."

Part II

# PUTTING IT ALL TOGETHER

B UT NOW HERE'S SOME BAD NEWS: YOU CAN'T CHOOSE at random from all of the above. You have to choose carefully, and interweave a Believe, Care, and Invest that cohere together organically.

You have to be aware that some Believe moments (such as showing that their job is mundane) will cause us to Care less. Some Care moments (such as showing a lack of confidence) will cause us to Invest less, and some Invest moments (such as giving them superpowers) might cause us to Believe less. As with creating a Dungeons & Dragons avatar, you have to balance out various traits to create a compelling character.

You have to be careful not to lose your audience. I can think of various recent winners of the Best Screenplay Oscar that received quite a bit of backlash from the screenwriting community. They'll say, "Sure, these characters are witty, but they're so witty that they're unbelievable. Is this an award for *best* written, or *most* written?" (Of course, some would say those other writers are just jealous!)

So how do you balance them out?

Ideally, you want to look for examples like Harry's scar, Irving's toupee in *American Hustle*, or the temperature information in *Gravity* that achieve Believe, Care, and Invest *all at the same time*.

The key here is that you want the character to be *compelling* and *intriguing*. Everything we read should make us want to read more. This character should get us on the hook. We should think, "I just have to see what this hero is going to do."

What we're going to focus on in Part II is a fourth element beyond Believe, Care, and Invest. You can't just overwhelm us with tricks designed to make us identify with a hero, or else the character will seem too sickly sweet and we will gag. The whole reason I've taught you all these sweeteners is that I'm assuming you'll have some sour, too. The fourth element is Liabilities.

You've come up with a perfect concept, but you're aware that your concept generates a hero who, for some reason, isn't *perfectly* likable. There's some reason we may have a hard time identifying with them. This is *good*. Your characters should not bend over backward to be liked. They should break some of the unbreakable writing rules, or else they'll be too predictable.

On SecretsOfStory.com, I've done 130 BCI breakdowns. Thirty novels, sixty-five movies, twenty-five TV pilots, and ten memoirs. For each one, I focused on what inherent liabilities this character had. What is there that makes this hero hard to identify with? I then looked at how BCI was used to overcome those hurdles. I originally intended to include all 130 here, but that would of course be ridiculous. So let's look at just twenty examples: five novels, five movies, five TV pilots, and five memoirs. I picked out those twenty examples and decided to reserve them for Part II, so for the most part I haven't referenced them in the first half.

I don't want to overwhelm you with too many, I just wanted a quick roundup to show you how a complete BCI works. This is just a sampling of what you'll find at the website.

Throughout this section, I have tried to represent a diversity of genres and backgrounds of the authors. But I am going to stick to examples written in English, because I want to talk a little about the authors' language and I can't do that if I'm not reading the original words.

Okay, let's start with . . .

## Believe, Care, Invest: Novels

Different types of writers disagree on who's got the hardest job, but I personally think novel writing is the most challenging type of writing. First and foremost, there's the issue of quantity: Novelists simply have to write more words than any other writers. Then there's the issue that novelists never get to hand their work off to anyone else, as a screenwriter does. You have to be in charge of props, costume, hair, makeup, and lighting. You have to provide every nuance of every actor's performance, you have to frame every shot, you have to time every edit. And you have to do it all on the page.

And only novelists have to worry about the most dreaded word of all, "voice." Whether first-person or third-person, you're supposed to have personality not just in your dialogue, but in your *descriptions*. You can't even set the scene without having the quality of your writing judged! It's maddening.

And no one has to hit the ground running as hard as novelists. Asking someone to read a whole novel manuscript is a big ask. We might give a screenplay or TV script twenty pages to achieve BCI, just because they're quick to read, but slogging through ten pages of a novel we're not digging is more than enough to get us to bail. We're looking for *any* excuse to put your magnum opus down unless the hero totally grabs us right away.

So you've got a lot of work to do.

When choosing which examples to highlight in this book, I've looked for ones where the writers had particular challenges. I'm not exactly looking for "pure" BCI, but rather focusing on ones where the BCI was unusual in some way. On the blog, you can find more typical ones.

## Our Choice of Heroes in George R. R. Martin's *A Game of Thrones*

*The fantasy kingdom of Westeros: Three rangers patrol north of the Wall and encounter ice zombies. One survives and flees, but he is caught south of the Wall and executed for desertion by Lord Eddard Stark. We see this through the eyes of Eddard's young son Bran. On the way home, the Starks find a litter of direwolves and adopt them.*

*Massive spoilers for the book series and TV show follow. Skip to the next example if you don't want to know what happens!*

It's fascinating to reread this first chapter, knowing how it all ends. For the past twenty years, readers have been saying to themselves, "Why do we start with Bran?? He's such a minor character!" Little did we suspect . . . Maybe Martin knew what he was doing all along.

But before we get to Bran, we start with a prologue. These pages are not yet identified as Chapter 1, so we sense that we need not fall in love with these characters, but this prologue is long-ish, so if we didn't find the characters and situation compelling we'd probably stop reading.

Ultimately, we will realize that these opening pages prefigure the whole series. Our POV character watches as a grizzled old veteran ranger, whose sword is "nicked from hard use," is led into disaster by a "lordling" whose sword has never "been swung in anger" (the ultimate insult in this manly world). Over the course of the next three books, both the North and South of Westeros will be led into disaster by too-young lords that are ill-prepared for leadership.

We never find out enough about the prologue's POV character, Will, to Believe, Care, Invest, but we certainly do so for the veteran, Gerad, who gets lots of details, suffers mightily, and shows his clever skills. We even come to appreciate the lordling, Royce, who, in a nice ironic turn, dies bravely. We sense that these aren't our heroes, and don't really invest our hopes and dreams in them, but we can tell from these pages that Martin *can* make us identify with heroes, if he wants to, and we trust him going forward.

Another thing this intro establishes is Martin's greatest strength: his ability to put the audience on an emotional roller coaster. Over and over in this series, Martin will fool the reader into thinking that the heroes will triumph, only for something awful to happen. The most essential line in this prologue is this:

*For a moment, he dared to hope.*

That's a dead-simple trick that any writer can use: Lift the reader up, then cut them down. Martin has a curiously sadistic relationship to his readers. Perhaps more than any other popular writer, he really likes to torture his heroes (to death), which also tortures the readers who love those characters . . . but we wouldn't have it any other way. He triggers a pleasurable masochism within the reader. Every time Martin tricks us into daring to hope, then viciously punishes us for it, we get a thrill.

But we still haven't met any main characters, so let's move on to Chapter 1, which is named "Bran." Right away, we start getting a little nervous: We find out in the first paragraph that Bran is seven years old! Is this a kids' book? It doesn't seem so from the page count. Martin is basically counting on us to flip ahead and see that the book's seventy-two chapters will be credited to eight different third-person POVs, and Bran will only get seven of those chapters. We sense that Bran is *not* going to solve the book's big problems, so we need not fully invest our hopes and dreams in him.

So Martin has a tricky task: We're meeting our main cast now, but we're meeting them through the POV of a (seemingly) minor character. His goal in the first real chapter is to get us to believe in and care for this *family*, and then, through Bran's eyes, search for some member of the family *other* than Bran that we can invest our hopes and dreams in.

## Believe

After reading the prologue, we already believe in the reality of this world. Martin is mostly Italian American and grew up in a New Jersey housing project in the 1960s, and yet he convinces us that surely he must have lived in medieval England at some point with his wealth of detail.

And Bran is a believable seven-year-old: eager to be included in adult things but anxious about what he might see. We are told it's been summer for nine years but winter is coming, so seven-year-old Bran is about to know the cold for the first time, which is a metaphor for the chilling step into reality we all must take on the brink of adolescence.

## Care

Bran is not suffering all that much. Sure, he feels cold, and he's being forced to watch a man being beheaded, which disturbs him. Later, he almost has to watch some wolf-puppies put to death. But the *real* reason we care about Bran is because we sense, from reading the prologue, that the ice zombies we've met in the prologue will eventually come for him, and he's so terribly unaware of this. (In fact, they will come *just* for him, though those who stick to the books may never find that out.) We care for him because we can see what he can't see.

The novel's multiple-POV structure ensures that we will always know more about what's going on than any of the POV characters we're reading about, not just plot-wise, but also morally. We know from the prologue that the deserter had a good reason to flee, which none of the Starks bother to elicit. Each POV jump for the rest of the book will follow this pattern. There will never be a character who understands this world as fully as the reader does. Only we can see the ironic contrasts between these points of view. Only we know how tragic all of these events truly are. We care about these characters in an almost godly way: What fools these mortals be.

## Invest

We're in an odd position: We discover that we were correct not to invest our hopes in any of the characters from the prologue, and we can't really invest in a seven-year-old boy, but we can tell that the Starks are going to be our main characters, so we examine them through Bran's eyes, looking for a hero.

The most obvious choice is Eddard, who seems like a manly and responsible Lord in his insistence on being the one who swings the beheading sword himself. And if we've flipped ahead, we know that he will have the most POV chapters. But we also can see that Eddard has a limited perspective. He dismisses what Will has to say without really listening, leaving his kingdom eventually vulnerable to ice zombie attack. And of course, as fantasy readers, we're conditioned to seek out young heroes so we're also looking at his sons, whether adopted, blood, or bastard.

It's easy to dismiss Theon Greyjoy, Eddard's ward:

> *The head bounced off a thick root and rolled. It came up near Greyjoy's feet. Theon was a lean, dark youth of nineteen who found everything amusing. He laughed, put his boot on the head, and kicked it away.*

But it's not so easy to choose between Eddard's bastard son, Jon, and his official heir, Robb:

> *"Ass," Jon muttered, low enough so Greyjoy did not hear. He put a hand on Bran's shoulder, and Bran looked over at his bastard brother. "You did well," Jon told him solemnly. Jon was fourteen, an old hand at justice.*

> *It seemed colder on the long ride back to Winterfell, though the wind had died by then and the sun was higher in the sky. Bran rode with his brothers, well ahead of the main party, his pony struggling hard to keep up with their horses.*

> *"The deserter died bravely," Robb said. He was big and broad and growing every day, with his mother's coloring, the fair skin, red-brown hair, and blue eyes of the Tullys of Riverrun. "He had courage, at the least."*

> *"No," Jon Snow said quietly. "It was not courage. This one was dead of fear. You could see it in his eyes, Stark." Jon's eyes were a grey so dark they seemed almost black, but there was little they did not see. He was of an age with Robb, but they did not look alike. Jon was slender where Robb was muscular, dark where Robb was fair, graceful and quick where his half brother was strong and fast.*

*Robb was not impressed. "The Others take his eyes," he swore.
"He died well. Race you to the bridge?"*

In the introduction it was easy enough to choose between the two men that were being described: Gerad was full of manly virtues and the lordling Royce was not. Here, it's harder: Robb and Jon offer two different visions of manhood that both seem equally appealing at this point. Ultimately, we (correctly) invest more in Jon, because he perceives more of what we know, and shows more compassion to Bran, but it will take three long books before we can be sure we've made the right choice.

Of course, on some level, the moral of the prologue lingers in our minds: Don't trust lordlings.

As with any fantasy author, Martin is asking a lot of his readers: He's asking us to commit to a long book with lots of characters. In the end, this book will not end satisfactorily, demanding we read the next and the next in a search for satisfaction that will never end, because it's more than two decades later and it seems likely Martin will never finish the book series.

There's only one good reason to read this series: Because it is pleasurable to read each chapter. Martin will not honor the pledges that most authors make to their readers, but we will forgive him for that, because the books are so enjoyable.

## Meg Murry in Madeleine L'Engle's *A Wrinkle in Time*

*A small town in Massachusetts in 1962: Twelve-year-old Meg Murry cowers in her bed from a midnight storm. She thinks about what all has gone wrong with her life, including her father disappearing. She*

*laments that she got in a fight when she heard someone insulting her*
*odd little brother. She eventually decides to get up and make herself a*
*sandwich.*

This is one of the trickiest books we'll look at, because this is a rare kids' novel that does not ask us to fully identify with the heroine. We will judge Meg as much as we identify with her. Let's walk through it.

L'Engle begins with a very odd choice: She intentionally starts off with the most clichéd opening in literature (though kids may not know that): "It was a dark and stormy night." L'Engle's puckishly laying down a gauntlet: I can win you over after first getting you to roll your eyes! We then meet Meg as she huddles in fear from that storm and L'Engle has to get us to identify with her . . .

## Believe

L'Engle perfectly captures the thought patterns of a twelve-year-old in a way we recognize and identify with:

*—A delinquent, that's what I am, she thought grimly.—That's*
*what they'll be saying next. Not Mother. But Them. Everybody*
*Else. I wish Father—*

*But it was still not possible to think about her father without the*
*danger of tears. Only her mother could talk about him in a natural*
*way, saying, "When your father gets back—"*

*Gets back from where? And when? Surely her mother must know*
*what people were saying, must be aware of the smugly vicious gossip.*
*Surely it must hurt her as it did Meg. But if it did she gave no out-*
*ward sign. Nothing ruffled the serenity of her expression.*

*—Why can't I hide it, too? Meg thought. Why do I always have to
show everything?*

Good dialogue allows scene partners to step all over each other's sentences, but here we see that a lone heroine can also do
that to herself in her own head. Short, choppy sentences with
lots of em dashes, a brain anxiously circling downward in a miserable spiral of self-pity. We get to know the specific details of
her situation in a rhythm and syntax we recognize as similar to
our own inner voice.

In later chapters we'll get a physical description of Meg that
many young readers will identify with ("Automatically she pushed
her glasses into position, ran her fingers through her mouse-
brown hair"), but we're already identifying with her intensely,
because of her very recognizable internal voice.

## Care

Here's where things get tricky. L'Engle invites us to be a little judgmental of her heroine. Meg's afraid of the storm raging outside, and
afraid of tales of a "tramp" threatening the neighborhood . . . but
we're not as worried as she is. We can sense that the storm isn't so
bad, and she's just projecting her inner turmoil onto it. And we
suspect that the "tramp" might not be such a threat. We certainly
feel bad for her for being so afraid for her own safety, but we do so
without sharing her external fears. L'Engle is doing something so-
phisticated: trusting her readers, young and old, to have a little distance from Meg and see things she doesn't see.

So why do we still care so much for her, despite the fact that
we don't fully identify with her external fears? Most obviously
because her father has disappeared, but it's more than that. We
all identify with characters who have unfair expectations put on
them, and that's very true of Meg:

*That morning one of her teachers had said crossly, "Really, Meg, I
don't understand how a child with parents as brilliant as yours are
supposed to be can be such a poor student. If you don't manage to do
a little better you'll have to stay back next year."*

Being in her head, we can intimately see things the world
refuses to see about her. We understand how unfairly she's being
treated, and burn with indignation for her. And, of course, the
most unfair assumption people make about her situation is when
they assume her father ran off with another woman, so that
brings it all together.

### Invest

Once again, we're allowed to be a little judgmental of Meg.
L'Engle knows she must get us to invest in Meg's ability to tackle
whatever challenges she might face, and she does so in a classic
way: Right away, we find out that, earlier in the day, Meg has
launched into a fight, fists first, to defend the good name of her
odd kid brother. But that night, Meg has already figured out that
she was once again projecting her inner turmoil onto an outward
source, and she shouldn't have done it . . . and we agree. She's
showing that we'll be able to invest in Meg, but she's not asking
us to fully identify with her hero's pugnaciousness.

Nevertheless, we fall totally in love with this very sophisti-
cated book. We love Meg, though we don't fully fear for her
nor fully cheer for her. Even young readers understand their so-
phisticated relationship to her. Readers of all ages come to understand that Meg is projecting her problems onto the world,
and we hope that she will come to see herself as completely as
we see her. As we wait for her to do that, we come to fully Believe, Care, and Invest, even though, by design, we don't fully
identify.

# Various Heroes in Toni Morrison's *Beloved*

*A rural area outside Cincinnati, Ohio, in 1873: Escaped slave Sethe is haunted by her baby's ghost. Baby Suggs, the mother-in-law who originally owned her house, has died and her two sons have run away in fear of the ghost, leaving her alone with her quiet eighteen-year-old daughter, Denver. Paul D, an old acquaintance from her plantation days, stops by and quickly realizes the house is haunted. He banishes the ghost and moves in.*

Like all of the other books in this section, this was a bestseller, but unlike those, it won its writer a Pulitzer and Nobel Prize. It's a tough read about the most painful fact of American history, but it's also a compelling ghost story. It has horrific atrocities, but it's also, in some ways, an uplifting romance. You can read it in high school or a book group, but you can also write a dozen doctoral theses about it.

The biggest reason it may be hard to identify with any one hero of this book is that it's hard to tell who the hero is. In the Invest section, we will look at how we have to shift who we identify with as the book progresses.

## Believe

Morrison has a lot of big jobs in front of her. As with any novelist, she must describe things with unique similes we haven't read before (a gravestone is "pink as a fingernail," Sethe shoots Paul D "a look of snow"), then she must make the nineteenth century come to life with details unique to that century (slop jars, a kettleful of chickpeas, a "keeping room" in the house), then she must make the horrors of slavery come alive (the scars on Sethe's back are in the shape of a "chokecherry tree"). Ideally she can do all three in one phrase, such as when we hear that one of Sethe's memories is "as lifeless as the nerves in her back where the skin buckled like a washboard"

Morrison's utterly unique character descriptions are perfect models of efficiency. Here's how Paul D sees Sethe: "A face too still for comfort; irises the same color as her skin, which, in that still face, used to make him think of a mask with mercifully punched out eyes." Here's how Sethe sees Paul D: "Except for a heap more hair and some waiting in his eyes, he looked the way he had in Kentucky. Peachstone skin; straight-backed."

One way to make characters feel unique is to give them things they won't normally do, and then we know the significance of a change in that behavior. Denver notes that Paul D is "someone her mother wanted to talk to and would even consider talking to while barefoot." Sethe has unique values that define her, and then she makes an exception, showing how these events are shifting her world.

Morrison uses the classic trick of setting the sexually charged second scene in the kitchen: "The last of the Sweet Home men was there to catch her if she sank . . . The stove didn't shudder as it adjusted to its heat." Morrison then finds a good thing about sex that I don't think anyone has ever pointed out before: "What she knew was that the responsibility for her breasts, at last, was in somebody else's hands."

Already in these first ten pages, we totally believe in the reality of this world. We sense that Morrison surely must have been there in person to have noticed all these odd little details that no one could just make up.

## Care

On the one hand, these characters are very easy to care about. They are, after all, the victims of America's greatest atrocity.

Who in our history has suffered more than they? But Morrison knows that it's hard to conceive of the horror of slavery. Many of her readers had seen *Roots* ten years earlier, so they knew about the vicious whippings, the omnipresent rape, and having your children sold away from you, and they were somewhat inured to it. But of course slavery is an unending fount of horror, and Morrison used her research to gouge through the calloused skin of her readers and make the wounds fresh.

Sethe's mother-in-law, Baby Suggs, has had all eight of her children taken from her. How can we conceive of the magnitude of that? The horror comes alive when she says, "My first-born. All I can remember of her is how she loved the burned bottom of bread. Can you beat that?" The fact that she only has one memory of the toddler who was taken from her is staggering, but the memory is fascinatingly bizarre (and thus convincing).

Likewise, Morrison knows she must confront the reality of rape, but she must make the horror fresh. For Sethe, what made it so horrific was that she was nursing at the time and "they took my milk." A horrifically unique detail.

In the modern-day story, things are going better for Sethe, as a lover emerges as if from nowhere and eases her burden a little, but we only believe it because it's not as easy as it should be. Sethe is amazed to see Paul D and asks, "Is that you?," to which he honestly answers, "What's left." Later, she says, "You could stay the night, Paul D," and he parries with "You don't sound too steady in the offer." Neither feels entitled to happiness and they're wary of it. She recalls that he's always "treated her to a mild brotherly flirtation, so subtle you had to scratch for it." Even when the romance develops quickly, as it does in this book, always make your heroes scratch for it a bit, and we'll care about the relationship so much more.

## Invest

Of course, the ghost story also needs unique details, to separate it from a million other ghost stories. Here the ghost-baby picks on their poor dog, which is named Here Boy, and Denver remembers Sethe's disturbing strength:

> *And when the baby's spirit picked up Here Boy and slammed him into the wall hard enough to break two of his legs and dislocate his eye, so hard he went into convulsions and chewed up his tongue, still her mother had not looked away. She had taken a hammer, knocked the dog unconscious, wiped away the blood and saliva, pushed his eye back in his head and set his leg bones. He recovered, mute and off-balance, more because of his untrustworthy eye than his bent legs, and winter, summer, drizzle or dry, nothing could persuade him to enter the house again.*

We will find out more and more as we read of the remarkable (and occasionally disturbing) resilience Sethe has shown over the years . . . but do we really invest our hopes and dreams in Sethe in these opening pages? Not really. And we're right not to. About half of the book takes place in flashback, and in those sections "iron-eyed" Sethe will show epic heroism, but in the modern-day story, Sethe has lost all willingness to stand up to the vengeful ghost that rules her house, and she will continue to cling desperately to it even past the climax where the ghost, Beloved, is finally banished.

No, in these opening chapters, we invest our hopes in Paul D, which is easy enough to do, as he shows traditionally heroic traits and stands up to the ghost right away:

> *A table rushed toward him and he grabbed its leg. Somehow he managed to stand at an angle and, holding the table by two legs, he bashed it about, wrecking everything, screaming back at the screaming house.*

*"You want to fight, come on! God damn it! She got enough without you. She got enough!" The quaking slowed to an occasional lurch, but Paul D did not stop whipping the table around until everything was rock quiet.*

That's pretty easy to invest in. As it will turn out, Paul D, too, will eventually prove to be unequal to the task and it is meek Denver who will do what is necessary to purge Beloved from the house, but we don't sense that yet, which is fine. As long as we have characters to root for early on, we don't mind if the real hero turns out to be one we didn't pick from the start.

*Beloved* is probably the most acclaimed book of the last fifty years, and with good reason. It's both powerfully important and wonderfully readable.

## Rahel in Arundhati Roy's *The God of Small Things*

*The Indian Province of Kerala in 1993: Thirty-one-year-old Rahel returns after many years away to help her troubled twin brother, Estha. She quickly becomes overwhelmed with memories of different times, including the death of a girl named Sophie Mol in 1969, when Rahel and Estha were seven.*

This novel requires the most out of its readers of any of those we're looking at. Postcolonial writers have literally had the ground ripped out from under their feet, leaving them unmoored in time and space, and modern literary authors like Roy capture that condition in prose. Complex literary fiction challenges the reader, but in a masterful book such as this one, those readers who rise to the challenge are richly rewarded.

## Believe

We've already covered Believe for this one, in the first half. First we talked about how the setting truly comes alive when Roy says, "May in Ayemenem is a hot, brooding month," and "the countryside turns an immodest green."

Then we looked at how Rahel's odd thoughts capture the weird logic of childhood, thinking that Sophie Mol must still be alive in her coffin.

## Care

It will take us a while to understand every trauma that happened in two terrible weeks in 1969, but right away we do get just a sense in these first ten pages of the various traumas that still have both Rahel and Estha in their grip:

1. The Orangedrink Lemondrink Man did something to Estha (which we can already correctly guess to be molestation).

2. Their cousin Sophie Mol drowned, and perhaps they're to blame.

3. A man named Velutha seems to have died because of Sophie's death, and perhaps the kids are to blame for that as well due to some further sin of theirs.

4. As a result of all of the above, the closer-than-close twins were sent to live in different cities until now.

5. Estha stopped speaking not long thereafter and has never spoken since.

Of course, it will take us until the end of the book to figure out the five points above, but we get hints of all five very early on. These traumas have fractured Rahel's sense of self, and they've also fractured her perception (and therefore our perception) of these events, so we get passages like this:

*In those early amorphous years when memory had only just begun, when life was full of Beginnings and no Ends, and Everything was Forever, Esthappen and Rahel thought of themselves together as Me, and separately, individually, as We or Us. As though they were a rare breed of Siamese twins, physically separate, but with joint identities.*

*Now, these years later, Rahel has a memory of waking up one night giggling at Estha's funny dream.*

*She has other memories too that she has no right to have.*

*She remembers, for instance (though she hadn't been there), what the Orangedrink Lemondrink Man did to Estha in Abhilash Talkies. She remembers the taste of the tomato sandwiches—Estha's sandwiches, that Estha ate—on the Madras Mail.*

*And these are only the small things.*

From such tangles of memory we have to pick out the salient details and arrange them into a timeline, and we are increasingly horrified as it all falls into place.

## Invest

Like any good hero, Rahel shows up on page one on a heroic mission. Her brother has finally come home, there's something wrong with him, and she must come home as well to try and fix him. Most of the pages will be devoted to her fractured memories of what happened to them in those two terrible tragic weeks in 1969, but we will regularly check in on her modern-day attempts to get through to Estha, which she will do . . . in a fashion. It is only because we are invested in this modern-day mission that we are willing to do the hard work of piecing together their past.

But of course, as with most literary fiction, we are really rooting for Rahel to deal with her own pain. As she and we sort through the shattered pieces of her traumatized psyche, we feel a shared sense of accomplishment. We have to struggle to piece together a coherent story, which can make for a frustrating reading experience, but ultimately, those who do the work the novel requires will feel all the more bonded to the heroine, because she is undergoing the same struggle. She and we are working together to make sense of her life, and we feel a shared sense of accomplishment as the jigsaw pieces slowly click together. Of course, as with any old jigsaw puzzle, we'll never find all the pieces, but we'll have enough in the end to get a sense of the whole picture.

## Various Heroes in Celeste Ng's *Little Fires Everywhere*

*We meet the wealthy Richardsons of suburban Shaker Heights, Ohio, as they watch their house burn down. Lexie, Trip, and Moody all suspect it was burned down by the fourth, missing sibling, Izzy. Then we move across town to another house owned by the Richardsons, and we meet the poor mother and daughter who rent it, Mia and Pearl Warren.*

We meet a ton of characters in these ten pages and we're not at all sure who will be the main protagonist . . . and even when the novel's over, it will still be hard to say. This is a true ensemble novel, even more diffuse than *A Game of Thrones*, because it puts us in more heads.

There's also the question of POV. We're hopping into a lot of heads, but there's another POV to take into account. When we meet Lexie, we jump into her thoughts:

> *She glanced at her brothers, at her mother, still in her bathrobe on their tree lawn, and thought, They have literally nothing but the clothes on their backs.*

. . . then there's a comment:

> Literally *was one of Lexie's favorite words, which she deployed even when the situation was anything but literal. In this case, for once, it was more or less true.*

Who is saying that literally is one of Lexie's favorite words? Lexie probably wouldn't say that about herself, and she certainly wouldn't say that she misuses it. So whose head are we in right here? The omnipotent narrator's. As with Vernon Dursley in the first Harry Potter book, we are meeting these suburbanites from a jaundiced point of view, and that POV is the author's own.

## Believe

First Ng has to get us to believe in the Richardsons. This is tricky because, as I said above, we're looking down on them judgmentally. On a certain level we're supposed to scoff, roll our eyes, and say "typical suburbanites." But they also have to seem real in very specific ways. Ng grew up in Shaker Heights in the '90s, so she has fun facts readily at hand.

For instance, she features an object we remember from our

childhood but probably haven't thought about much since: intricately folded notes . . .

> *Now Lexie watched the smoke billow from her bedroom window, the front one that looked over the lawn, and thought of everything inside that was gone. Every T-shirt in her dresser, every pair of jeans in her closet. All the notes Serena had written her since the sixth grade, still folded in paper footballs, which she'd kept in a shoebox under her bed; the bed itself, the very sheets and comforter charred to a crisp.*

My own memories of many classroom notes folded into footballs came flooding over me and the book tapped into my real emotions.

It's also hard because she's pretty much introducing this six-member family all at once. That's always super risky. I thought, "Oh, no, I'll never get these characters straight." But I needn't have worried. As with Martin, Ng is a master at lightning-fast, fully realized characterization. In the second chapter, we looked at how Ng, like Louisa May Alcott, has several paragraphs in the first ten pages that list what each member of the family does in the same situation.

Then she has to get us to believe in the Warrens. Once again, we do so not by jumping into their heads, but by looking at them with jaundiced eyes, in this case the eyes of the Richardsons:

> *They knew there was no Mr. Warren, and that Mia was thirty-six, according to the Michigan driver's license she had provided. They noticed that she wore no ring on her left hand, though she wore plenty of other rings: a big amethyst on her first finger, one made from a silver spoon handle on her pinkie, and one on her thumb that to Mrs. Richardson looked suspiciously like a mood ring.*

The wealth of detail makes it easy to believe in the reality of these eight characters (and more to come).

## Care

Again, we'll start with the Richardsons: We sense right away that these may be clueless, overprivileged white people, but hey, their house just burned down. As Lexie observes, everyone but her has only the clothes on their backs. We don't know yet if they deserve this to some extent, and we suspect they might, but even so, it's an outsized humiliation. No fair court of law would sentence you to have your house burnt down.

As for the Warrens, we meet Mia and Pearl through the judgmental eyes of the Richardsons and we sense that these judgments are unfair, so we're inclined to feel for them. We then get a chance to bond with Mia in a way that we haven't really bonded with anyone, when we jump into her head to share her fright at this freaky world.

> *Large motor scooters, each piloted by a man in an orange work suit, zipped down each driveway to collect the garbage in the privacy of the backyard, ferrying it to the larger truck idling out in the street, and for months Mia would remember their first Friday on Winslow Road, the fright she'd had when the scooter, like a revved-up flame-colored golf cart, shot past the kitchen window with engine roaring.*

## But What About Invest?

Ng does an amazing job in these ten pages of introducing this world, these characters, and a compelling flash-forward toward a climax that implies a big mystery, but she doesn't have time to introduce a problem to be solved, so we don't *really* invest in anyone yet. In a book with a large ensemble, we search for the character who wants something, but no one wants much in these ten pages. In the next ten pages we'll get our first character who really wants something, Moody, who will come to want Pearl. But we don't really invest in him, either.

To a certain extent, this is not a book about the solving of a large problem. There will eventually be a unifying plot involving a contested adoption, but it will take almost a hundred pages for it to coalesce.

Ng's Shaker Heights will ultimately have certain things in common with another nearby municipality: Sherwood Anderson's *Winesburg, Ohio*. The flash-forward to the fire will give this book a lot more structure than that one had (or at least the *illusion* of structure), but they're doing something similar: Putting us in a dozen Buckeye heads and inviting us to feel the weight of the modern condition.

In a Barnes & Noble podcast, Ng says of her book, "Everyone has thoughts about what's going on, but nobody in the book has all the pieces, and I guess even when you've got all the pieces it's not always easy to figure out what's right." That's the goal of all truly omniscient narrators, whether it's George R. R. Martin or Leo Tolstoy or Ng. Ultimately, the large problem is life itself, and the only hero who can attempt to solve that problem is the reader, because only we have all the facts.

**THERE ARE A** lot more novel BCI breakdowns on the blog. Go there to see:

• *A is for Alibi* by Sue Grafton

• *Americanah* by Chimamanda Ngozi Adichie

- *Catch-22* by Joseph Heller

- *Emma* by Jane Austen

- *The Fault in Our Stars* by John Green

- *The Firm* by John Grisham

- *Go Tell It on the Mountain* by James Baldwin

- *Gone Girl* by Gillian Flynn

- *Harriet the Spy* by Louise Fitzhugh

- *Harry Potter and the Philosopher's Stone* by J. K. Rowling

- *The Hitchhiker's Guide to the Galaxy* by Douglas Adams

- *The Hobbit* by J. R. R. Tolkien

- *Holes* by Louis Sachar

- *The House on Mango Street* by Sandra Cisneros

- *The Intuitionist* by Colson Whitehead

- *Invisible Man* by Ralph Ellison

- *Jane Eyre* by Charlotte Brontë

- *Killing Floor* by Lee Child

- *Little Women* by Louisa May Alcott

- *Matilda* by Roald Dahl

- *Moby-Dick* by Herman Melville

- *Slaughterhouse-Five* by Kurt Vonnegut

- and *White Noise* by Don DeLillo

This list probably won't be that surprising to you, because you've seen me mention most of them in Part I, but there were probably places where you said, "Wait, Matt told me how they got me to fear for this hero, but he didn't mention the book again. How was 'fear for' balanced with 'cheer for'?" You can check out the full BCI for each example to see how they all came together.

Now let's move on to . . .

## Believe, Care, Invest: Movies

Movies are very different from books: Reading is an individual experience with individual meaning. Moviegoing is a collective experience with collective meaning. Obviously, this is partially due to the fact that we read books while we're alone, and we view movies (ideally) while we're gathered together. (Of course, COVID has accelerated a move away from collective moviegoing, but I still think it's an essential element of how we think about the artform.)

You may read a book and then insist that your friend read it, too, but you probably won't be that offended if they don't like it. That usually just leads to a friendly debate in which you describe why *you* liked it. If, on the other hand, you see a movie with someone, and you're sitting there loving it, and you walk out only to discover that your friend was sitting there hating it the whole time, you feel oddly betrayed. There is an assumption that everyone should react to movies in the same way.

This is why the Oscars are televised and the Pulitzers will never be. The Oscars are the validation of our collective consciousness, a moment for America to come together and say, "We all see the same value in the same movies!" Even when you totally disagree and hate the Oscar choice, they're still fun to watch, because you get to yell at the screen: "How dare they get it so wrong?? Don't they realize that *Brokeback Mountain* was obviously better??" A bad Oscar choice only reinforces our conviction that we should all share the same taste in movies. By contrast, we may respect the work of the Pulitzer committee, but we don't actually expect it to affirm our own individual taste in books.

Why do we expect our movies to have so much shared meaning? Is it merely a result of the collective viewing experience? I think it has something to do with how they're made . . .

Movies are collaborative. *Extremely* collaborative. Novelists who try to cross over are always shocked to discover that nobody in moviemaking is allowed to say, "I chose that setting because it had a special meaning to me." By the time the movie gets made, too many people are going to have to spend too much money re-creating that time and place, so you have to be able to justify why that setting is essential to the meaning of your story (especially if it's an expensive setting).

But it goes further than that. On the most fundamental level, the screenwriter can't even say, "That plot turn happens that way because I decided to do it that way." There is no "I" in film. There is only "we." Eventually, you will have to justify and explain the meaning of every single choice, from character to setting to theme, not only to your artistic collaborators but to everyone putting any money into the project. The only way to justify your choices is to explain that your choice serves the story. The story is never allowed to serve your choice.

This creates a weird situation in which you have several artists all putting their fingers on the Ouija board and attempting to collectively divine what the story wants, without anyone seeming to push it in any particular direction. Because every decision has to justify itself to the movie's theme, this results in movies being far more thematically "pure" than books. This is also one reason why movies have more collective meaning than books: because every decision the moviemakers made already had to have collective meaning to the team that made it.

And yet, you might think that this would result in an audience bonding more with a movie than with a book, but you'd be wrong. It all comes down to this: A book is a friend. A movie is a stranger with a problem.

You invest more of yourself (i.e., more money) in a book, you invite it into your house, you visit it multiple times for multiple hours, you have to actively commit to it in order to keep the experience going. But a movie is totally different: You invest less; you meet it socially, in a neutral location; you only agree to sit down with it once; and you can just sit there passively and judge the story, without committing to it. Therefore the movie (the stranger) must stick to the point, in a way that a book (your friend) doesn't have to do.

Every scene in a movie has to be (at least tangentially) about one problem. After all, if you agree to sit down with a stranger to talk about their problem, then you will become very impatient if they suddenly start talking about something else from their life unrelated to that. There is an understanding that you're only there to hear about one thing. Friends, on the other hand, can jump around and talk about a bunch of different problems or just make idle chit-chat about what they did all day. You like the sound of their voice, and if they drop a random tangent they can always finish it up at a later time.

So the screenwriter has a very peculiar task. The movie viewer has made less commitment, so the writer has to work harder to win them over, and has fewer tools with which to do so. Screenwriters have to hit the ground running even harder than novelists.

Once again, this will be an idiosyncratic selection of the movies I've analyzed the BCI for . . .

## Jeffrey Beaumont in *Blue Velvet*, Written by David Lynch

*On a beautiful day, a man has a heart attack while watering his lawn. His son, Jeffrey Beaumont, takes time off from college to come home and help run the family hardware store. Walking home from the hospital, Jeffrey spots a severed ear in a field, and takes it to Detective Williams, who tells him he must not ask for any more details. Jeffrey decides to investigate anyway on his own, striking up a relationship with Williams's daughter, Sandy, to ask her more about the case.*

In most stories, this challenge is something the hero needs to do because external circumstances are providing the hero with a big motivation to get involved. The hero usually hesitates to commit, until a further external impetus makes it clear that this is something they must do. Jeffrey is very different. He finds the ear by accident, but as soon as he does, he's compelled to pursue this case on his own, not because it's something that must be done, but because of his volatile internal psychology. Jeffrey is just tremendously odd. We will find out as the story goes on that he's a born voyeur. In fact, the script began with Jeffrey still in college, peeping on a couple, when he gets the news about his father. The finished movie chooses to let Jeffrey's addiction to voyeurism come out more gradually.

Why do we Believe? In some ways Jeffrey is hard to care about because he's so odd, but it helps that he's odd in specific ways. He's the sort of person who says, "I used to know a kid who lived there, had the biggest tongue in the world."

He's nervous on a first date, which is something we've all experienced, but his volatile personality reacts in a way we never have. He suddenly, apropos of nothing, says to his date, "You know the chicken walk?" Then he gets a big grin on his face and begins to, well, do a bizarre chicken walk in the street. She feels both weirded out and charmed watching this, and we feel both of those things as well. This is a unique character. He feels what we feel, but he doesn't react how we would react.

As for giving the hero a convincing world, the setting and the economic activity certainly could not be more thoroughly established. We begin with a sign reading WELCOME TO LUMBER-TON while voices sing, "Logs, logs, logs!" A DJ then says, "It's a sunny, woodsy day in Lumberton, so get those chainsaws out." We will soon see Jeffrey working in the hardware store, and he begins his investigation by borrowing pest control equipment from the store and pretending to inspect a suspect's apartment.

It's easy to Care about Jeffrey. His father seems to be dying, and we see the anguish on Jeffrey's face as he watches his father crying piteously in the hospital room, unable to speak. We'll soon realize that Jeffrey's had to give up on college for the foreseeable future, and a hardware store is not enough of an outlet for his curiosity.

We know we're in a thriller and so we want the murder solved, and we share Jeffrey's enormous frustration at being shut out from the case. "You found something that is very interesting to us. Very interesting. I'm sure you must be curious to know more. But I'm afraid I'm going to have to ask you not only not to tell anybody what you found, but also, not to ask any more about the case. One day, when it's all sewed up, I'll let you know the details. Right now, though, I can't."

It's not so easy to Invest in Jeffrey. He's a somewhat hapless hero, but he has an air of determination, and that goes a long way. Jeffrey's response to Williams is "I understand, I'm just real curious like you said." We like curious heroes. We also like volatile heroes, and Jeffrey certainly has an unexpectedly volatile reaction to this situation. It strikes a dark chord within him.

We also like heroes that have good eyes. Jeffrey can see things others can't. We sense that only he would have spotted that ear. And we like that Jeffrey is willing to be wily, even a little sketchy, in pursuit of his goal, possibly just pretending to be interested in Sandy to get her to help him.

*Blue Velvet* was that rare beast: An art film that broke through to mainstream audiences. The movie is defiantly weird, but utterly compelling.

## Mookie in *Do the Right Thing,* Written by Spike Lee

*On the hottest day of 1989 in the Bed-Stuy neighborhood of Brooklyn, a young pizza delivery man named Mookie counts his previous day's money, talks with his sister, Jade, then heads to work at Sal's Pizzeria. Sal and his sons, Vito and Pino, arrive, already bickering with each other. There's a dispute about who will sweep up outside, and the task eventually falls to local bum Da Mayor. At lunchtime, Mookie's friend Buggin' Out demands that Sal put some pictures of Black people on the wall, and Sal has Mookie kick him out. Mookie is told by Da Mayor, "Always do the right thing."*

This movie is indeed scorching. Every frame literally pops with color (cinematographer Ernest Dickerson painted some walls bright red) and sizzles with personality. On one level, this is a vivid portrait of a fun-loving neighborhood at its best, but growing anger and resentment builds, quietly at first, then loudly, until it erupts in the final moments.

In the beginning, Lee has a lot of characters to introduce to us, and it would have been easiest to introduce them all from Mookie's point of view, but he introduces most of them to us separately, though Mookie does interact with each one eventually. This means that we bond with Mookie less than we might if he was our strict POV character.

In fact, there are lots of reasons Mookie might be hard to identify with. He's essentially a passive protagonist for most of the movie. Like Jake Gittes walking a beat in *Chinatown*, he's trying to keep the peace by doing as little as possible. He shuts down Buggin' Out, deflects Vito's provocations, humors a man who has autism named Smiley, and compliments the intimidating Radio Raheem on his rings. He's not especially resourceful and he doesn't really show any special skills, but we don't get frustrated with him because it seems like he is indeed doing the right thing and successfully keeping the peace.

Why do we Believe? We first believe in Mookie when we see him joshing around with his sister in a friendly way. We always like friends, and his relationship with his sister is not exactly like others we've seen before (sharing a Brooklyn brownstone apartment as adults with their parents out of the picture).

Then he announces his initial motto: "Gotta get paid!" Later, he will get an alternate motto, when Da Mayor gives him the titular advice. Ultimately, he will have to choose between these mottoes. (It's ironic, of course, that this advice comes from an old drunk.) It will be up to the audience to decide if Mookie does the right thing by initiating the destruction of the pizza place, but he clearly did it with Da Mayor's words ringing in his ears.

When Mookie arrives at work, we see how the job of sweeping the front of the pizza place is handed down from Sal to Pino to Vito to Mookie to Da Mayor, establishing the pecking order quickly as an actual object symbolizing power passes from hand to hand.

We Care, first of all, because it's the hottest day of the year and nobody's air conditioning is working. Sal says, in reference to his agitation from the heat, "I'm gonna kill somebody today," which turns out to sort of be true.

But then our caring becomes acute when Mookie must kick out Buggin' Out. Pino tells Mookie, "Talk some brother talk to him." Mookie tells Buggin' Out, "I gotta work here, you're fucking my shit up," only to be told, "Stay Black," and we empathize with how painful that is to hear.

Then Sal, who is generally a nice guy and likes Mookie, reveals his real character when he tells Mookie, "There's no free here, I'm the boss. No freedom, I'm the boss."

I had to search around to figure out when we Invest in Mookie. Then I found it. As he leaves his brownstone to go to work, he's approached by two Jehovah's Witnesses, proselytizing their religion. Without breaking his stride, he barks "Hell no!" and keeps on going. Now we love him. After that, at work, Mookie insists that he's just a delivery man, and won't do other jobs, so he has a sense of self-respect. "Fuck that shit, I deliver pizzas, that's what I get paid for."

And, of course, as I talked about before, we like heroes who bestride two worlds. Only Mookie is welcome in both the Black and white worlds. Everyone in the neighborhood knows and respects him. We like heroes with a reputation.

Ultimately, it's not a problem that this movie has a fairly

passive protagonist, because it's a movie that's not about the solving of a large problem. The movie isn't structured around Mookie's internal journey, and it misses many of the steps you would normally expect to see in a movie structured around the solving of a large problem, such as a midpoint disaster. Mookie never has a big crash that causes him to rethink everything and get on the right track. This is a movie in which everyone, including our hero, *ignores* a large problem as it grows, until it finally erupts. That's an equally satisfying form of storytelling.

## Chris in *Get Out*, Written by Jordan Peele

*In 2017, we see a Black man, lost in suburbia, get kidnapped into the trunk of a car. Then we meet Chris, in his nice apartment surrounded by his street photography. He nicks himself shaving, then goes through the photos on his high-end camera. His white girlfriend, Rose, brings him croissants, then talks about their upcoming trip to visit her parents. As they drive up there, Chris speaks on the phone with his friend Rod, who will be taking care of their dog. Rose hits a deer and calls the cops, who demand to see Chris's license, but Rose shuts them down.*

On my blog, I apply a checklist of 122 questions to lots of stories, to see how they do. According to the checklist, Chris seems like a rather deficient hero in *Get Out*. I was shocked at all the ones that Chris didn't check:

**Does the hero have a consistent metaphor family (drawn from their job, background, or developmental state)?**
*Just very slightly. He has a bit more personality with Rod than he does with Rose ("Yo, you at work?") but for the most part he speaks*

*without much individuality. He's code-switching, and around white people he's careful to be generic in his metaphor family.*

**Does the hero have a default argument tactic?**
*Not really, and he loses every argument he has in the movie. When Rose throws his cigarette out the car window, he protests, "That was a dollar, you just threw a dollar out the window," but it's a half-hearted attempt and she ignores it.*

**Is the hero's primary motivation for tackling this challenge strong, simple, and revealed early on?**
*His motivation is that Rose is all he has in the world (other than his dog and Rod), but we don't understand that until halfway through. Before he admits that, we wonder why he's putting up with this.*

**Does the hero have a false or shortsighted goal in the first half?**
*He's not very goal oriented. In retrospect, we can figure that he might have seen this as an opportunity to have a family again, but he mainly just pastes on a smile in the first half and doesn't try hard to impress. He's very polite but not eager to please.*

**And is the hero willing to let others know that they lack the hero's most valuable quality, subtly or directly?**
*He gently points out to Rose her seeming naivete, but mainly just reacts to everyone with pointedly quizzical looks. He laughs off Rod when Rod sees something very wrong in this situation.*

**Does the hero have (or claim) decision-making authority?**
*Absolutely none, as her father jokingly points out. And she drove, so he can't leave without her approval.*

IN THE DVD commentary, writer/director Jordan Peele points out something interesting: "I could talk all day about how amazing Daniel [Kaluuya, who plays Chris] is. I mean, at some point we realized, y'know, Chris doesn't have very many *lines* in this. And it's true. His role is to just kinda get out of here without the shit hitting the fan . . . He's just trying to minimize the awkwardness and make it through the weekend and get out, so that's why he's not gonna pop off, and, of course, he's in love, so we understand why you're on your best behavior at your love's parents' house."

Eventually, Chris will get hypnotized by Rose's mother and sent to "the sunken place," a void deep inside his subconscious. But already from the beginning, Chris is hiding inside himself, and we understand that, so that's one reason we find him compelling, despite his lack of some of the surface traits we typically crave. He's somewhat self-less (but not selfless) and generic, but we sense more under the surface of Kaluuya's performance, so we don't reject him.

There are lots of reasons to Believe in Chris: I've talked about the importance of including real-life national pain in any story, and the intro, which is strongly reminiscent of the murder of Trayvon Martin, certainly qualifies. This movie was made by a studio called Blumhouse, which turns out a lot of low-budget horror quickies, but with this scene, we realize with discomfort, "Uh-oh, this isn't the standard Blumhouse horror movie, this one is set in *our* world, and it'll hit us where we live."

For all the reasons I listed above, Chris is somewhat lacking in personality, but putting his beautiful, raw street photography on the wall (and showing him sorting his new photos in his digital camera) goes a long way to getting us to see inside his mind and his soul. We see that he has a unique perspective on the world, which makes him an individual.

Chris doesn't just ask Rod to take care of his dog while he's away, he has to warn Rod that the dog has IBS, which is a specific detail that makes this situation come to life.

So why do we Care about Chris? First and foremost because we sense early on that he's being gaslit. Even the title is screaming at him to get out, but his girlfriend keeps convincing him there's nothing wrong, and subtly mocking his attempts to piece it all together.

But there are more reasons:

• When we first see him, he nicks himself shaving, foreshadowing bloodletting to come.

• Chris goes to check on the deer, and finds it's dying and clearly feels anguish. We won't realize until much later that he's thinking of his mom, who was also hit by a car, but we can see some of that anguish on Chris's face.

• When they arrive, Chris is jokingly told by Rose's dad that his role as boyfriend is to say, "She's right, I'm wrong," as often as possible, but of course there's a racial component to that as well. Chris is expected to say that to every white person. (When the cop arrives, the Black man is in deadly peril, but the white girl has power over the cop, which she happily flexes.)

We don't Invest in Chris very much, because he's easily cowed, but there are a few elements that help us: It keeps coming up that his most valuable quality is his eyes, and we like good eyes.

And we like that he's wary, even though he chooses to ignore his own wariness. He never stands up to Rose, but he does give her a lot of momentary side eye, before assuring himself over and over that he should trust her.

He has a bit of a "save the cat" moment when he checks on the deer to see if it's suffering, but he's powerless to save it, which prefigures a lot of the powerlessness he will feel in the movie.

Ultimately, Chris will find the strength inside him to triumph in this situation, but it's not clear to us right away that we can invest in him to do so. To a certain extent, this is the nature of horror movies. I've talked about how writers always have to balance "cheer for" and "fear for," but horror movies tip toward the latter. It's inherent to the genre that the heroes seem more helpless. The more we fear for them, the more we enjoy ourselves.

Peele specifically establishes that Rose's brother is good at sports and Chris is not, so when things come down to a physical contest between them, we think that Chris will surely fail. This is the opposite of what non-horror movies do. (Or is Chris just *claiming* that he's bad at sports because he doesn't want to confirm the brother's stereotypes?)

Ironically, the one personal quality that causes Chris to succeed in the end when all has failed (the "secret weapon in the cave," as Joseph Campbell would say) is that he naturally claws at chairs he sits in (which is established early on the first time he is hypnotized). Minor spoiler warning: When he's trussed up at the end, he nervously scratches open the leather chair he's in. Only when he's done that does he realize he's saved himself. He picks the cotton stuffing out, plugs up his ears, and attacks them when they think they've hypnotized him.

(It's also noteworthy that, in the original ending, Chris *didn't* triumph: He killed the family only to be immediately arrested for their murder, and seemingly ended up on death row. After Trump's election, Peele thought people needed to see a win, and shot a new ending in which Chris and Rod get away clean.)

# Fern in *Nomadland*, Written by Chloé Zhao, Based on the Book by Jessica Bruder

*In 2012, aging drifter Fern empties out her rented storage space and throws most of the stuff out. She hits the highway, peeing by the side of the road when she needs to. She goes to work at an Amazon warehouse. She shows off her van to one of her coworkers. Amazon lays everybody off and she's back on the road.*

This 2020 Best Picture is based on a nonfiction book called *Nomadland: Surviving America in the Twenty-First Century*, and is only lightly fictionalized. The leads, played by Frances McDormand and David Strathairn, are fictional, but many of the other characters are played by real nomads, using their real names.

As for why it might be hard to identify with Fern, this movie came in for some ironic criticism: The film was written and directed by Chloé Zhao, and made her the first Asian woman to win Best Director, but it was criticized for showing but not calling out white privilege. We come to realize that, while Fern has clearly suffered unjustly in various ways, she's ultimately chosen to be homeless (or "houseless," as she prefers to put it), which is a choice that's much easier to make when you're white. You're certainly less likely to get shot for parking (and going to the bathroom) on other people's land.

There is certainly no shortage of reasons to Believe in Fern: Cowriter Jessica Bruder, who wrote the nonfiction book, had observed hundreds of details of van life, and life in an Amazon plant. One of Fern's Amazon coworkers is covered in tattoos of lyrics by The Smiths, which is certainly a memorably unique detail.

Of course, usually, a character's possessions make them come alive. Fern just has a few, but they're memorable. Her dishes were handed down to her by her father (and eventually get broken by her love interest).

As I mentioned before, this is one of two 2020 movies in which the hero has named their beloved van (she's named hers Vanguard). In both cases, the van is the love of their lives, and of course it means that this love will be tested. In *Onward*, Barley must sacrifice his van (which is replaced with a new one at the end). In this one, she's told not to bother repairing it when it breaks, but goes to great lengths to save it.

So why do we Care? She's very much suffering real-life national pain. We begin with a title card straight out of the book: "On January 31, 2011, due to a reduced demand for sheetrock, US Gypsum shut down its plant in Empire, Nevada, after 88 years." We think, "Well, I guess that's sad," but then the second half of the title card fades up: "By July, the Empire zip code, 89405, was discontinued." That last detail drives home in one sentence how complete the devastation was. We can't help but wonder what we would do if our entire way of life disappeared.

Scenes where people must throw away most of their stuff always get to me. It seems as if one of the items in storage might have belonged to her dead husband, from the way she hugs it. Her feelings for him will not be mentioned a lot in the movie, but starting with that moment drives home that he's never far from her mind.

She's embarrassed to run into a woman with kids she used to tutor, who is clearly concerned for her. "If you need a place to stay, you can come over and stay with us. We're worried about you." She is embarrassed by the offer, and says no. When the daughter repeats the offer, she gamely responds, "I'm not homeless, I'm just houseless. Not the same thing, right?"

It's always good to foreshadow doom for the hero, of course, and one way to do that is with parallel characters: Introduce other characters in a similar situation to the hero, and show how things turned disastrous for them. Fern never seems to succumb to despair, but she meets a woman in her situation who turned suicidal, and it drives home that Fern is walking a tightrope over the same abyss:

*Before I moved into the Squeeze Inn, I was out looking for work and putting in applications . . . 2008, and it was just tough. And I got to a really, really low point. And I thought about suicide, and I decided I was gonna go buy a bottle of booze, turn on the propane stove . . . and I was gonna drink that booze until I passed out. And if I woke up . . . I was gonna light a cigarette, and I was gonna blow us all up. And I looked at my two sweet little trusting dogs, my cocker spaniel and my little toy poodle, and I just couldn't do that to them. And I thought, well, I can't do that to me, either. So, I was getting close to sixty-two and I went online to look at my Social Security benefit. It said $550. Fern, I had worked my whole life. I'd worked since I was twelve years old, raised two daughters. I couldn't believe it.*

We know that Fern could easily end up in the same spot (and we wonder about our own Social Security nest egg).

I've ended up choosing movie examples where we only Invest a little. We don't have much reason to invest in Fern, and indeed she'll have a hard time taking care of herself throughout the movie, but we admire her ingenuity. She describes her van: "The guy who had the van before, he just had a mattress in the back but I didn't want to keep it that way, I wanted to build the bed up so I could have storage underneath." She shows a little cabinet she's made: "You see that? This was my husband's old fishing box, I put this little latch on it. Open it, the stopper holds it and creates more counter space."

And we do see that she's smart—smart enough that we

wonder how she ever got in this dire situation. We find out she taught the girl Shakespeare, so she's upsetting our expectations of drifters.

In the end, we deeply identify with Fern, though we never cease to be frustrated with her unwillingness to provide a stable life for herself. We are much more aware than she is that she's only able to live this way because of the inherent safety of being a white woman, but I think that Zhao herself never forgets that. In the end, Fern is somewhere between the Joad family in *The Grapes of Wrath* and Sal Paradise in *On the Road*: She's driven out onto the road due to economic desolation, but she stays out there, despite some tempting offers to settle, because of existential longing.

## The Title Character in *WALL-E*, Written by Jim Reardon, Based on an Original Story by Andrew Stanton and Pete Docter

*We see a broken-down robot compressing garbage into cubes and making huge piles of them in an abandoned city. His cockroach friend seems to be the only other sentient thing left on Earth. Eventually, he finds a plant, and then a fetching robot named Eve arrives to collect it. WALL-E falls in love instantly, and tags along when Eve returns to space.*

I thought it would be interesting to look at an intro with no dialogue. WALL-E doesn't speak for the first nineteen minutes of this movie, so the filmmakers have a lot of work to do silently. Every day for a year they watched Chaplin and Keaton movies at lunchtime to relearn the language of silent cinema.

This was the last of the movies that the Pixar gang conceived in the early days of the studio, before they were sure they would be able to create skin or hair. We judge movie heroes by how human they seem, but what about a silent, shambling mass of metal? How do you make that come alive? Can we ever hope to identify with a garbage compactor?

Amazingly, we do. WALL-E ended up being one of the most lovable heroes of all time. They endow him with a profound level of humanity. How do they do that?

First and foremost, we Believe in WALL-E because he has a very complex setting. We piece it together: We see that every store and bank was called Buy N Large. We see a newspaper in which the CEO of Buy N Large said Earth had to be abandoned. We see holographic ads in which the CEO suggests to humans that they leave the earth for a five-year cruise in a starliner, while WALL-E cleans up. We see on the side of WALL-E's home base that his name stands for Waste Allocation Load Lifter Earth-Class. Now we're all caught up, simply and organically.

We quickly see that he has all sorts of human traits. He's making his own collection of his favorite junk, just for fun. As director Andrew Stanton said on the DVD commentary: "I always thought of him as somewhat of a beachcomber . . . It was a great way, story-wise, to just show his curiosity, show how he's evolved some sort of sensitivity and emotion, and it's just appealing. It was very easy for us in art or story to call back on things that fascinated us as a kid."

(I criticized Stanton's *John Carter* a lot in the last book, so it's nice to get to praise his masterpiece here.)

WALL-E loves to watch a VHS tape of *Hello Dolly* on TV, sings along, and imagines what it would be like to hold hands with a love interest (which we can see because he's holding his own hand). It turns out that he brought home a hubcap so he can pretend it's a hat when he dances along to the video. We always love to see emulation.

Once we've seen his fascinating stuff, we're eager to see his process as he goes out to get more. He shows his unique and amusingly unexpected values: He finds a ring box with a beautiful diamond ring inside, then throws away the ring and keeps the box.

We Care for WALL-E at first because he's totally alone (except for his cockroach friend) on an abandoned planet, doing an especially demeaning task. As Stanton says: "I don't know why, I can't remember where the idea came from, I think we always wanted a character that compacted trash. I don't even remember there being debate about that. It just seemed so sad, sort of lowest on the totem pole, almost sort of like a janitorial job, we never even questioned that."

He's feeling what we've all felt, but magnified on a planetary scale: "He's really the ultimate definition of futility, for me. That's really what WALL-E was. I think that's why I really could relate to him and people hopefully start to relate to him. If you're doing the same thing, day in and day out, year after year, at some point you have to just start asking the question, 'Is there more to life than what I'm doing?' And I think because we take WALL-E to such an extreme, even though he's just a machine, you can't help but imbue him with that thought process. You can't help but empathize and assume he must be thinking that."

We sense that his human masters were supposed to come back a long time ago and never did. He's old and broken down, just barely keeping himself alive.

But I think the movie pushes that situation as long as it can. If WALL-E was alone any longer, we might have gotten too frustrated. Luckily, EVE arrives just when the story needs her. But of course that brings a new problem, as he falls for her at first sight, and she's initially uninterested. Unrequited love is one of the world's most universal emotions.

We primarily Invest in WALL-E because he's good at his Sisyphean job: We see him complete one massive tower and begin a new one. We also see that he's resourceful: He repairs himself by taking parts from old dead Wall-E robots. Stanton calls him "the ultimate personification of perseverance."

It's also important that he's kind. He feeds his cockroach buddy a Twinkie. When he rolls over the roach, he feels awful, but of course the insect is fine, because they can survive anything.

The filmmakers had a momentous task, but the result is one of my favorite movies of all time. I feel for WALL-E more than any other animated character. The filmmakers made this mostly silent robot abundantly human.

OKAY, THAT'S JUST five movies, but if you want more, you'll find an absurd number of movie BCI breakdowns on the blog, including:

- *The 40-Year-Old Virgin*, written by Judd Apatow and Steve Carell

- *Aladdin*, written by Ron Clements, John Musker, Ted Elliott, and Terry Rossio

- *American Hustle*, written by Eric Warren Singer and David O. Russell

- *An Education*, written by Nick Hornby, adapted from the memoir by Lynn Barber

- *The Babadook*, written by Jennifer Kent

- *Back to the Future*, written by Robert Zemeckis and Bob Gale

- *Batman Begins*, written by David S. Goyer and Christopher Nolan

- *The Big Short*, written by Charles Randolph and Adam McKay, from the book by Michael Lewis

- *Birdman*, written by Alejandro G. Iñárritu, Nicolás Giacobone, Alexander Dinelaris Jr, and Armando Bó

- *Black Panther*, written by Ryan Coogler and Joe Robert Cole

- *Blazing Saddles*, written by Mel Brooks, Norman Steinberg, Andrew Bergman, Richard Pryor, and Alan Uger

- *The Bourne Identity*, written by Tony Gilroy and W. Blake Herron, from the novel by Robert Ludlum

- *Bridesmaids*, written by Kristen Wiig and Annie Mumolo

- *Captain America: The First Avenger*, written by Christopher Markus and Stephen McFeely

- *Casablanca*, written by Julius J. Epstein, Philip G. Epstein, and Howard Koch, from the play by Murray Burnett and Joan Alison

- *Chinatown*, written by Robert Towne

- *Donnie Brasco*, written by Paul Attanasio, from the book by Joseph D. Pistone and Richard Woodley

- *Dr. No*, written by Richard Maibaum, Johanna Harwood, and Berkely Mather, from the novel by Ian Fleming

- *Elf*, written by David Berenbaum (with an uncredited rewrite by Jon Favreau)

- *The Farewell*, written by Lulu Wang

- *The Fighter*, written by Scott Silver, Paul Tamasy, and Eric Johnson

- *Frozen*, written by Jennifer Lee, Chris Buck, and Shane Morris

- *The Fugitive*, written by Jeb Stuart and David Twohy

- *Ghostbusters*, written by Dan Aykroyd and Harold Ramis

- *Gravity*, written by Alfonso Cuarón and Jonás Cuarón

- *Groundhog Day*, written by Danny Rubin and Harold Ramis

- *Guardians of the Galaxy*, written by James Gunn and Nicole Perlman

- *How to Train Your Dragon*, written by William Davies, Dean DeBlois, and Chris Sanders, based on the book by Cressida Cowell

- *In a Lonely Place*, written by Andrew Solt and Edmund H. North, from a novel by Dorothy B. Hughes

- *The Invisible Man* (2020), written by Leigh Whannell

- *Iron Man*, written by Mark Fergus, Hawk Ostby, Art Marcum, and Matt Holloway

- *It's a Wonderful Life*, written by Frances Goodrich, Albert Hackett, Frank Capra, and Jo Swerling, based on the book by Philip Van Doren Stern

- *Jaws*, written by Peter Benchley and Carl Gottlieb, based on the novel by Benchley

- *Juno*, written by Diablo Cody

- *Lady Bird*, written by Greta Gerwig

- *The Little Mermaid*, written by John Musker and Ron Clements

- *Ma Rainey's Black Bottom*, written by Ruben Santiago-Hudson, from the play by August Wilson

- *Mean Girls*, written by Tina Fey, based in part on a book by Rosalind Wiseman

- *Moana*, written by Jared Bush, from a story by Ron Clements, John Musker, Chris Williams, Don Hall, Pamela Ribon, Aaron Kandell, and Jordan Kandell

- *Moonlight*, written by Barry Jenkins, from the play by Tarell Alvin McCraney

- *Pirates of the Caribbean: The Curse of the Black Pearl*, written by Ted Elliott, Terry Rossio, Stuart Beattie, and Jay Wolpert

- *Raiders of the Lost Ark*, written by Lawrence Kasdan, George Lucas, and Philip Kaufman

- *Raising Arizona*, written by Ethan Coen and Joel Coen

- *Rear Window*, written by John Michael Hayes, from a short story by Cornell Woolrich

- *Rushmore*, written by Wes Anderson and Owen Wilson

- *Selma*, written by Paul Webb with an uncredited rewrite by Ava DuVernay

- *The Shining*, written by Stanley Kubrick and Diane Johnson, based on the novel by Stephen King

- *Sideways*, written by Alexander Payne and Jim Taylor, from the novel by Rex Pickett

- *The Silence of the Lambs*, written by Ted Tally, from the novel by Thomas Harris

- *Snowpiercer*, written by Bong Joon-Ho and Kelly Masterson

- *Soul*, written by Pete Docter, Mike Jones, and Kemp Powers

- *Spider-Man*, written by David Koepp

- *Star Wars*, written by George Lucas

- *Sunset Boulevard*, written by Charles Brackett, Billy Wilder, and D. M. Marshman Jr.

- *Thor*, written by Ashley Edward Miller, Zack Stentz, and Don Payne

- *Toy Story*, written by Joss Whedon, Andrew Stanton, Joel Cohen, and Alec Sokolow

- *Vertigo*, written by Alec Coppel and Samuel A. Taylor, from the novel by Boileau-Narcejac

- *Wendy and Lucy*, written by Kelly Reichardt and Jonathan Raymond

- and *The Wizard of Oz*, written by Noel Langley, Florence Ryerson, and Edgar Allan Woolf, from the novel by L. Frank Baum

Now let's move on to . . .

## Believe, Care, Invest: TV

Novel writing is the hardest type of writing, but I think TV pilot writing is a close second, much harder than movies. You have to do all the same work as writing a feature and more, but in a much shorter time frame. You have to cram a dramatic feature into an hour (forty-two minutes for network) or a comedic feature into a half hour (twenty-one minutes for network)!

But, you might ask, wouldn't it be easier in some ways, since you have so much more time over the course of a season to get to know these characters? Nope, if you want to sell the pilot, you can't hold anything back for later. We have to get to know (and love) these characters just as well as feature characters, lightning fast, and then plunge them right into the plot a minute later.

In fact, we have to love them even more than we love feature characters. Features are only asking for a two-hour commitment, so we're more forgiving toward cookie-cutter heroes. We're far more wary of TV heroes, though, since they're asking us to make a much longer commitment.

Yes, but at least you don't have to transform the characters! In fact, these characters are forbidden from *ever* transforming, so you don't have to build an arc, right? Well, it is true that a TV hero is not going to be fundamentally transformed in the way that a movie hero is. A movie (or play, or novel) is about the most important thing that will ever happen to your hero. Obviously, you can't do that on TV . . . There's no way every week can be the most important week in their lives!

But the art of TV is the art of the small transformation. Our heroes very rarely change their philosophy, but they almost always have to change their perspective to get what they want. Over the course of a one-hour show . . .

1. Our hero has a long-standing problem that becomes acute (Teaser): Dr. House has been kicked out of the hospital again. He's going crazy . . .

2. He gets a new opportunity to fix it (Act 1): His interns secretly bring him a case that they can't solve . . .

3. That opportunity leads to an unforeseen conflict (Act 2): Cutty finds out and tries to block him from the case . . .

4. So first he tries to resolve that conflict the easy way, which leads to a midpoint disaster (Act 3): House makes a cocky diagnosis, which accidentally puts the patient in a coma . . .

5. Then he tries the hard way, which leads to a realization (Act 4): House stays up all night, but can't fix it, then he notices they forgot the lemon juice in his iced tea . . . Wait, that's it!

6. . . . Which allows them to solve the problem (Act 5): He runs across the hospital just in time to save the patient with the correct diagnosis: It's scurvy! Cutty reluctantly restores his privileges . . .

Like I said, all the same stuff that happens in a movie, except in half the time. Plus, a TV show is more likely than a movie to have unrelated subplots interwoven with the above. Movies are far more linear, focused like a laser on the hero's journey, whereas TV almost always presents a broader, messier picture.

The above is true for almost every episode, but in a pilot you have to do all that while introducing the setting and the characters in a way that's so compelling that the audience will want to commit for the long haul. It's insanely hard.

There are two types of pilots: center-cut pilots show you a sample day in the life of the hero; premise pilots show the characters launching into a new situation. Let's start with some center-cut pilots, then do some premise pilots . . .

# Phil and Elizabeth Jennings in *The Americans* Pilot, Written by Joseph Weisberg

*Washington, DC, 1981: Soviet spy Elizabeth seduces a Reagan official. Later, she joins her husband, Phil, to kidnap a Soviet defector named Timoshev off the street. They try to put him on a slow boat bound for Russia, but they're late and the boat has taken off without them, forcing them to keep the man in the garage of their idyllic suburban Virginia house, where they live with their unsuspecting kids, Paige and Henry.*

TV Networks love to hire people with real-world experience. They love to make doctor shows created by doctors (Michael Crichton's *ER*) and law shows by lawyers (David E. Kelley's *L.A. Law*, *Ally McBeal*, *The Practice*, and *Boston Legal*). *The Americans* was the first spy show created by a spy, former CIA Officer Joe Weisberg.

And indeed this is the first show that shows what life is actually like for a spy. On most spy shows, the spies are doing all the sneaking around themselves, but in real life, the job more often involves acting as a handler for the assets you recruit, either through temptation or blackmail.

But Weisberg makes the fascinating decision to write about the other side, not his own. One obvious reason is that spies are forbidden to operate in their own countries, so if you want to make a real spy show set in America, it has to be about foreign spies. But the main reason, of course, is irony. Pretending to be an ideal American family while working for the KGB is deeply ironic, and it's an irony we all recognize from our own lives. Every family man such as myself feels at times like we're just playacting the American Dream, not really believing in it. We've all felt imposter syndrome, and this show takes that feeling and makes it quite literal.

There was no shortage of antihero shows at the time, but few where they served masters as evil as the KGB. I find it interesting that Phil and Elizabeth don't kill any innocent people in the pilot, and won't until the sixth episode or so (all the more shocking because it's so casual). They're easing us in.

This is an interesting example because it has two coequal heroes, and neither one is very easy to care about. Let's look at our two heroes separately. Why might Phil be hard to identify with? He's a violent KGB sleeper agent. He's kidnapping a defector, and usually we're predisposed to like defectors (though this one will turn out to be more evil than the agents trying to forcibly repatriate him back to Russia). So they definitely had some hurtles to overcome with BCI.

So why do we Believe in Phil? He's not an inhuman KGB robot: He's tempted by the offer of three million dollars to defect. He's grown used to the comforts of American life. "What's . . . what's so bad about it, you know? The electricity works all the time. Food's pretty great. The closet space . . ."

He's humanized by playing around with his children, playing a game called Ice Cream Olympics that involves bopping them on the nose with soft serve (and hints at his KGB training): "Take your time. Eyes on the cone. Be the cone. Eyes . . . eyes on the cone. Don't feint too early. Don't feint too early! Know your distance . . . Know your distance . . . Oh, no!"

Why do we Care about Phil? First and foremost, he's in a lot of danger, with Timoshev trying to kill him, and mortally wounding his colleague Rob. Then we feel for his tough dilemma: Save Rob or complete his mission on time. Finally, we share his frustration at missing the boat. Even if we sharply disapprove of a hero's actions, whenever we watch someone trying hard to do something, and fail through no fault of their own, we share their consternation.

And, on a more universal level, any co-parent has felt frustration at not being listened to on parenting decisions from time to time, and in Phil's case, those disputes take on life-or-death stakes.

Phil is pretty easy to Invest in. He's a total badass: We meet him as he's talking to Rob about Timoshev, assuring him that Timoshev won't be so hard to grab:

Phil: *You know how guys like him kill people? They plan it for weeks, and they always come up from behind. Fighting face-to-face, that's a different story.*

Rob: *I heard once he got in a bar fight with the entire Japanese Olympic judo team. Took out four of 'em before the rest of 'em ran.*

Phil: *Which year? Because '64 to '72 were pussies. They didn't even medal.*

Then Timoshev runs for it and they chase him down. When he's cornered, he pulls a knife, and Phil is unarmed, but Phil still wins the fight. Timoshev says, "I know you're not supposed to kill me." Phil responds, "I don't think you understand how unpopular you are. I could deliver you in a hundred pieces and they'd give me a separate medal for each one."

We love to watch anyone do spy stuff. He switches license plates quickly and skillfully. Later, he keeps cool when cops are running toward him, and even makes his dead drop while one of the cops is watching him.

We see the FBI talking about people like Phil and Elizabeth in awed tones: "Super-secret spies . . . They look like us, they speak better English than we do." We think, "Hell yeah, I'd watch a series about that."

Now let's look at Phil's wife, Elizabeth. Why might Elizabeth be hard to identify with? Her job involves having sex with strangers, which we traditionally find a little off-putting. Later, we see that she's even more committed to the KGB than her husband.

So how do they get us to Believe in Elizabeth? To their credit they also make her a bit mean-spirited as a mom, saying about her daughter's teacher: "I don't know how you can look at him all day with that harelip." It would have been easier to say, "Oh, isn't it ironic that this perfectly sweet and innocent American mom is actually a merciless Soviet spy?," but instead they asked, "What would she actually be like? No matter how dedicated she is to her cover, wouldn't a little of her real merciless personality slip out?"

We really come to Care for her when she recalls being beaten up and then raped by her recruiter back in the Soviet Union while Timoshev looked on. Of course, this makes us far more frustrated with her, that she would stay with the KGB after that kind of treatment. It's intensely sympathetic, but it tests our identification with her.

Why do we Invest in her? When we first meet her, she's wearing a leather dress, a wig, and sexy lingerie. This is a super-sexy spy. We will soon see that she's tougher than her husband: He wants to save Rob's life but she says, "The mission comes first!" When Phil points out the defector got three million dollars, she responds, "He can buy himself a diamond-plated coffin."

Of course, if we don't want to root for Phil or Elizabeth and their KGB mission, we can simply root for their neighbor Stan, who works for the FBI Counterintelligence squad. So with that less loathsome option on the table, why do we identify more with the Jenningses? I think it ultimately comes down to irony. Stan is what he seems to be, which is less ironic and thus less compelling. Phil and Elizabeth have a huge gap between their public and private identity, and so we're naturally drawn to them, even though we find their profession evil.

## Gil Grissom in the *CSI: Crime Scene Investigation* Pilot, Written by Anthony E. Zuiker

> *In Las Vegas in 2000, crime scene investigators Gil Grissom and Jim Brass show up at a crime scene where someone appears to have shot himself in the bathtub. Gil finds a maggot on the corpse and learns a lot from it. They find a suicide audiotape, then play it for his family. His mother says that's not her son's voice. After the credits we meet new CSI Holly Gribbs on her first day on the job. Brass has Gil take her along to an autopsy.*

*CSI*, when it first debuted, was a mix of the ultra-realistic with the ultra-unrealistic. On the one hand, it would be the first show to actually take the time to explain the workaday science of forensics to Americans, showing the what, how, and why of each test, and stressing the capabilities and limitations of each.

On the other hand, in order to turn these scientists into the primary heroes of their cases, it had to massively falsify many realities of the job. Why? Because heroes (and especially TV heroes) must have (or seem to have) decision-making power: Audiences don't want to watch the activities of a hero who is merely a cog in a larger machine, making contributions every week to decisions that will ultimately be made by other people offscreen.

This is why Aaron Sorkin had to reluctantly make the president a character (and ultimately the main character) on *The West Wing*, and why Jack gradually became the co-hero of *30 Rock*. Ultimately the weight of most stories falls on the shoulders of the decider, not the contributor.

So how do you make a story about CSIs? Let's look at all the things they can't and/or don't do:

- They don't have guns or badges.

- They can't interrogate the criminals.

- They can't declare that it's time to make an arrest or make the arrest themselves.

In short, the show can't deliver many of the traditional pleasures of a cop show. So how do they deal with this? In some ways, they proudly own up to these differences:

- We begin with Neanderthal detectives at the crime scene, staking out their territory but not noticing anything important. They then roll their eyes and scoff when the CSIs show up, saying, "Here comes the nerd squad." But Grissom smirks right back and blows past them dismissively. He then spots all of the clues they missed: The nerd squad are the real heroes.

- Grissom brags about not doing interrogations: "Why ask the criminals? They'll just lie. The evidence never does."

- When the CSIs refer to the actual arrests, they talk as if that's mere mopping up after the real work is done.

But the show also loses the courage of those convictions rather quickly, and begins cheating right away in the pilot to create the impression that our heroes do have those powers:

- They create a rare situation in which they can use guns: One is called in to help another secure a crime scene from an uncooperative victim who pulls a gun, so she brings a gun to force the victim to stand down.

- They allow the CSIs to do interrogations at the crime scene as they're doing their DNA swabs, and then later, they simply have the CSIs show up at interrogations and ask the detective in charge if they can jump in and ask a few questions. (To which the detectives always shrug and step away, letting the CSI take over from then on.)

- They have the CSIs unrealistically show up for the arrest, standing on the sidelines looking smug and/or righteous as the faceless detectives lead the suspects out in handcuffs.

The creators of *CSI* discovered a huge treasure trove of untapped drama: the hard work, neat gadgets, and brilliant deductions of the forensics squad, but in order to tap into it, they had to find ways to deal with the fact that this squad was in many ways not an ideal subject for a satisfying police drama. Sometimes they did so by openly defying those expectations and other times they did so by distorting reality to match those expectations. This combination worked well, and soon viewers learned to reset their expectations and embrace the sort of drama that only this unique setting could create.

Okay, so let's focus in on Gil. Why might Gil be hard to identify with? Gil was, like many TV heroes of his era, inspired by Sherlock Holmes. He's somewhat nicer than Dr. House, but he's still kind of an asshole. He demands a pint of Holly's blood before she's even clocked in. She asks why, and he says, "So many reasons." We'll later find out he just wanted it for a blood splatter re-creation. When she then feels light-headed, he tries to trick her into eating a grasshopper.

So why do we Believe in Gil? After Holly turns them away in disgust, he does eat one of the grasshoppers himself, so he certainly has individual tastes. His particular interest in bugs makes him stand out from other CSIs.

And of course we love mottoes to show what a hero believes in. We've already listed one of his mottoes above, but this is network TV, so they drive the point home many times. Later, he says to a CSI named Warrick, "Forget about the husband, Warrick, forget about the assumptions, forget about your promotion, these things will only fool you. Think about what cannot lie, the evidence."

And finally, we like that he's got a unique POV. The camera zooms into bullet wounds when he looks at them, which was the first time anyone had seen anything like that on TV. (Another element *House* borrowed.)

So then, how do they make us Care? As I pointed out above, he's disrespected by his colleagues ("Here comes the nerd squad"). In the pilot, Brass is his boss and also treats him with a lot of disrespect. (In future episodes, Brass would be reconceived as a nonscientist, and Gil would be the boss, which is another example of how every series trends in that direction.)

He's embarrassed when a coworker reminds him they went on a date that fizzled. They find a mix of chemicals on the tape recorder and Gil wonders:

Gil: *If latex rubber and cooking spray went on a blind date, how would the night end?*

Charlotte: *A lot better than ours did.*

Gil: *I know. Pink Floyd's not your thing.*

Charlotte: *I have on cowboy boots, I work in a lab, What makes you think* Dark Side of the Moon *synched to* The Wizard of Oz *is going to warm my damn barn?*

Gil: *I just thought it'd be something different.*

Charlotte: *You want to be different? Pin me up against a wall; lay one on me like you mean it.*

He's clearly a little too nerdy for that.

We Invest, most obviously, because he's great at his job. He's got good *eyes*. When he plucks the maggot off the corpse, he says to Brass:

Gil: *Pupa, stage three.*

Brass: *English. I'm not an entomologist.*

Gil: *It's the third stage of larva metamorphosis. This guy's been dead seven days.*

We've never seen a cop on TV spot something like that before.

Also, though he's a little awkward around women, he can also loosen up and be funny when the moment demands it. When Holly gets scared by a room full of dead bodies, he comforts her and then yells "You assholes!" at the corpses.

Ultimately, audiences loved Gil, but they loved the format even more. If you count the spin-offs, there were more seasons without him than with him, but I think that, before we could fall in love with the idea, we had to fall in love with this character as our doorway into this world.

## The Unnamed Heroine of the *Fleabag* Pilot, Written by Phoebe Waller-Bridge

*A young woman has a late-night assignation with one man, then flirts with another man on the bus the next morning. She then interviews for a bank loan for her small café. Afterward, she meets her sister to attend a feminist lecture.*

This TV show is adapted from Phoebe Waller-Bridge's one-woman stage show, where she developed this character. Obviously, a one-woman show is all about direct address to the audience, and TV shows are all about dialogue, so how do you make that transition?

In the introduction to the published text of the show, she explained the dilemma she faced: "In theatre, people come to your characters. In TV, characters arrive in people's living rooms, their kitchen tables, and are often even taken into bed with them! . . . I was determined for the audience of the TV series to feel like they were having a personal relationship with *Fleabag*—hence the audience address."

Her solution was to do the comedy version of *House of Cards*. Unseen and unheard by her scene partners, she turns directly to the camera and gives us her running commentary on what's going on.

The effect is delightful. Voiceover can be alienating, but this feels like we're getting intimate confessions from the heroine. Of course, one big difference from other shows that have done this is that, though no one can hear what she's telling us, other characters increasingly notice that she's doing *something* ("Where'd you just go?," asks her biggest crush, the so-called hot priest). By choosing to only confide her secrets in us, she's harming her ability to achieve intimacy with anyone on her side of the camera.

For the heroes of both the UK and US *House of Cards*, confiding in us alone is probably a good idea. As Bob Dylan would say, if their thought-dreams could be seen, someone would put their heads in a guillotine. But the unnamed heroine of this show (The scripts just refer to her as *Fleabag*) will discover that her thoughts aren't so terrible that she only dare confide them with us. We bond with her because we get to hear her private secrets, but we ultimately realize that, in order to learn and grow, she'll have to break her connection to us and connect with the hot priests in her actual life.

So how does the show get us to connect with an unnamed, self-destructive heroine? We're always reluctant to commit to a heroine who doesn't respect herself, but we nevertheless wind up closely bonding with her.

Why do we Believe? Well, she's certainly got an interior life. As she's flirting with the guy on the train, she shoots us a quick look and tells us "I hate myself," then goes back to being flirty with him. We like an ironic gap between a character's external behavior and interior thoughts. We get to the point where all she has to do is shoot us a quick look to let us know that she's exasperated with various things over the course of the episode.

When she's with her sister, we realize that this is a very consistent character with predictable behavior: Her sister says, "Don't get drunk and scream through his letterbox again." She has various reputations she's trying to live down.

And she has a signature outfit: A tremendously stylish black trench coat, which every woman who watched this show immediately tried to find her own copy of. It really makes her pop as an individual.

There are lots of reasons to Care about her.

Her boyfriend has dumped her (because he caught her masturbating to a Barack Obama speech). She's not as upset about this as she could be, because she obviously has other options, but it bugs her more than she'll lets on. She tries to criticize him to the guy flirting with her but finds she can say nothing but great things about him:

Man: *You've got a boyfriend?*

Fleabag: *Er, no, er . . . No, we broke up quite recently, actually.*

Man: *Oh, my God. I'm so sorry-slash-really pleased. Er . . . How the hell did he manage to fuck that up?*

Fleabag: *Oh, he was just . . . really kind and supportive with my work. He'd cook all the time, run baths, hoover. He'd laugh at all of my jokes. He was really great with my family, my friends loved him. Plus, he was really fucking affectionate.*

Man: *Sounds like a dickhead.*

The pilot has a great moment of embarrassment: She accidentally flashes a banker interviewing her for a loan, and they've just had a sexual harassment case, so the banker says, "I'm sorry, that sort of thing won't get you very far here anymore. We take this kind of thing very seriously . . ." She responds, "I'm not trying to shag you— Look at yourself!" Suffice it to say, she doesn't get the loan.

One of her underlying sources of suffering is that she "grew up without a mother": "Dad's way of coping with two motherless daughters was to buy us tickets to feminist lectures, start fucking our godmother, and eventually stop calling."

She doesn't want to talk about her failing business. "The only thing harder than having to tell your super-high-powered, perfect, anorexic, rich super-sister that you've run out of money, is having to ask her to bail you out."

So why do we Invest? She's certainly resourceful and puts a lot of work into her pursuit of men: "You know that feeling when a guy you like sends you a text at two o'clock on a Tuesday night asking if he can come and find you and you've accidentally made it out like you've just got in yourself, so you have to get out of bed, drink half a bottle of wine, get in the shower, shave everything, dig out some Agent Provocateur business, suspender belt, the whole bit and wait by the door until the buzzer goes, and then you open the door to him like you've almost forgotten he's coming over?" No, I can't say that I do, but I'm impressed by the amount of thought you've put into this.

More important, she's confident. She can handle herself flirting on the bus. She can go toe-to-toe with her sister. She's brash. She's got a lot of attitude, in a way we can't help but admire.

Ultimately, we come to care deeply about this unnamed heroine, even though we can see how she ended up with that pejorative moniker. (Actually, only the scripts call her that, no one on the show does.) Everybody loved the first season, but they loved the second and final season even more, where she fell in love with that priest. As she tried to get him to stray, he tried to save her soul. She eventually succeeded, but he made some progress, too. The show ends not because she's solved her problems, but because she's decided to stop addressing the audience and be in the moment.

# The Four Family Members in the *Schitt's Creek* Pilot, Written by Dan Levy and Eugene Levy

*We begin with a servant answering the door in a ridiculously opulent mansion. An army of intimidating government agents is waiting for her. Looking nervous, the maid asks, "Immigration?" They respond, "Revenue." Soon the agents are tagging and confiscating every object in the mansion. We then meet the four members of the Rose family as they react. It turns out that their adviser, Eli, stole all their money. They end up in a town called Schitt's Creek, which they'd bought as a joke and forgot about. Town mayor Roland Schitt shows them their motel rooms, then ignores several hints to leave.*

So obviously this is a case, as with *Emma* and *Harriet the Spy*, where the heroes are rich and spoiled, and the creators will have an uphill job getting us to identify with them. But an advantage here is that these characters are instantly humiliated by the agents, then further humiliated by the residents of their new town, and, of course, each other.

First of all, why do we Believe? Because each one is oddly unique:

- Mother Moira: She names her wigs, and wraps each one up very carefully. She yells at a servant: "Did you put Kristen with Robin? They don't like each other!"

- Patriarch Johnny has a signature personality trait: Frustration. He finally snaps at the mayor, "Roland could you, Roland, could you get the fuck out?!," then instantly becomes deeply embarrassed and stammers, "That was an overreaction. That was uncalled for."

• Son David: He has an eye-popping fashion sense (shorts and a leather coat) and a characteristic high dudgeon: "I have asked you thrice now for a towel." He also has a fear that reveals a general inability to live in the world: He's afraid of moths.

• Daughter Alexis: She has a rather unique argument tactic. David asks, "What kind of sociopath abandons her family in some vomit-soaked dump, to gallivant around the world with her dumb shipping-heir loser boyfriend she's known for three months?!" She responds, "Um, David, it will be four months next month." It's hard to argue with that.

We Care for them all for the same reason: They're losing everything.

• Moira: "I've been gutted. John, I've been stripped of every morsel of pleasure I've earned in this life. My very soul has been kidnapped, there's no ransom, no one's coming to save me." We may have some contempt for a woman who worries more about her wigs than her children, but it's hard not to sympathize with that situation.

• Johnny: "Well, how do you think I feel, Moira, Eli was family, for God's sake! 'Leave your finances to me,' he said! Son of a bitch!" Personal betrayals always hit hardest.

• David: "I'm still trying to wrap my mind around what kind of a sick person wants to get paid to

destroy another person's life! Destroy another person's
life!"

- Alexis (talking to a friend on her phone): "Baby, it's
crazy, people are just like, taking our stuff! [Realizes her
friend can't hear her] I said, they're taking our stuff!
Can you just step out of the club for a second, please?"

As their family portrait is hauled away, their lawyer tells
them that they'll have to move to Schitt's Creek. Moira says she's
sure there are other options, but the lawyer responds, "Well,
homelessness is still on the table." They've literally lost everything they can't carry.

There's not much reason to Invest in these four, and they'll
be pretty hapless throughout the whole series, but they do have
some meager skills. They do what they can to keep their stuff.
Alexis tries tricks and traps: "Hold on, hold on! Those bags are
not for you, my boyfriend bought those for me, so, theoretically,
they are his!" David tries defiance: A revenue agent asks, "Please,
sir, can you step aside?" but David stands in his way, shaking
pearls in his face: "No! You step aside, YOU step aside!" When
they arrive in town, they start fending for themselves admirably.
("Apparently in hell, there's no bellman.")

It should be pointed out that *Schitt's Creek* is a show that took
a long time to build an audience. Its first season failed to garner
much attention, but then it made it onto streaming services and
got a reputation for getting better and better as it went along. By
the time it got to the final season, it swept every conceivable
Emmy. The show is already appealing in this pilot, but it was
only after these characters settled down in this town in later seasons, and gradually deepened, that we really came to love them.

# Tony Soprano in the *The Sopranos* Pilot, Written by David Chase

*In 1999 New Jersey, mobster Tony Soprano reluctantly tells his problem to a therapist named Dr. Melfi: He's been passing out from panic attacks. We see his obsession with the ducks that live in his pool, which his family finds strange. He relates that his Uncle Junior wants to kill a man in Tony's friend's restaurant, and he wants to stop it.*

Like the heroes of *The Americans,* Tony might be hard to identify with because he's evil. Eventually, at the end of the series, Dr. Melfi will realize that she needs to quit treating Tony because she's just making him a more effective psychopath. He begs for sympathy, but he doesn't deserve any. By that point, many of the viewers agreed, but in this pilot, creator David Chase is including just enough elements to make us sympathetic to this evil man.

Let's start by talking about Believability. Obviously, the best way to make a character believable is to have lots of great details, but where will those details come from? In the DVD commentary for the pilot, Chase discusses where each of his ideas come from, and shows how important it is to draw from your own life and your own research, as opposed to simply using your imagination.

Chase says that he, like all of us, often feels like a criminal. He was a successful screenwriter, but he was putting his own mean-mouthed mother in a home and she was heavily guilt-tripping him. He thought, *I'm such a monster.* He decided to do a show about what it felt like to be a rich guy putting his mother in a home. Except, in the TV version, instead of the meek TV writer he was, he would portray himself as the monster (aka mobster) he felt like.

Chase cites the fact that Tony's mother, Livia, won't answer the phone after dark as a detail right out of his own life, as well as several other bits of dialogue. But it goes much further than that:

- Chase had a real Uncle Junior, and you can see him standing next to the fictional Uncle Junior in his first scene.

- The story Tony tells Dr. Melfi about stonecutters in his family was from Chase's history.

- Chase had an alienated teenage daughter.

- He was in therapy.

- Tony's dream about unscrewing his bellybutton and his penis falling off came from one of Chase's friends.

- Surprisingly, the story about blowing up the restaurant came not from his research, but from a family story: "My cousin Tony Pasquale told me about it."

But there are also elements that come strictly from mob research:

- The method that Tony uses to take control of the HMO.

- There really were gangsters named Big Pussy and Little Pussy in the 1940s.

That leaves one big detail that came solely from Chase's imagination, and left him feeling embarrassed: the ducks. When it came time to shoot the crucial shot of the ducks flying away, Chase's duck handler informed him such a thing could never happen: Ducks need at least a twenty-foot taxiway to take off; they can't lift straight up and fly out of someone's pool. Chase was mortified. They had to fake the shot.

Does that mean that he shouldn't have included the ducks? Of course not. It's a powerful metaphor, even if it couldn't actually happen that way. But it strengthened his commitment to drawing most of his details from real life.

So let's talk about why we Care about Tony. We would loathe Tony if he wasn't suffering panic attacks that sent him into humiliating therapy. He describes them memorably: "At first it felt like ginger ale in my skull." As we discussed in Part I, Tony is told by his wife as he's sucked into an MRI machine, "What's different between you and me is you're going to hell when you die." Audiences have a limited tolerance for malaise, but he describes it memorably: "Lately, I'm getting the feeling that I came in at the end. The best is over." Melfi responds, "Many Americans feel that way."

And of course he has a horrible mother, which always makes unsympathetic characters more likable. In fact, Tony finds disrespect everywhere he looks. Even his likable behavior, like watching baby ducks try to fly, is looked down upon by his family. That seems very unfair, and he's understandably wounded.

As we discussed before, Tony is fairly easy to Invest in. ("I'm the person who says how things go, that's who I think I am!") In the commentary, Chase says that in the original script, Tony engaged in no violence, because Chase was worried that would be too unsympathetic, but he found out the opposite was true:

Studio executives suggested he add some violence in. Chase added the scene of Tony (with upbeat doo-wop music playing) running down someone with his car and he became more likable. He's active and good at his job!

And of course we admire that Tony is willing to see a therapist, which *seems* to show that he does have a soul (though, along with Melfi, we will come to doubt if he really does over the course of the show). We always admire heroes who are willing to put their jobs at risk, and this certainly qualifies. It's hard to observe *omertà* in a psychiatrist's office.

**YOU'LL FIND LOTS** more TV pilot BCI breakdowns on my blog, including:

- *24*, written by Robert Cochran and Joel Surnow

- *30 Rock*, written by Tina Fey

- *Avatar: The Last Airbender*, written by Michael Dante DiMartino and Bryan Konietzko, with Aaron Ehasz, Peter Goldfinger, and Josh Stolberg

- *Black-ish*, written by Kenya Barris

- *Breaking Bad*, written by Vince Gilligan

- *Cheers*, written by Glen Charles and Les Charles

- *Community*, written by Dan Harmon

- *The Good Place*, written by Michael Schur

- *House*, written by David Shore

- *How I Met Your Mother*, written by Carter Bays and Craig Thomas

- *Insecure*, written by Issa Rae and Larry Wilmore

- *Mad Men*, written by Matthew Weiner

- *Master of None*, written by Aziz Ansari and Alan Yang

- *Modern Family*, written by Steven Levitan and Christopher Lloyd

- *Scandal*, written by Shonda Rhimes

- *The Simpsons*, written by Mimi Pond, based off characters created by James L. Brooks, Matt Groening, and Sam Simon

- *Stranger Things*, written by Matt Duffer and Ross Duffer

- *Supernatural*, written by Eric Kripke

- *Transparent*, written by Joey Soloway

- and *Twin Peaks*, written by David Lynch and Mark Frost

# Believe, Care, Invest: Memoirs

So there you go: five novels, five movies, and five TV pilots. But to round it out and make it an even twenty, let's look at five memoirs, too.

Obviously a lot of the rules are different here. These writers can't invent incidents or dialogue. They have to work with what life has given them. But they still have a tremendous amount of storytelling latitude. They can arrange things however they wish, snipping here and there, selecting out only the best bits, then stitching them together in a way that has nothing to do with chronological order.

Even more than prose fiction writing, memoir writing really comes down to voice. Yes, your reader wants to hear about compelling incidents, but no memoir has ever sustained itself by just being a series of events. What readers really want to know is, even if there's nothing extraordinary going on, will you have a unique perspective on everyday life? Do you have a properly skewed point of view, showing amusing and perceptive insights that surprise us, but still feel true?

In a great memoir, each chapter has to be a great story on its own. Memoirs are, by their nature, very episodic. Each chapter will jump months or years ahead to the next anecdote. Nobody wants to read a memoir and say, "Well, we've had a hundred pages of nothing but downward trajectory, so I sure hope this is going somewhere at some point." They want to read constant ups and downs, constant ironies, constant dilemmas, constant decisions, constant conflict with shifting power dynamics.

A great memoirist is a great storyteller, which means you know how to tell one big story and lots of little stories. If you have a great memoir, you can read any chapter from it at a storytelling showcase, like The Moth, and satisfy the audience.

I've only analyzed five prose memoirs and I've cited them all a lot in Part I, so let's do something new for Part II: Let's look at some *comics* memoirs.

# Believe, Care, Invest: Cece Bell in her Memoir, *El Deafo*

*In 1974, four-year-old Cece Bell gets meningitis and loses the ability to hear. She soon gets a powerful hearing aid and decides that she is now a superhero called El Deafo.*

Cece Bell was a successful creator of children's books when she decided to try something riskier, telling the story of her childhood illness and the resulting disability but turning everybody into rabbits. It's an epic story spread over many years, with many ups and downs, but it remains utterly compelling throughout. The result is a book that is a great introduction to disability for very young readers (both of my kids loved it when they were still in preschool) but is also abundantly readable by adults. Everybody loves this book.

Why Cece might be hard to identify with: It's a little hard to identify with a four-year-old, since most of us have lost all our memories of that age. It's pretty odd that it seems to take her days or maybe even weeks to figure out she's gone deaf—I believe it, because this is obviously a very honest memoir, but it just makes me think, "How could a four-year-old not notice that? They're so weird!"

But I think that this book may have the best one-two punch of Believe and Care that I've seen in any of the 130 works I've examined. Here's the first page:

- Panel one: "I was a regular little kid. I played with my mom's stuff." We see four-year-old Cece scribbling designs on her mom's bureau mirror with lipstick.

• Panel two: "I watched TV with my big brother, Ashley, and my big sister, Sarah." She sits between two much bigger kids while the TV blares "Batman!"

• Panel three: "I rode on the back of my father's bicycle."

• Panel four: "I found caterpillars with my friend Emma."

• Panel five: "And I sang." She holds a carboard tube and belts out "We all live in a yellow submarine—"

So right away we've got many reasons to Believe:

• First and foremost, in all five of these panels Cece wears the same two-piece polka-dotted swimsuit, every day, even when other people are dressed in normal clothes. Distinctive wardrobe choices really help us Believe, and, to the extent that we remember being four, that's so perfectively indicative of that age's peculiarities.

• Drawing on the mirror fits with our memories of that age and is emblematic of her personality because we know that Cece will eventually become an artist (thus this book).

• Watching Batman on TV establishes the setting and her family situation (and foreshadows that she will emulate Batman later when she gets her own very cool gadget).

• We love to watch people enjoy things fully, and her sheer look of joy on the back of her dad's bike is infectious.

- It's always good to give your hero friends and an activity to do with that friend that we haven't seen a million times.

- And finally, song lyrics! We love song lyrics, and singing into a cardboard tube makes it tactile and unique.

So, boom: We totally believe in this four-year-old hero in one page. Then what happens on page two to make us Care? She almost dies! We cut to one instant later as she trails off the lyrics and collapses mid-song. Her parents realize she's very sick and rush her to the hospital.

Because we totally Believed on the first page, we now totally Care on the second page.

At the hospital, she's taken from her parents and has a needle put in her back. We hear (but she doesn't) the doctor tell her parents: "The fluid from her spine tells us she has meningitis. Her brain might swell—" Her mom replies, "But she's only four!" Cece wakes up in pain. She notices that the other girl in her room got ice cream and she didn't (and only much later figures out she didn't hear when they offered it to her). When she tries to get up, she can't stand or walk.

Of course, she's only four and quickly becomes very helpless, so she's hardly badass when we first meet her, but we finally get the chance to see how awesome she can be starting on page twenty-two, when she gets a hearing aid and starts to realize that this makes her kind of a kickass bionic woman. Now we know we can full Invest in her to overcome her problems. Then she goes to school and gets an even more powerful hearing aid, connected to a microphone her teacher wears at all times (and forgets to take off). At first, she feels self-conscious about it, and enters a "bubble of loneliness," but then she realizes that she can hear so much more than the other kids. She can hear her teacher going to the bathroom, and gossiping about the kids in the teachers' lounge ("That Jimmy Malone is making my life HELL!"). She thinks, "I have amazing abilities unknown to anyone! Just like Bruce Wayne uses all that crazy technology to turn himself into Batman on TV." Once she lets her secret be known, the other kids think she's cool. She now sees herself as a superheroine called El Deafo. The bubble pops (though it will return intermittently as we move through several years of story).

This book is a great example of how the more specific a story is, the more universal it becomes. She goes through trauma that hopefully most of us can't imagine (and we're fascinated by all the odd, specific details of that life), but she's experiencing emotions we've all felt. We've all felt distanced from those around us. We've all been trapped in that bubble of loneliness, and we've all felt that maybe we were willing to put up with overly annoying friends in order to pop it.

## Believe, Care, Invest: Alison Bechdel in her Memoir, *Fun Home*

*Alison Bechdel tells us about her life before and after her father's death by suicide in 1980. Her father spends all his time renovating their house, and also runs a funeral home. (The central irony: They shorten "funeral home" to "fun home.")*

Bechdel is another passive hero. Her central action in the story is getting a phone call telling her that her father has died. She will find out some of her dad's secrets before his death, and some after, but she mostly learns them because her mom drops them unexpectedly, not because Alison is actively pursuing the mystery. This book's primary appeal is that it's thoughtful. She has, in retrospect, given a lot of thought to her relationship with her dad and now she's got 242 pages of fascinating insights. That's not an easy sell, but the book turns out to be easy to love simply because it's so well written (and well drawn, but the art's not the main focus).

She could have structured the book by building up to the shocking reveal of her father's death, or the shocking reveal that the seemingly accidental death was probably suicide, or the shocking reveal that her father was pursuing affairs with adolescent boys, but all three of those facts are mentioned very early on. We move outward in concentric circles from these central facts, adding a series of layers to the narrative.

So Bechdel had a lot of work to do with BCI. She had to get us to connect with a passive heroine on an inner quest that doesn't build to any catharsis in real time. How did she do it?

There is no shortage of reasons to Believe in this character and this world. Bechdel has the ideal material of every memoirist: She kept extensive diaries as a girl and still has them. That means she has hundreds of details readily at hand. The diaries themselves are fascinating: She becomes increasingly unsure of herself and starts to add a qualifying "I think" in tiny letters after every sentence. Eventually she just creates a shorthand symbol to express this, and soon she's scrawling the symbol on top of every single word.

Some other ways she gets us to Believe:

- Characters usually reveal themselves in what they compliment in others, but her backhanded compliments toward her father show what she *doesn't* value: "He was an alchemist of appearance, a savant of surface, a Daedalus of décor."

- In response to her unloving father's obsession with interior design, she develops a motto: "When I grow up, my house is going to be all metal, like a submarine."

- Sense memory always makes a character come alive. She remembers one of the few times she felt close to him: "My mother must have bathed me hundreds of times. But it's my father rinsing me off with the purple metal cup that I remember most clearly. The suffusion of warmth as the hot water sluiced over me . . . the sudden, unbearable cold of its absence." Later, she has to remind herself, "He really was there all those years, a flesh-and-blood presence steaming off the wallpaper, digging up the dogwoods, polishing the finials, smelling of sawdust and sweat and designer cologne."

- We see the books he's reading and often they're red flags to his secrets.

Obviously, the main reason to jump ahead and reveal her father's death early on is that it makes it easier to Care about her right away. If she had waited to wallop us with it later, we might not have gotten as involved with the narrative. Other ways she gets us to Care:

- Foreshadowing through the use of parallel characters: In a moment that is fairly typical of the book's philosophical bent, she remembers her father lifting her up on his feet, and tells us that she now knows that it's called Icarian games in acrobatics. She then talks about how Icarus and Daedalus became parallel characters for her and her father. (And this leads to a discussion of Joyce's character Stephen Dedalus.)

- Her father calls a room he's decorated "slightly perfect." Nothing is ever good enough for him.

- Her father insists on pink and flowers for her room though she hates both. She hasn't figured out yet that they're both gay.

- Her father hits both her and her mother, and at one point she flees the house in fear of violence.

- "I grew to resent the way my father treated his furniture like children and his children like furniture."

- Everything is a risk: "If we couldn't criticize my father, showing affection for him was an even dicier venture."

We never fully Invest in Bechdel to solve the book's mysteries. In the end, she gives it all a lot of thought, and reaches some fascinating conclusions, but she has no big breakthroughs or catharsis. It's a gentle, melancholy book. Nevertheless, here are some reasons we Invest:

- She's defiant: "I was Spartan to my father's Athenian. Modern to his Victorian. Butch to his Nelly. Utilitarian to his aesthete."

- She rides a bike: "I bicycled back to my apartment, marveling at the dissonance between this apparently carefree activity and my newly tragic circumstances."

- She's brave: She comes out to her parents as soon as she figures out she's gay, though she has reason to suspect they won't approve.

- She's a classic book-taught amateur: When she comes out, it's still totally hypothetical. She then reads every book ever written on lesbianism (braving potentially disapproving librarians) and launches into her first relationship fully informed.

Here, too, Bechdel forges a universal story out of observations that are very specific to her odd circumstances. It's the ultimate testament to this story's fundamentals that it was able to be translated into a hit Broadway musical, despite having none of the elements one generally associates with that art form.

## Believe, Care, Invest: John Lewis in *March: Book One*, Written by Lewis and Andrew Aydin, Illustrated by Nate Powell

*We begin on the Edmund Pettus Bridge in 1965. John Lewis and Hosea Williams lead a group of marchers across the bridge and get attacked by the local police. We then jump to the morning of President Obama's inauguration in 2009 as a much older John wakes up and prepares for his day. He goes to his office, where a family peeks in and he offers to show them around. One of the boys asks why he has so many pictures of chickens. He describes growing up in Alabama as the son of a sharecropper who eventually bought his own farm.*

Obviously John Lewis is one of the great American heroes of the twentieth century, so we certainly admire him right away. You might think that his monumental edifice would make him hard to fully identify with, but Lewis is delightfully humble and human here, allowing us to Believe, Care, and Invest right away.

As with any good memoir, we primarily Believe because of all the specific details of his life. It's fascinating to compare this book to Lewis's prose memoir, *Walking with the Wind*, because there are many differences. The most obvious is that the titular incident of that book is not in this one! That book gets its title from a time that his family's modest farmhouse almost blew over, and his family had to walk en masse from corner to corner to hold it down. This comics memoir, written ten years later, seems to say, "Well, that was a pretty good metaphor for my life, but we've got limited space here and we just don't have room for it." Instead, he focuses on his childhood relationship with his chickens, which bonds us more, partially just because it's so odd.

He has great kid logic: "When the hens began laying their eggs, I'd mark each one with a lightly penciled number to help keep track of its progress during the three weeks it took to hatch. The numbers were always odd. Never even. I had been told never to put an even number under a setting hen. It was bad luck."

He has distinctive syntax: He says of his family's cabin, "My father bought it in the spring of 1940 for $300. Cash." That period tells us about the lifetime of hurt they would have been in for if they hadn't paid for the house all at one time.

His dreams are represented by an object: "I always hoped to save enough money for an actual incubator, like the $18.95 model advertised in the Sears-Roebuck catalog. We called that our wish book."

And of course, we love his iconic, odd outfit on that bridge in Selma: He was wearing the standard suit and tie of the movement, but over it he has a trench coat and a backpack, which emphasizes his young age and his preparation for going to prison.

As far as getting us to Care, this book does the classic trick of beginning with the most brutal moment in Lewis's life (it's actually just one of the many police beatings he'll receive in the story, but it's the only time he's clubbed into unconsciousness). On Bloody Sunday in Selma, he could not be more trapped; the bridge behind him is filled with marchers pushing him forward, and they discover a weapon-wielding mob waiting for them at the far side of the bridge. Williams nervously asks him, "Can you swim?" He says, "No." Williams responds, "Well, neither can I, but we might have to."

Let's look at other reasons we Care:

- As a child, he's very poor, going to substandard "separate but equal" schools using the broken-down, discarded bus of the white kids, and their discarded old schoolbooks as well.

- He takes a road trip with his uncle and he becomes aware they could be killed at any time for driving through all-white areas. We hear racist epithets from the whites eyeing them, for the first of many times in the book.

- He's expected to eat the chickens he loves. "Worse, though, was watching my mother or father kill one of the chickens for a special Sunday dinner. They would either break its neck with their hands, spinning it around until the bone snapped, or simply cut the head off. Then they would drain the blood from its body and dip it in boiling water, scalding it to loosen its feathers for plucking. I was nowhere to be seen at those family meals."

Obviously, Lewis is easy to Invest in. He's tremendously badass. When the cops swarm on them, he just says to Williams, "We should kneel and pray, Hosea." This infuriates the cops, who attack them all the more viciously.

In the present, he certainly has decision-making authority as a congressman. (The framing sequence is set on the day that his party takes over all three branches of government.)

He's a precociously smart and determined child. He can read the Bible on his own at age five. On the days when his father tells him he must stay home from school to help on the farm, he hides until the bus comes by and then bolts for it just as it's leaving, getting away to school before his father can stop him. "When I got home, my father would be furious. I was certain he would tan my hide. But he never did whip me—not over that."

He's also a uniquely sensitive child with good eyes: "No one else could tell those chickens apart, and no one cared to. I knew every one of them by appearance and personality. They were individuals to me. Some I even named."

In seminary, Lewis tells of coming across the story of Martin Luther King told in comic book format, and what a powerful tool that was. He published his memoirs in prose form but then he chose to reach out to another audience with this comics version—cowritten with Andrew Aydin and illustrated by Nate Powell—and the result is a stunning success.

# Believe, Care, Invest: Art and Vladek Spiegelman in Art's Memoir, *Maus*

*We begin with an emblematic incident from the hero's youth—in Rego Park, New York, in 1958, young Art Spiegelman skins his knee and goes to his Holocaust-survivor dad, Vladek, for sympathy, but gets none. We then jump forward to a modern-day framing sequence—in the late '70s, Art visits his dad for the first time in years to get out of him details of his life for a Holocaust comic using mice—before jumping further back into a harrowing past, where Vladek tells of the 1930s in Poland, when signs of impending doom were everywhere.*

Neither Art nor his father is very easy to identify with. Art is an unsuccessful underground comic book creator, which isn't any reader's favorite profession. He hasn't visited his father in two years, until he decides to come ply him for comic book material. He smokes constantly and feels no compunction about getting ash everywhere. Vladek is not a great dad in the 1958 sequence, unkind to his new wife in the modern-day framing sequence, and a bit caddish and mercenary in his flashbacks. So the book has some hurdles to overcome with BCI.

Let's look at Art and Vladek separately. Here are some of the reasons we Believe in Art:

- In 1958, Art has an object unique to the time: skates that attach to his shoes.

- We get just a brief mention of Art's French American wife Francoise, but we can tell that such a wife makes him unique in Rego Park.

• He has a signature piece of clothing: the vest he always
  wears.

There are lots of reasons to Care about Art:

• In 1958, he's abandoned by his friends: "I-I fell, and my
  friends skated away w-without me." His father responds,
  "Friends? Your friends? If you lock them together in a
  room with no food for a week . . . then you could see
  what it is, friends!" We instantly get that it would suck to
  have to beg for sympathy from someone who survived
  the Holocaust.

• In the present, we realize that Art's mother has died by
  suicide.

• His father doesn't respect his job: "Better you should
  spend your time to make drawings what will bring you
  some money."

• His father is exasperating, telling him great stories and
  then insisting they not be in the book. We're glad Art
  breaks his promise to leave them out.

As for Investing in Art, the quality of the comic itself is the
ultimate testament to his skills. His goal of commemorating the
Holocaust is noble, and he does push to get the story against
strong resistance. Neither Art nor Vladek can suspect that this
comic will make Art one of the first comics artists to become rich
and famous. His stepmother correctly points out, "It's an important book. People who don't usually read such stories will be
interested."

But this is really Vladek's story. Let's look at why we Believe in him:

- He has very distinctive syntax: "It's a shame Francoise also didn't come." "I don't want you should write this in your book."

- In the flashbacks, he's got a nicely mundane job buying and selling textiles.

- He knew his current wife back in Poland before he met his first wife, which is a nicely complicated situation.

- And, of course, he has that horrifying number tattoo.

There is no shortage of reasons to Care, even before we get to his time in the concentration camps:

- In the present, his wife has died by suicide, a tragic death for a Holocaust survivor, and he doesn't get along with his new wife.

- He has a unique complaint to his new wife: "A **wire** hanger you give him! I haven't seen Artie in almost two years—we have plenty **wooden** hangers." Shades of Joan Crawford!

- In the flashback, he finds one girlfriend more attractive than the richer girl he actually wants to marry, which is a caddish problem, but we still sympathize.

So why do we Invest in Vladek?

• Crucially, he rides an exercise bike while he tells his son of his past. We love exercise and bikes!

• When we get the flashback, he's a great lover: "I had a lot of girls what I didn't even know that would run after me. People always told me I looked just like Rudolph Valentino." We admire his confidence and charm.

• It's always a great superpower when the hero understands a second language and then others use it around him, not knowing he understands it: "The next morning we all met together. My cousin and Anja spoke sometimes in English." The cousin asks, "How you like him?" Anya replies, "He's a handsome boy and seems very nice." Vladek explains to Art: "They couldn't know I understood."

Spiegelman is acutely aware of the ironies of this story. He overcomes the urge to present his late, long-suffering father as saintly, and instead presents him flaws and all. He worries to his stepmother that unflattering aspects of his portrait might seem to confirm some stereotypes. But ultimately, he has to trust himself. The more three-dimensional the story is, the more powerful it will be, and the more it will impact every reader.

## Believe, Care, Invest: Marjane Satrapi in her Memoir, *Persopolis*

*Marjane Satrapi recalls being nine years old in 1979 when the Islamic Revolution takes over Iran. The next year, the girls at school are all forced to wear veils, but they take them off and play with*

*them. She recalls wanting to be a prophet as a child, even before the
revolution.*

For the last example in the book, I'll break my rule and do just
one book in translation. The author is an English speaker who
supervised the translation, so I'm going to let myself get away
with it, and I just love it too much not to use it.

Marjane is in an ironic situation: As a small child, living in a
secular country, she is intensely religious, in a way that somewhat disturbs her teachers and parents. She even has a close,
personal relationship with God, who comes to her and has long
conversations into the night. Then, of course, religious fanatics
slowly begin to take over her country. Now it's her turn to be
disturbed by religiosity. Soon, she has completely reversed herself, adopting a precocious form of Marxism, though it means
that her friend God now refuses to visit her.

We Believe because she's got beliefs and she's written them
down: "I wanted to be a prophet because our maid did not eat
with us, because my father had a Cadillac, and above all, because
my grandmother's knees always ached." Her grandmother says
to her, "Come here, Marji, Help me to stand up." Marjane helps
her and says, "Don't worry, soon you won't have any more pain,
you'll see," then reads to her from the Holy Book she's written:
"Rule number six: Everybody should have a car. Rule number
seven: All maids should eat at the table with the others. Rule
number eight: No old person should have to suffer."

The book captures how children process things: Marjane is
told that her communist grandfather was put in a cell filled with
water for hours. That night she insists on taking a long bath. "I
wanted to know what it felt like to be in a cell filled with water.
My hands were wrinkled when I came out, like Grandpa's." Using her childhood logic, she falsely associates one with the other.

She's stubborn: When she tells her teacher she wants to be a prophet, the other kids laugh at her and her teacher says to her parents, "Doesn't this worry you?" They tell the teacher it's fine, but she still decides to lie about it, even to them. Her father says, "So tell me, my child, what do you want to be when you grow up?" She thinks, "A prophet," but says, "I want to be a doctor." There is now a gap between her public persona and her private beliefs. She won't let the world change her yet.

As with most of our other examples, Marjane is caught up in a historical tragedy, so she's easy to Care for: She is forced to wear a veil she doesn't want to wear. Her coed French school is eventually shut down and she is sent to an all-girls religious school.

She is caught between the shah and the revolutionaries, both of whom are horrible. Her parents are political, so she has even more reason to worry about them. A picture of her mom taken at an anti-veil protest goes global, putting her life in danger. "She dyed her hair, and wore dark glasses for a long time."

There are lots of reasons to Invest in Marjane:

She's got a pretty badass attitude for a ten-year-old: "I wanted to be justice, love and the wrath of God all in one."

She's smart: "To enlighten me, they bought books. I knew everything about the children of Palestine, about Fidel Castro, about the young Vietnamese killed by the Americans, about the revolutionaries of my own country . . . But my favorite was a comic book called 'Dialectic Materialism.'"

She dresses up with a (presumably toy) machine gun and bullet sash, then marches around in her garden: "Today, my name is Che Guevara! Down with the king! Down with the king!"

In the end, Marjane will not lead a counterrevolution, but we trust in the opening pages that she could. Eventually, she will make her way to the West and publish this memoir (later turned into an equally excellent animated movie) and get her story out to the world.

**OKAY, IF YOU** want to read more, you can read write-ups of these prose memoirs on the blog:

- *Angela's Ashes* by Frank McCourt

- *The Autobiography of Malcolm X*, as told to Alex Haley

- *Born a Crime* by Trevor Noah

- *Educated* by Tara Westover

- and *Kitchen Confidential* by Anthony Bourdain

**NOW FEEL FREE** to do an analysis of your favorite story openings and see how they *really* won you over. I think you'll find it had nothing to do with the plot, and everything to do with how the writer got you to Believe in, Care for, and Invest in the hero.

That just leaves one more piece of advice . . .

# WHERE DO YOU FIND BELIEVE, CARE, AND INVEST MOMENTS?

S O RIGHT NOW, YOU'RE SAYING, "OH, CRAP! I NEED TO add a lot more Believe, Care, and Invest moments to my manuscript!"

So what do you do? Well, obviously, you can do what I've been doing for the past five years: reread your favorite novels and memoirs and rewatch your favorite TV shows and movies. You can find great examples of Believe, Care, and Invest, and shamelessly pilfer them.

Or, better yet, you can use your imagination to dream up new twists on each example you find: odder Believe moments, more painful Care moment, more badass Invest moments. That's fine, too.

But neither of these is ideal. For any writer, even if you're not writing a memoir, your best material is your real life. You may have a fertile imagination, but it's no substitute for lived experience. Keep a notebook! Or at least have a document on your computer and add to it every night with things you've seen or heard or felt during the day.

You'll find no shortage of Believe moments. Here's one from my life:

Readers love song lyrics, especially original ones. My daughter, like many little girls in her generation, grew up with the lyrics to Hamilton memorized, and eventually, at age nine, started writing her own rap musicals, with rapid-fire lyrics such as these: "There are bunnies building burrows / In what used to be your heart / They're living on pixie sticks and churros / Their tunnels are like art." It's emblematic of her generation, and it couldn't be more delightfully bizarre. Anyone is going to subconsciously think, "That must be from real life, that can't be made up."

And plenty of Care moments:

A friend of mind called her dad's workplace, trying to reach him. She said, "Is [Dad] in? This is his daughter." The woman running the desk said, "Oh, his daughter, he talks about you all the time! You did [amazing achievement], [amazing achievement], and [amazing achievement]! He's so proud of you!" She then said, "No, I'm his other daughter, the one he's apparently never mentioned." It was a painful moment.

And you can find Invest moments, even for people not as tough as Jack Reacher. My wife and I both had somewhat misleading moments in the opening week of our relationship that gave us an inflated sense of the other's badassery.

I had been living in Minneapolis for a while and she had just moved to town. We were drinking in a fancy bar downtown when I said that the people there would go driving on the frozen lakes. She had been raised never to trust the ice and said she would never step on one. It had been below freezing for a week, so I said "C'mon, there's a lake outside this bar, let's go stand on it right now." We left our friends inside with our drinks, and she reluctantly followed me outside, where I waltzed out to the center of the lake and beckoned her to follow me. She very reluctantly stepped out onto the ice until she joined me in the center, feeling exhilaration at overcoming a childhood fear.

A week later, we were with a group of friends barhopping on St. Patrick's Day (we weren't lushes, I swear). We arrived at a bar's tent party, and our friends quickly decided it was lame, so they wanted to move on, but my future wife had just ordered a beer, and was too poor to abandon it. So she tucked the full pint glass under her arm in her jacket and said, "Let's go." I thought that was so cool. In fact, she's never done anything like that again in the intervening twenty years, but at the time, I thought, "This girl is wild."

My wife and I started to fall for each other at first sight, but before we fell *hopelessly*, we needed to *admire* each other. My wife said, "I trust this person with my life." I said, "I trust this woman to be fearless." We each thought, "This is a person who can face the challenges of life with me." We invested in each other. Within a year, we were engaged, and we've been together ever since.

So start keeping your Believe, Care, Invest notebook now. Look for odd behaviors that make you say, "That's better than anything I could make up." Look for painful moments that make you say, "Ouch!" Look for badass moments that make you say, "I would go anywhere with that person."

Use this book as evidence of what kinds of moments to look for, and then find them in your real life. Happy hunting!

# NOW YOU JUST HAVE TO WRITE THE REMAINING 95% OF THE STORY!

**G**OOD NEWS! THEY LIKE THE FIRST TEN PAGES, SO THEY say, "Send me the rest!" This is the point where you admit, "There *is* nothing else. The only writing book I've ever read is *The Secrets of Character* by Matt Bird and he just showed me how to write ten pages."

To your surprise, they aren't happy to hear this. They think you've wasted their time. Well, don't panic! Just tell them, "Wait, I'll write the remaining 95% of it in the next two days." They're dubious, but they *really* like the first ten pages, so they say, "All right, McWilliams, you've got two days!" (Your name is McWilliams in this scenario.)

So now what do you do? Easy: You run out and get my *other* book, *The Secrets of Story: Innovative Tools for Perfecting Your Fiction and Captivating Readers.* That'll give you more advice on writing the whole thing. Good luck, McWilliams!

## ACKNOWLEDGMENTS

Many of the ideas in this book were developed along with the cohost of The Secrets of Story podcast, James Kennedy, so his ideas are liberally sprinkled throughout this book. Many thanks.

Thanks, of course, to my agent, Stephen Barbara, who makes these books happen. And thanks to Betsy, for everything.

# INDEX